a handbook of
canadian
film

a handbook of canadian film

eleanor beattie

peter martin associates limited
in association with 'take one' magazine

Cloth edition: ISBN 0-88778-073-3
Paperbound edition: ISBN 0-88778-074-1

Printed in Canada by Web Offset

Design: Diana McElroy

General Editors: Peter Lebensold, Joe Medjuck

The Take One Film Book Series is published by Peter Martin Associates Limited, 35 Britain Street, Toronto, Ontario M5A 1R7, in association with *Take One* magazine, Post Office Box 1778, Station B, Montreal 110, Quebec.

preface

A Handbook of Canadian Film *is an attempt to bring together and to make accessible all information about film and filmmaking in Canada. Furthermore, by its very organization, the book is meant to point up areas which need critical investigation and to encourage the use of our resources. I have chosen not to repeat the work of others, but rather to refer to it and indicate where it can be found; the whole book is, in fact, a kind of dictionary, an open-ended listing which invites additions. And while the book does not pretend to be a work of criticism, it does carry a critical point of view which has influenced the particular subject matter.*

This book is the result of the cheerful collaboration of many filmmakers and of the people who help to produce and distribute their films. I take all responsibility for the errors and omissions in the book and acknowledge the generous help of the Canadian Film Development Corporation, Joe Medjuck, Sandra Gathercole, Raymond Gordy and Peter Lebensold; Carol Faucher and La Cinémathèque québécoise, Robert Daudelin and Le Conseil québécois pour la diffusion du cinéma, Michelle Bischoff, Colin Neale, Lyle Cruickshank, David Novek and the National Film Board, Dényse Morrow and Faroun Films. I also thank the Quebec Government and the Canada Council who made this book financially possible.

Eleanor Beattie

contents

NOTES

Financing of Films: CFDC

10.   (1)   The objects of the Corporation are to foster and promote the development of a feature film industry in Canada, and without limiting the generality of the foregoing, the Corporation may, in furtherance of its objects,

   (a) invest in individual Canadian feature film productions in return for a share in the proceeds from any such production;
   (b) make loans to producers of individual Canadian feature film productions and charge interest thereon;
   (c) make awards for outstanding accomplishments in the production of Canadian feature films;
   (d) make grants to filmmakers and film technicians resident in Canada to assist them in improving their craft; and
   (e) advise and assist the producers of Canadian feature films in the distribution of such films and in the administrative functions of feature film production.

Canadian Film Development Corporation Annual Report, available from:

   800 Place Victoria, Suite 2220, Montreal 115 (Tel: 283-6363).
   Toronto: 96 Bloor St. W. (Tel: 966-6436).

Variety, November 17, 1971, PR. 28-60, a special issue on "Canada's 'Nervous' Film Boom."

The Feature Film Industry in Canada, a thesis submitted by R. Jock to the School of Business Administration, University of Western Ontario, London, Ontario, in April, 1967. Available from the Centre de documentation cinématographique (Bibliothèque Nationale), 360 McGill Street, Montreal 125 Quebec.

an introduction to canadian film

John Grierson founded the National Film Board on a political and cultural ideal which serves as a solid base for our growing film industry. The Canadian Film Development Corporation has given that industry its financial base. Together they have created an environment that has made possible such films as Claude Jutra's **Mon Oncle Antoine**, Don Shebib's **Goin' Down the Road**, Gilles Carle's **Red**, Claude Fournier's **Deux Femmes en or**, Allan King's **A Married Couple**, Gerald Potterton's **Tiki Tiki**, Jean-Pierre Lefebvre's **les Maudits Sauvages**, Paul Almond's **Act of the Heart**, Eric Till's **A Fan's Notes**, Peter Carter's **The Rowdyman**, Jacques Godbout's **IXE-13** and many others.

The existence of a Canadian film industry is no longer in question; the question now is whether this industry is in danger of betraying its heritage. The direction which it chooses at this point will determine its future. If it develops as a supermarket cinema; if it trades on commercialism; if it is essentially derivative; then it will be merely a branch-plant industry, flaccid and faceless. But if it is rooted in this country's historical and immediate experience; if it gives a face to our unique aspirations; if it draws on the resources of the congregation which is Canada; then its appeal will be distinct, dynamic — and international. The films of Sweden, Italy, France; of Bergman, Fellini, Godard, bear this out.

The National Film Board has gone a long way toward developing an attitude and feeling for Canada, with millions of people having seen their productions in schools and halls across the country. Now as Canadian filmmaking moves into a commercial context, it is subject to pressures not experienced by the Film

NOTES

Statistics Canada, *Annual Catalogue #63-206, on Motion Picture Production*, available at Information Canada bookstores.

"Sex Is Out", an article by Marc Gervais, in *The Montreal Star*, July 24, 1971, discusses the record of the CFDC and interviews the CFDC chairman, Gratien Gelinas, and executive director, Michael Spencer.

Le Cinéma: autre visage du Québec colonisé, a manifesto of l'Association professionnelle des cinéastes du Québec, available on request from that association at 3466 St. Denis, Montreal 130, Quebec.

"Donner un cadre à une industrie", by Luc Perreault, *La Presse*, June 19, 1971. An interview with François Cloutier, Quebec Minister of Cultural Affairs on the problems of developing a national cinema of Quebec.

L'Etat et l'industrie du cinéma by André Poirier, January, 1963, Ecole des hautes études commerciales, University of Montreal. Available from the Centre de documentation cinématographique (Bibliothèque Nationale), 360 McGill St., Montreal 125, Quebec.

L'Industrie du cinéma dans la province du Québec, by Jacques St. Laurent, March 25, 1962. Available from the Centre de documentation cinématographique (Bibliothèque Nationale), 360 McGill St., Montreal 125, Quebec.

How to Make or Not to Make a Canadian Film (Comment faire ou ne pas faire un film canadien). André Paquêt, editor, La Cinémathèque canadienne, 1967. The most complete historical description of cinematic events in Canada, listed chronologically from 1898 to 1967.

The annual reports of the Department of Trade and Commerce in the Dominion of Canada and later Canada (1917-1941) have sections on film in the country. Any large library should have these books and they are available at the Centre de documentation cinématographique (Bibliothèque Nationale), 360 McGill St., Montreal 125, Quebec.

Board. Although we do not have control of the distribution and exhibition of Canadian feature films, we do have many resources which can provide a widening base of support.

Above all, we have the resource of our filmmakers, many of whom have been trained by the National Film Board and by private companies throughout Canada; this is the backbone of our industry. We have, too, a Canadian public which has invested more than ten million dollars in the development of an autonomous cinema and is taking an increasing interest in its results. There is a growing understanding that an appreciative milieu is of utmost importance for the development of our indigenous cinema. For the first time students are using Canadian productions in film study courses and they are assisted by film study centres. Hundreds are studying filmmaking at universities and community colleges across the country. Out of this have grown cooperatives — in Vancouver, Edmonton, Calgary, Regina, London, Toronto and Montreal — to assist the independent filmmaker in the production and distribution of his films.

It is clear that despite the present centralization of facilities, filmmakers are no longer content to work only in the major centres, but experience a growing desire to remain in the communities which fostered them. The Secretary of State has already acknowledged the need to decentralize both the Film Development Corporation and, particularly, the Film Board, in order to make their facilities available to a broader cross-section of the filmmaking community. With the proper use of these resources and the increasing awareness of Canadian audiences, Canada has the opportunity to create a unique experience with film.

Little of the early cinema in Canada was indigenous: the exotic snowy plains and Eskimos brought Robert Flaherty to the Hudson Bay area in 1922 to film **Nanook of the North**; so, too, the western plains and the legend of the RCMP attracted all the large Hollywood companies.

Another attraction of the Canadian setting was that beginning in 1930, Great Britain's quota system on films considered any

NOTES

The *Canadian Moving Picture Digest,* is a good source of historical information. The following issues tell something of the "Carry On Sergeant" disaster: January 12, February 2 & 23, 1929.

Sparling's extraordinary experiences in early Canadian cinema are documented in his article, "The *Short* Way to Canadian Entertainment", in *How To Make or Not to Make a Canadian Film* (see above).

Parts I & II of *Canadian Feature Films 1913-69* lists chronologically all known films shot in Canada by indigenous and foreign companies between these years. Edited by Peter Morris. Canadian Filmography Series 106 & 107, The Canadian Film Institute, 1970 & 1972.

Homage to John Grierson, La Cinémathèque canadienne on the occasion of the National Film Board's 25th Birthday, 1964. Out of print, it is available in film study libraries and contains testimonials and a filmography.

"John Grierson: 1898-1972" *McGill Daily Supplement,* Monday, February 28, 1972. Edited by Ronald Blumer.

A valuable collection of Grierson's writings have been edited by Forsyth Hardy, *Grierson on Documentary,* London, Collins, 1946.

production filmed and produced in a Commonwealth country as British-made. Out of this situation developed one of the first so-called Canadian talking feature films, **North of '49**, directed by Neal Hart and produced by the short-lived British Canadian Pictures Ltd.

Although Canadian companies and distribution outlets were set up, most collapsed; for in the field of entertainment films, Canada was simply an extention of the American distribution-exhibition system. **Carry On Sergeant**, directed by Bruce Bairnsfather, and purported to have cost $500,000, was released in 1928, silent — while American films enthralled Canadian audiences with sound.

One of the assistant directors on **Carry On Sergeant** was Gordon Sparling, who later joined the Montreal branch of New York's *Associated Screen News;* his "Canadian Cameos" series lasted from 1931 to 1954, producing over 80 films, among them **Grey Owl's Little Brother** (1932) and **Rhapsody in Two Languages** (1934). Some indigenous films did grow out of the need to build and populate the country; the Canadian Bioscope Company was founded in 1900 to make films for the Canadian Pacific Railways directed toward the stimulation of British immigration to the West. This same company produced (in 1913) Canada's first feature film, **Evangeline**, directed by E. P. Sullivan and W. H. Cavanaugh. Similarly, the Canadian Government Motion Picture Bureau (founded in 1921 out of the Exhibits and Publicity Bureau and later incorporated into the National Film Board) was introducing one part of the country to another through the medium of film. Among their productions: **Lest We Forget** (1935) on Canada's role in World War I, and **Heritage** (1939), directed by J. Booth Scott, concerning the ten year drought in Western Canada.

The National Film Board was the result of John Grierson's coming to Canada in 1938 to advise the Government on its film policy. The National Film Board Act states the duties of the Commissioner: ". . . to advise upon the making and distribution

NOTES

For recent interviews with Grierson see "John Grierson: 'I derive my authority from Moses' ", an interview with Ronald Blumer, *Take One*, Vol. 2, No. 9. Also see "John Grierson: The 35mm Mind", interview with Darlene Kruesel, *McGill News*, March, 1971.

"Political Film". A talk by John Grierson followed by a panel discussion recorded from *Ideas*, CBC, Nov. 25, 1970. Cat. No. 546L. One hour. Available from *CBC Learning Systems*, Box 500, Terminal A, Toronto 116, Ontario.

"Le coeur et l'esprit", Roger Blais and Françoise Jaubert. *Le Devoir*, February 26, 1972.

The National Film Board of Canada: The War Years, edited by Peter Morris. Canadian Filmography Series No. 103, Canadian Film Institute, Ottawa, 1965. p. 32. Second edition, 1972.

Hye Bossin, editor of the *Canadian Film Weekly* which started in 1942 and continued into the 60s, recalls the participation of Canadian Jews in those early days in his *Stars of David*, The Canadian Jewish Congress, 1965.

Pierre Savignac, *Historique du cinéma canadien*. Mimeographed. Written for *Semaine du cinéma canadien*, January 1965. Available for reference at the NFB library, Montreal, and the Canadian Film Institute, Ottawa.

See Tom Daly's article of personal reminiscences "From 'World in Action' to 'Man in His World' " in *How to Make or Not to Make a Canadian Film*, La Cinémathèque canadienne, 1967.

The National Film Board's Publicity Department has published in mimeographed form, *A Brief History: The National Film Board of Canada*, by James Lysyshyn, and also assembled a special edition of *News Clips* dated April, 1968 on the history of the Board. Both are available by writing: Information Division, National Film Board, P.O. Box 6100, Montreal 101, P.Q.

Rodney James has written a thesis, *The National Film Board of Canada and its Task of Communication*. Published in 1968 by the US Department of Health, Education and Welfare, Washington, it is available from them and also available for reference at the National Film Board library in Montreal.

of national films designed to help Canadians in all parts of Canada to understand the ways of living and the problems of Canadians in other parts." Grierson's formulation of the documentary film as a powerful tool for the discovery and illumination of the ordinary world shaped and continues to influence Canadian cinema.

The war years brought an accelerated need for propaganda and information films; Britain needed support and America was being encouraged to enter the war. Grierson, as first film commissioner, invited a number of foreign directors to the Board: Stuart Legg directed the Board's first film, **The Case of Charlie Gordon** (actually produced under the old Motion Picture Bureau in 1939); he then created the "Canada Carries On" and "World In Action" series. Such films as **The War for Men's Minds** (the Allies' answer to Leni Riefenstahl's **Triumph of the Will**), **Churchill's Island** and **The Gates of Italy** attempted to supply mass education for a democratic world. Joris Ivens, the great Dutch filmmaker, came to make **Action Stations!** (1942); Evelyn Spice-Cherry (who continues to work in Regina) and Norman McLaren (who likewise still delights us) came and stayed. Other directors included Raymond Spottiswoode (**Quebec – Path of Conquest**), George L. George (**Handle with Care**) and Ernest Bornemann (**Target Berlin**). It is estimated that the "World in Action" films were seen by an international audience of thirty million people.

Canadians, too, were drafted to the film front of the war effort: Sydney Newman, present film commissioner, came from Toronto to make **Trainbusters** (1943), a film about the fighter plane pilots; Tom Daly, a brilliant editor, worked with Stuart Legg in piecing together stock-shots, newsreel and captured footage; Julian Roffman, Michael Spencer, James Beveridge, Gudrun Parker, Guy Glover – all began making their great contributions during this vital period. Budge and Judy Crawley – who had won an award in New York for their short **Ile d'Orleans** in 1938 – received contracts from the National Film Board during the war

NOTES

"The Private Film Industry in Canada and its Relation to Government",
F. R. Crawley. A speech given to the Conference on Canadian Information,
November 12, 1971. Available from Crawley Films, Ottawa, Toronto, or
Montreal. Judith Crawley, *The Quality of a Nation*, Crawley Films, 1962,
18 pp.

For a complete description of this period in Quebec, see the following
publication: *Vingt Ans de cinéma au Canada français*, Robert Daudelin,
Ministère des Affaires culturelles, Québec, 1967; the section on the
history of Quebec cinema was reprinted in *Objectif*, May 1967, pp. 18-20.

The complete story of the work produced by the filmmakers in Unit B
at the NFB, their search for, and indeed, the building of more manageable
equipment, the development of their new approach and its cross-fertilization in France and the United States has yet to be thoroughly investigated
by film historians. The following articles are, however, available:

"A Note on Candid Eye", by Wolf Koenig, in *How To Make or Not To
Make a Canadian Film*. La Cinémathèque canadienne, 1967.

Terence Macartney-Filgate: The Candid Eye, edited by Charlotte Gobeil,
Canadian Filmography Series No. 104, Canadian Film Institute, Ottawa
1966. (Out of print; available at film study libraries.)

"En courant derrière Rouch" Parts 1, 2 & 3, by Claude Jutra, *Cahiers
du cinéma (Paris)*, #113, November 1960, pp. 32-43, #115, January 1961,
pp. 23-33, #116, February 1961, pp. 39-44.

"Le Cinéma direct nord-Americain", by Louis Marcorelles, *Image et Son*,
No. 183, April, 1965, pp. 47-54.

years. After the war, the Crawleys became heavily involved in sponsored films (their all-time hit being **The Loon's Necklace** (1948) made for Imperial Oil) while at the same time giving rise to a whole new generation of professional personnel.

After the war, production companies began to mushroom across the country — among them, Parry Films and Trans-Canada Films Company in Vancouver, and Chetwynd Films in Toronto. But the biggest boom took place in Quebec. There, in addition to the founding of Peterson Productions and Les Films Lavoie, Quebec Productions and Renaissance Films — two large studios — were built, producing such films as **un Homme et son péché** (Paul Gury, 1948), **le Gros Bill** (René Delacroix, 1949) and **Tit-Coq** (Gratien Gelinas and René Delacroix, 1952).

This period of feature film production ended with the introduction of television in 1952 but it stimulated the growth of the film society movement (the Canadian Film Institute was founded out of the old National Film Society), the concept of Canadian film awards, amateur film production (Claude Jutra won first prize in the 1949 Canadian Film Awards for **Mouvement perpetuel**) and film criticism (*Découpages,* a Montreal-based film magazine, had Pierre Juneau, Michel Brault and Marc Lalonde on its editorial board). With television came the demand for speedier production. The National Film Board began turning out series of half-hour films; film adapted to television brought new techniques for a fresh look at the everyday world: "Petites Médisances" was directed by Jacques Giraldeau with camera by Michel Brault, and Bernard Devlin produced "On the Spot" (Sur le vif). Perhaps best-known is the "Candid Eye" series produced by Tom Daly's Unit B; Wolf Koenig, Michel Brault, Roman Kroitor and Terence Macartney-Filgate directed such gems of craftsmanship and teamwork as **The Days Before Christmas, The Back-breaking Leaf, Glenn Gould** and **Lonely Boy**. Other members of the "Candid Eye" team were John Spotton, Georges Dufaux and Stanley Jackson. This unit was a training ground and inspiration for many young people who later formed

NOTES

"Michel Brault et Claude Jutra racontent Jean Rouch" (Interview with
R. Daudelin and M. Patenaude), *Objectif*, No. 3, December 1960, pp. 3-
16. "Entretien de deux cinéastes" (Brault and Jutra talk about Jean
Rouch and Norman McLaren), *L'Ecran* (Montreal), No. 2, pp. 7-15.

Movie (Britain), No. 8, April 1963 discusses *cinéma-vérité* and the role
which the National Film Board group, in particular, Brault, has played.

Liberté, Vol. 8, No. 2-3, March-June 1966. The whole issue is dedicated
to Canadian cinema carrying an article by George Dafaux and Jean-Claude
Labrecque, "Le fameux cinéma candide" p. 84-90.

Elements pour un nouveau cinéma, Louis Marcorelles, published by
UNESCO, Paris, 1970. 154 pp. Contains a section on the National Film
Board's Candid Eye Unit.

See *Homage to the Vancouver CBC Film Unit*, La Cinémathèque canadienne, 1964.

The Canadian Film Industry: Past, Present and Future, by Joseph Fox.
Thesis submitted to the School of Journalism, Carleton University.
Available for reference at the Canadian Film Institute, Ottawa.

See "Conversations on film with Arthur Hiller and Sidney Furie",
Canadian Cinematography, January-February, 1966, pp. 13-16.

the French Unit, such as Gilles Gascon and Jean-Claude Labrecque.

The National Film Board's animation department also became involved in television work. During the war years, Norman McLaren had gathered talent around him — George Dunning, René Jodoin, Jim McKay, Evelyn Lambert, Grant Munro, Robert Verrall and Maurice Blackburn — and most had stayed on. Television created another animation centre in the CBC's Toronto Graphics Department founded by David McKay; it employed such artists as Dennis Burton, Warren Collins and Carlos Marchiori.

With the formation of the French Unit at the National Film Board in 1959 (following the Board's move from Ottawa to Montreal), French-Canadian cinema was revivified. Those assertive efforts of Michel Brault, Gilles Groulx, Claude Jutra, Claude Fournier, Arthur Lamothe and Marcel Carrière resulted in such seminal films as **les Raquetteurs, la Lutte, Golden Gloves, les Bûcherons de la Manouane** and **Québec — USA**.

The demand for televised drama found the National Film Board producing a series for the French network entitled "Panoramique", produced by Guy Glover. The Vancouver CBC film unit, founded in 1953 by Stan Fox, Jack Long and Arla Saare, had been producing short documentaries by Allan King, Daryl Duke and Gene Lawrence. With Ron Kelly's **A Bit of Bark** in 1959, they began to produce dramatic shows, most particularly, the series "Caribou Country", written by Paul St-Pierre and directed by Philip Keatley. Harvey Hart returned to Canada to head up "Festival", a dramatic series at CBC Toronto in 1962 and the dramatic productions of Eric Till, Arthur Hiller, Harvey Hart and Paul Almond became familiar to the Canadian public.

An outgrowth of the intense television production was the renewed activity in feature-length films: Julian Roffman directed **The Bloody Brood** (1958) and Canada's first and only 3-D feature, **The Mask** (1961); Norman Klenman and William Davidson co-directed four of Morley Callaghan's stories in **Now That**

NOTES

Some fascinating background on the large theatre chains and distributors in Canada can be gleaned from an old government report, *Investigation into an Alleged Combine in the Motion Picture Industry in Canada,* 234 pp. Department of Labour, April 30, 1931. Available at the Centre de documentation cinématographique (Bibliothèque Nationale), 360 McGill Street, Montreal 125, Quebec.

It must be noted that the case was heard in the Ontario Supreme Court, without jury, and on March 18, 1932 the accused were discharged.

April's Here (1958) and Sidney Furie made two films in 1959, **A Dangerous Age** and **A Cool Sound from Hell**. The attempts to establish a viable commercial film industry met with little success; the years following found many of our filmmakers departing for either Hollywood or England.

But young people in the universities organized film crews and found professional help. **Seul ou avec d'autres** (1962) was made at the University of Montreal with the co-operation of Michel Brault; directed by Denis Héroux, Denys Arcand and Stephane Venne, it found limited commercial distribution. At the University of British Columbia in 1963, Larry Kent directed his first feature, **Bitter Ash**, which was banned in British Columbia and became a *cause célèbre* as it moved from university to university on the underground circuit. In 1965, David Sector found commercial and critical success with **Winter Kept Us Warm** made with a cast and crew from Ryerson and the University of Toronto. But perhaps the independently-made film which had the strongest effect was Claude Jutra's **A tout prendre** (1963), an intensely personal film using Jutra's skills as an actor, combining the qualities of fiction and the documentary.

The first feature films made by the National Film Board came in the midst of this independent activity: **Pour la suite du monde** grew out of the thirteen half-hour shows produced for the CBC by Crawley Films about the isolated French-Canadians who live on the north shore of the St. Lawrence River. One of the writers of the series, Pierre Perrault, went on to make two other films, **le Règne du jour** and **les Voitures d'eau**, completing a now classic trilogy of great poetic strength. Another feature film produced in this same year, **The Drylanders** (1963), was also a thematic investigation of a man's relationship to his land and country; directed by Don Haldane and produced by Peter Jones, it told a story of the pains and joys of western pioneer life. Starring Frances Hyland and Don Francks, the film had moderate success.

But while **Pour la suite du monde** and **The Drylanders** looked

14

"I am going to take you back to 1949 when Mr. C.D. Howe became quite alarmed about the dollar drain out of this country, and about where all that money was going. When he looked around he found that a large proportion of it was going out through Famous Players. Mr. Howe asked Mr. Fitzgibbons, who was then the President of Famous Players, to come up here to Ottawa and have a little chat about that. He thought that perhaps some of that money should stay in the country and they should perhaps use it to build up a Canadian film industry or make some of those films inside the country.

"To cut a long story short . . . , Mr. Fitzgibbons came out laughing with an agreement referred to as the Canadian Co-operation Project which said that they were not to get involved in the Canadian film industry because it was too young and it could not do the job anyway. However, because of the money they were taking out of the country, they agreed to do a big job of propaganda for us . . . 'to make sure that every time we have a feature film that makes reference to your country, we will spread it around the world'. What this meant in effect was that in a particular script, instead of the man coming from Canton, Ohio, they wrote in that he came from Moose Jaw, Saskatchewan. That was their Canadian contribution."

—From Minutes of Standing Committee on Broadcasting, Films and Assistance to the Arts, 1969-70.

to rural and traditional values, two young men — one from
Toronto, the other from Montreal — found intense challenge
in urban life. In **Nobody Waved Goodbye**, Don Owen told a
story of embattled youth. Taking a critical yet sympathetic
stance towards his characters, who were coping with a society
which operates on confused values, Owen summed up the
spirit of a generation. His successful efforts encouraged another
young filmmaker in Montreal, Gilles Groulx; his hero Claude, a
young québécois, and Barbara, a Jewish Montrealer, verbalize
layers of personal, social and political complexities. Robert
Daudelin describes the appearance of **le Chat dans le sac** as
"a moment of intense joy . . . At last we were confronted by a
film which really belonged to us, one in which we were happy
to recognise ourselves and see ourselves close to. **Le Chat dans
le sac** was (and remains) the image of our most recent awaken-
ings, as much through its stripped-down form as through its
voluntarily confused subject."

The year 1964 also brought the first efforts of Jean-Pierre
Lefebvre, poet and critic on the now-defunct film review,
Objectif; and the following year, Gilles Carle delighted popular
audiences with the Christmas story of a snowplow driver in his
la Vie heureuse de Léopold Z.

Television news programs such as "Document" and "This Hour
Has Seven Days" brought an intensification of the production of
film documentaries; Patrick Watson, Douglas Leiterman and Beryl
Fox produced such memorable films as **The Mills of the Gods**,
The Chief and **Seven Hundred Million**. Ron Kelly's document on
the depression, **The Thirties: A Glimpse of a Decade** won him
his first Wilderness Award. The kind of public, non-personal
documentary evolved by the Candid Eye Unit gave way to much
more intense and intimate portraits; CBC refused to telecast
Dick Ballentine's **Mr. Pearson**, as well as Allan King's **Warrendale**,
which went on to gather popular success in independent commercial houses.

With the founding of the Canadian Film Development Corpora-

NOTES

Proposals for Canada's Film Policy, a brief presented to the Secretary of State, May, 1972, by the Canadian Film-makers' Distribution Centre, available for reference in film libraries, or Canadian Film-makers' Distribution Centre, Rm. 204, 341 Bloor St. W., Toronto.

Liberté, "Cinéma si," Vol. 8, No. 2-3, March-June, 1966. A special issue on Canadian cinema with reprints of reports by the L'Association professionnelle des cinéastes du Québec to the Quebec government, recommendations by that body to the Federal Government, and many other articles by filmmakers reflecting on the industry.

Cinéma-Québec, summer, 1971, Vol. 1, No. 7. Special issue on production, distribution, and exhibition of Canadian films, particularly Quebec films.

La Société de développement de l'industrie cinématographique à l'heure du choix by Jean-Pierre Tadros, p. 15, *Le Devoir*, Sept. 12, 1970.

The Private Film Industry in Canada and its Relation to Government, a speech by F. R. Crawley to the Conference on Canadian Information at the Chateau Montebello, November 12, 1971. Available from Crawley Films Limited in Ottawa, Toronto, or Montreal.

Minutes of Proceedings and Evidence of the Standing Committee on Broadcasting, Film and Assistance to the Arts, House of Commons, Issue No. 7, May 6, 1971. These minutes from the annual accounting of the CFDC to the Committee contain some fascinating exchanges and arguments on the direction of the industry, and particularly on the "crucial problem" of distribution. (Available from Information Canada.)

Minutes of Proceedings and Evidence of the Standing Committee on Broadcasting, Film and Assistance to the Arts, House of Commons, February 26, 1970. Representatives of Le Syndicat général du cinéma present and discuss their brief to the Committee on problems in the industry. (Available from Information Canada.)

tion in 1967, Canada made a serious commitment to feature film production: this organization was allotted ten million dollars of public money "to foster and promote the development of a feature film industry". As a result, Canada has seen a breakthrough in the area of production; more than 80 feature films have been made with the assistance of the CFDC within the last 5 years. Many have received international recognition. However, there has been no corresponding breakthrough in the area of distribution-exhibition of these films.

In setting out the guidelines for the establishment of the CFDC in the House of Commons on June 20th, 1966, then Secretary of State Judy Lamarsh said: "Many countries, in order to encourage the distribution of their own films have applied quotas. We have chosen, however, not to introduce this kind of restriction in the Bill at this time. Canadian films must therefore make it on their own merits. But in rejecting quotas, we are counting on film distributors and cinema chains to give more than ordinary support to the aims of this program."

Every film-producing country in the world has some form of protection — usually a quota — for its indigenous productions. Ms. Lamarsh's decision to ignore their experience, coupled with the fact of Canada's vulnerability to the American culture, has meant that Canadian films have been denied an audience. Famous Players Canadian Corporation Limited and Odeon Theatres (Canada) Limited, two multinational, basically foreign-owned corporations, own or control more than two-thirds of the commercial cinemas in Canada: over 80% of the feature film distributors in Canada are branches of the American Seven — Twentieth-Century Fox, Metro-Goldwyn-Mayer, Paramount, Columbia, Warner Bros., United Artists, Universal — with little power to distribute films other than those which come from the parent company. Canada has become a "dumping ground" for the films of American companies which earn over 100 million dollars a year on the Canadian market. The result is that only a small percentage of the films produced in this country ever reach a Canadian

18

Motion Picture Theatres and Film Distributors, annual catalogue
#63-207, available from the Dominion Bureau of Statistics, gives the
statistics on film revenues, number of films exhibited in Canada and the
percentage of Canadian films exhibited in Canada and the percentage of
Canadian films exhibited in Canada (1% in 1969).

Rapport sur la distribution du film, Institut canadien d'éducation des
adultes, September 1967. Available from that organization at 506 St.
Catherine St. East, Suite 800, Montreal 24, Quebec.

audience. When they do, they are generally exhibited without proper promotion, in independent theatres in major centres only. Without access to the exhibition network, films produced by the Canadian industry are costing us many millions of dollars with very little cultural or economic return. This is a fraud.

We can no longer accept the argument that Canadian films are lacking in excellence — excellence is certainly not the criterion for the selection of films now exhibited in this country. Nor can we accept the argument that Canadian films are not viable at the box-office — too many of our recent features have disproved that myth. No, the problem is not excellence or lack of excellence; it is not a problem of box-office economics. It is a problem of changing needs which the existing distribution-exhibition machinery is failing to accommodate.

1. filmmakers

The following section is an alphabetical listing of filmmakers containing a short biography, a filmography and a bibliography in each case.

Where no other published material exists, all available information has been included; additional sources, if any, are indicated in the bibliography. Books listed are often sourcebooks on Canadian film and filmmakers; their authors, publishers and dates of publication can be found in section 23. BIBLIOGRAPHY, p.249. For further information on periodicals cited, see section 26. PERIODICALS.

In most cases, the filmographies list only those films directed or co-directed by the filmmaker; films on which he has worked in other capacities are mentioned in the biography. Filmographies are complete unless otherwise stated (in which case only television productions have been omitted). Where the production of a film is independent, a distribution source is given.

ALMOND, PAUL

Paul Almond was born in Montreal in 1931. After studying at McGill University he worked on his BA and Master's at Oxford, actively involved as president of its poetry society and editor of a literary magazine. After graduation, he travelled with a repertory company in England, joining the CBC in Toronto in 1954 as a director. He directed many dramas, in particular with the "Festival" series — among them, **Point of Departure**, **Shadow of a Pale Horse**, **Under Milkwood**, **Julius Caesar**, **Romeo and Jeannette** and **The Hill** which he wrote and produced, winning the 1957 Ohio Award. He later directed a number of episodes in the Canadian series "Wojeck", "RCMP" and "Forest Rangers" and in the American series, "Alfred Hitchcock Presents". Almond has written and produced his own feature material.

FILMOGRAPHY (incomplete)

1961 **Backfire**. Prod: Merton Park Production Co., England. 59 min. b&w.

1963 **The Dark Did Not Conquer**. Prod: CBC. 60 min. b&w.
Journey to the Centre. Prod: CBC. 60 min. b&w.

1964 **October Beach**. Prod: CBC for "Telescope". 30 min. b&w.
7 Up. Prod: Granada, England for "World in Action". 45 min. b&w.
Mother and Daughter. Prod: CBC "Telescope". 11 min. b&w.

1968 **Isabel** (Isabel). Prod: P. Almond, Quest Film Productions Ltd. 108 min. col.

1970 **Act of the Heart** (Acte du coeur). Prod: P. Almond, Quest Film Productions Ltd., 103 min. col.

1972 **Journey**. Prod: P. Almond, Quest Film Productions Ltd. 97 min. col.

BIBLIOGRAPHY

Paul Almond, by Janet Edsforth, Canadian Filmography Series #111, available from the Canadian Film Institute. It contains a complete filmography, an interview and criticism.

La Presse, June 3, 1967, p. 33, "Geneviève Bujold et Paul Almond: la lutte avec l'ange", by Luc Perreault. (Interview.)

The Montreal Star, September 26, 1970, pp. 21-22, "Life is Knowing How to Live It", by Martin Malina. (Interview.)

Séquences, October, 1970, pp. 4-8, "Entretien avec Paul Almond", by Léo Bonneville. (Interview.)

La Presse, September 26, 1970, p. D9, "L'Iceberg québécois", by Luc Perreault.

John Vernon in Almond's Journey.

ARCAND, DENYS

Called a filmmaker of "demystification", Denys Arcand brings a strong political and social argument to his work. His first film, **Seul ou avec d'autres** was made in a student group at the University of Montreal with the help of Michel Brault on camera; Arcand later collaborated on Brault's **Entre la mer et l'eau douce**. Arcand was born in Deschambault, Quebec in 1941, and studied history at the University of Montreal.

FILMOGRAPHY

1962 **Seul ou avec d'autres**. With Denis Héroux and Stephane Venne. Prod: Denis Héroux, Association Générale des Etudiants de l'Université de Montréal. 65 min. b&w.

1963 **Champlain**. Prod: André Belleau and Fernand Dansereau, NFB. 28 min. col.

1964 **La Route de l'ouest**. Prod: André Belleau, NFB. 28 min. col.

Les Montréalistes (Ville-Marie). Prod: André Belleau, NFB. 28 min. col.

1966 **Volley Ball** (Volleyball). Prod: Jacques Bobet, NFB. 13 min. b&w.

1967 **Parcs atlantiques** (Atlantic Parks). Prod: André Belleau and Jacques Bobet, NFB. 17 min. col.

Montréal un jour d'été. Prod: Raymond-Marie Léger, Office du Film du Québec and Les Cinéastes Associés. 15 min. col.

1970 **On est au coton**. Prod: Marc Beaudet, Guy L. Côté and Pierre Maheu, NFB. 120 min. b&w. Unreleased.

1972 **Québec: Duplessis et après** . . . . Prod: Paul Larose, NFB. 115 min. b&w.

La Maudite Galette. Prod: Cinak and Les Films Carle-Lamy. 108 min. col.

Rejeanne Padorani. Prod: Cinak.

BIBLIOGRAPHY

Cinéastes du Québec No. 8: Denys Arcand, 1971, CQDC. Contains a long interview with Arcand and others involved in the filming of **On est au**

coton with passages from the sound track; criticism by Réal La Rochelle, a filmography and bibliography.

Champ libre 11, November 1971, re: the censoring of **On est au coton.**

L'Action, Quebec, November 9, 1971, a letter from Sydney Newman to M. André l'Heureux, Directeur du secrétariat d'action politique, also concerning the censoring of **On est au coton.**

Le Cinéma québécois: tendances et prolongements, has a critique by Yvan Patry.

How To Make or Not To Make a Canadian Film, "Speaking of Canadian Film", by Denys Arcand.

BAIRSTOW, DAVID

Born in Toronto in 1921, David Bairstow joined the National Film Board in 1944. As a producer, Bairstow has been involved in a number of series — *Eye Witness* (1952-1954), a monthly theatrical screen magazine produced by the Board; "Perspectives" (1955-1958), a television series which dramatized social problems; "Frontiers" (1958-1960), half-hour documentary essays for television; and the "Netsilik" series in 1968-1969 which became the basis of a television series on Eskimo life, "The Stories of Tuktu". Bairstow spent the year 1969-1970 as exchange producer with the Australian Commonwealth Film Unit where he produced, among many others, the theatrical short, **Paddington Lace.** Some individual films which Bairstow has produced at the Board include Don Haldane's **Eternal Children**, Richard Notkin's **Autobiographical by A. M. Klein**, Josef Reeve's **Judoka** and most recently a film on John Grierson, directed by Roger Blais, **Art is a Hammer.**

FILMOGRAPHY (incomplete)

1952 **Royal Journey.** Prod: Tom Daly, NFB. 54 min. col.

1960 **Men Against the Ice** (Aux prises avec les glaces). Prod: D. Bairstow, NFB "Frontiers". 24 min. b&w.

1961 **Morning on the Lièvre** (Matin sur la Lièvre). Prod: D. Bairstow, NFB. 13 min. col.

1963 "Arctic Circle". Prod: D. Bairstow, NFB. Four films of 28 min. each.

1964 **Alexander Mackenzie — the Lord of the North** (Alexander Mackenzie–le maître du nord). Prod: Richard Gilbert, NFB. 28 min. col.

1965 **Max in the Morning**. Prod: D. Bairstow, NFB. 28 min. b&w.
Instant French. Prod: D. Bairstow, NFB. 21 min. b&w.

1967 **Twenty-Four Hours In Czechoslovakia**. Prod: Walford Hewitson, NFB. 57 min. col.

BIGGS, JULIAN

Born in Port Perry, Ontario in 1920, Julian Biggs joined the National Film Board in 1949 as Evelyn Cherry's assistant editor. His involvement in acting and directing while at the University of Toronto led him naturally into the first dramatic series produced by the Board for television. "Perspectives" ran three years, from 1955 to 1958, producing sixty-five half-hour dramas based on various social problems: **Monkey on the Back**, directed and edited by Biggs was a forerunner of films on drug abuse; **Go to Blazes** (retitled **Fires of Envy**) starred John Vernon in a W. O. Mitchell story of a Polish immigrant in rural Saskatchewan. This series, conceived by Tom Farley, was shot weekly on a single system; it used the talents of many writers — M. Charles Cohen, Charles Israel, George Salverson, Stewart Nutter, Arthur Hailey, Lister Sinclair, Joseph Schull and W. O. Mitchell, as well as a number of directors — Don Haldane, Bernard Devlin, Allen Wargone and Julian Biggs. The kind of training which this fictional and speedily-produced series provided in set and costume design, dramatic and technical competence allowed the Board and Julian Biggs to produce the dramatic series, "History Makers", many episodes of which were also directed by Biggs. In the early 1960s Biggs produced with Gordon Burwash a series called "Comparisons"; documentary material was used to relate peoples from around the world. Biggs has since produced a number of films, among them Owen's **High Steel** and **Nobody Waved Goodbye**, Potterton's **The Railrodder**, Spotton's **Buster**

Keaton Rides Again and Mason's **Paddle to the Sea**. He has been director of English Production at the Board, worked as a project director on a community development project for the United States government and, until his retirement in 1972, was a director-producer at the National Film Board. Julian Biggs died in 1972.

FILMOGRAPHY (incomplete)

1951 **The Son** (Le Fils). Prod: Michael Spencer, NFB. 27 min. b&w.

1953 **Herring Hunt** (Les Harenguiers). Prod: Guy Glover, NFB. 11 min. b&w.

1954 **Dresden Story**. Prod: Robert Anderson, NFB "On the Spot". 30 min. b&w.

1955 **The Shepherd** (Le Berger). Prod: J. Biggs, NFB. 11 min. b&w.

1956 **Monkey on the Back** (La Drogue). Prod: Grant McLean, NFB. "Perspectives". 30 min. b&w.

1957 **Journey from Etsa** (Marées au Ghana). Prod: David Bairstow, NFB "Perspectives". 29 min. b&w.

1958 **People of the Peace**. Prod: David Bairstow, NFB "Perspectives". 23 min. b&w.

1959 **Lord Elgin — Voice of the People** (Lord Elgin — La voix du peuple). Prod: J. Biggs, NFB "History Makers". 29 min. b&w.

1961 **William Lyon Mackenzie — a Friend to His Country** (William Lyon Mackenzie — l'ami de son pays). Prod: J. Biggs, NFB "History Makers". 28 min. b&w.

1963 **Three Grandmothers** (Trois Pays, trois grand-mères). Prod: Gordon Burwash & J. Biggs, NFB "Comparisons". 28 min. b&w.

1964 **23 Skidoo** (23 Skidoo). Prod: J. Biggs, NFB. 8 min. b&w.

1970 **A Little Fellow from Gambo**. Prod: Julian Biggs, NFB. 56 min. col.

BIBLIOGRAPHY

Dossiers de cinéma; 1, Fides, 1968. (Critique of **Le Berger**.)

L'Ecran et la vie #20, July 1965, pp. 32-36, "Connaissez-vous le berger?".

The Montreal Gazette, May 26, 1966, "Julian Biggs Named Director of Production at National Film Board". (Interview.)

The Montrealer, August 1966, p. 18, "Montreal International Film Festival, Filmmaker, Julian Biggs," by Martin Bronstein. (Interview.)

Le Cinéma canadien (references).

BONNIERE, RENE

Born in Lyon, France in 1928, René Bonnière worked in his native land in many aspects of film and television production, learning to edit with Henri Colpi who himself worked for Alan Renais. Bonnière joined Crawley Films in Ottawa in 1955 and worked closely with Pierre Perrault in directing thirteen half-hour films about the north shore of the St. Lawrence River called "Au pays de Neuve-France". Bonnière has worked extensively in both English and French television as well as in the feature film field. His **Amanita Pestilens** introduced Geneviève Bujold in 1964. His most recent film, **Hamlet**, is a youthful production photographed with a hand-held camera by Richard Leiterman. Bonnière works out of Toronto.

FILMOGRAPHY (incomplete)

1957 **Craftsmen of Canada** (Maîtres artisans du Canada). Prod: Crawley Films. 30 min.

1958 "Au Pays de Neuve-France" (St. Lawrence North). **La Traversée**
-60 **d'hiver à l'Ile aux Coudres** (Winter Crossing at Ile aux Coudres); **Attiuk** (Attiuk), **Le Jean Richard** (Jean Richard); **Tête-à-la-Baleine** (Whalehead); **L'Anse Tabatière** (Winter Sealing at La Tabatière); **Ka-Ke-Ki-Ku** (Ka-Ke-Ki-Ku); **Anse-aux-Basques** (Whalehunter at L'Anse-aux-Basques); **En revenant de St-Hilarion** (Soirée at St. Hilarion); **Diamants du Canada** (Canadian Diamonds); **Les Goélettes** (On the Sea); **Rivière du gouffre** (Turlutte); **La Pitoune** (Three Seasons); **Toutes Isles** (Land of Jacques Cartier). Prod. & Script: Pierre Perrault, Crawley Films for Radio-Canada, 30 min. each. col.

1961 **Abitibi**. Prod. René Bonnière, Crawley Films. 30 min. col.

1963 **Les Annanacks** (The Annanacks). Prod: R. Bonnière, Crawley Films for NFB. 1 hr. col.

Les Faux Visages (False Faces). Prod: R. Bonnière, Crawley Films. 60 min. col.

1964 **Amanita Pestilens** (Amanita Pestilens). Prod: F. R. Crawley, Crawley Films, 90 min. col.

1966 Over twenty "Telescopes" for CBC. Among them, **Gratien Gélinas**
-71 (1967); **Alex Colville** (1967); **Robert Charlebois** (1970); **Veronica Tennant** (1970); **Farley Mowat** (1970) and **Jean Gascon** (1971). Each 30 min. col.

1968 Directed a number of dramas in series "Wojeck", produced by Ron
-71 Weyman, "McQueen", also Ron Weyman, and "Anthology" produced by Ron Weyman and Dick Gilbert. Other dramas were produced for the series "Canadian Short Stories" (David Peddie) and "Five Years in the Life" (Michael Rothery).

1969 **Alexis de Tocqueville.** Prod: Lister Sinclair, CBC for Intertel. 60 min. col.

1970 **The Firebrand.** Prod: Alice Sinclair. CBC for Intertel. 60 min. col.

1971 **Four Day Wonder.** Prod: Ron Weyman, CBC "Anthology". 60 min. col.

1972 **Hamlet**. Prod: R. Bonnière, Crawley Films. Approx. 150 min. col.

BIBLIOGRAPHY

Objectif, October-November, 1964, pp. 47-49, "Bandes à part".

Objectif 61, pp. 21-22, "Dix-sept artisans du cinéma canadien" (with a descriptive filmography).

Objectif 9-10, pp. 22-23. (Bio-filmography.)

The Montreal Star, October 20, 1962, p. 43, "$200,000 Movie Being Produced Here", by Dusty Vineberg.

References in: *Vingt Ans de cinéma au Canada français, Jeune Cinéma canadien,* and *Le Cinéma canadien.*

BRAULT, MICHEL

Born in Montreal, 1928, Michel Brault began his film career while in university collaborating as cameraman with Claude Jutra on a number of shorts, and between 1950 and 1951 working on a film magazine, *Découpage*. His work as a cameraman both within and outside of the National Film Board has been impressive and influential; he had been cameraman for two television series, "Petites Médisances" and "Images en boîte" before joining the NFB's Candid Eye Unit with Koenig, Kroitor and Macartney-Filgate; he is credited as cameraman on **The Days Before Christmas** and **Festival in Puerto Rico** in that series. He later worked with Jean Rouch, the French anthropologist-filmmaker on **la Punition** and **Chronique d'un été** and with Mario Ruspoli on **Regards sur la folie, la Fête prisonnière** and **les Inconnus de la terre**. In 1962, Brault collaborated with Montreal students Denys Arcand and Denis Héroux to photograph **Seul ou avec d'autres**, and with Claude Jutra to film **A tout prendre**. In recent years Brault has photographed key Quebec films: **Faut aller parmi l'monde pour le savoir** by Dansereau, **Mon Oncle Antoine** and **Kamouraska** by Jutra, Groulx's **Entre tu et vous**, and le Temps d'une chasse, by Francis Mankiewicz.

FILMOGRAPHY

1958 **Les Raquetteurs.** With Gilles Groulx. Prod: Louis Portuagais, NFB. 28 min. b&w.

1961 **La Lutte** (Wrestling). With C. Jutra, M. Carrière, C. Fournier. Prod: Jacques Bobet, NFB. 28 min. b&w.

1962 **Quebec-USA** or **l'Invasion pacifique** (Visit to a Foreign Country). With Claude Jutra. Prod: Fernand Dansereau, NFB. 28 min. b&w.

1963 **Les Enfants du silence.** With C. Jutra. Prod: Fernand Dansereau and Victor Jobin, NFB. 24 min. b&w.

 Pour la suite du monde (Moontrap). With Pierre Perrault. Prod: Fernand Dansereau, NFB. 105 min. b&w.

1964 **Le Temps perdu** (The End of Summer). Prod: Fernand Dansereau, NFB, for "Temps Présent". 27 min. b&w.

 La Fleur de l'âge: section **Geneviève**. Prod: André Belleau and Victor Jobin, NFB. 28 min. b&w.

1966 **Québec . . . ?** with Gilles Groulx. Prod: Les Cinéastes Associés Inc. for Office du Film du Québec. 30 min. b&w.

1967 **Entre la mer et l'eau douce.** Prod: Pierre Patry, Cooperation. 87 min. b&w.

Conflicts. Prod: Crawley Films for the Canadian Pavilion, Expo 67. 4½ min. Two screens. col.

1968 **Les Enfants du néant.** Prod: Pyranha Films, France. 60 min. b&w.

Eloge du chiac. Prod: Guy L. Côté, NFB. 28 min. b&w.

1971 **L'Acadie, l'Acadie.** With Pierre Perrault. Prod: Guy l'Côté and Paul Larose, NFB. 117 min. b&w.

BIBLIOGRAPHY

Cahiers du cinéma in English, No. 4, p. 42, "10 Questions to 5 Canadian Filmmakers". (Interview.)

La Presse, June 22, 1968, p. 37, "Michel Brault: Pourquoi veut-on parler français?", an interview with Luc Perrault.

La Presse, June 29, 1968, "J'ai perdu l'espoir du monde. . . ", by Michèle Favreau.

Le Petit Journal, January 23, 1966, an interview with Michèle Gelinas.

La Patrie, Montreal, September 12, 1971, "L'ONF poursuit sa politique de censure", by Robert Levesque.

Le Devoir, December 12, 1961, "Opinion de Jean Rouch: le Canadien Michel Brault est le meilleur opérateur du monde".

Objectif, No. 3, December 1960, pp. 3-16, "Michel Brault et Claude Jutra racontent Jean Rouch", an interview with Robert Daudelin and Michel Patenaude.

L'Ecran (Montreal) No. 2, pp. 7-15, "Entretien de deux cinéastes".

Le Soleil, November 7, 1970, "Michel Brault: mettre le pays sur pellicule", by Paul Roux. (Interview.)

Séquences No. 68, February 1972, pp. 4-14, "Entretien avec Michel Brault". (Interview.)

La Presse, February 8, 1969, *"Les Enfants du néant* de Michel Brault en *Quinzaine",* by Louis Marcorelles.

Québec-Presse, February 13, 1972, *"L'Acadie, l'Acadie* s'adresse plus aux québécois qu'aux acadiens. . . ".

Extensive criticism in *Vingt Ans de cinéma au Canada français, Le Cinéma canadien* and *Jeune Cinéma canadien;* numerous references in *Essais sur le cinéma québécois.*

Cinéastes du Québec No. 11: Michel Brault. CQDC. Introduction by Gilles Marsolais. Interview by André La France, Yves Leduc and Gilles Marsolais. Filmography and bibliography.

Louise Marleau and Geneviève Bujold in la Fleur de l'âge, *a co-production with France, Italy and Japan, presenting four stories of adolescence. Brault directed the Canadian segment,* Geneviève.

BRITTAIN, DONALD

Born in Ottawa in 1928, Donald Brittain worked as a journalist, then in 1954 joined the National Film Board as a writer. As well as scripting most of his own films, Brittain wrote and animated **The One Man Band that Went to Wall Street** for the New York Stock Exchange; scripted and co-produced with Joseph Koenig "Canada At War" (thirteen documentaries); wrote the commentary for **Stravinsky** (Koenig and Kroitor), the animated spoof **What On Earth** (Pindal and Drew), **The Railrodder** (Potterton), **Labyrinth** (Low) and **Helicopter Canada,** among others. In 1970 he worked with Georges Dufaux and Roman Kroitor on **Tiger Child** for the Fuji Group Pavilion at Osaka. Presently with Potterton Productions in Montreal, Brittain produced Larry Kent's **The Apprentice.**

FILMOGRAPHY

1958 **Setting Fires for Science** (Les Incendiares). Prod: Peter Jones, NFB. 20 min. col.

1960 **A Day in the Night of Jonathan Mole.** Prod: Peter Jones, NFB for the Department of Labor. 29 min. b&w.

1963 **Fields of Sacrifice** (Champs d'honneur). Prod: D. Brittain, NFB. 38 min. col.

1964 **The Campaigners.** Prod: D. Brittain, CBC "This Hour Has Seven Days". 35 min. b&w.
Bethune. (Bethune, héros de notre temps). With John Kemeny. Prod: J. Kemeny & D. Brittain, NFB. 59 min. b&w.

1965 **Mosca.** Prod: D. Brittain, CBC "This Hour Has Seven Days". 10 min. b&w.

1966 **Ladies and Gentlemen, Mr. Leonard Cohen.** With Don Owen. Prod: John Kemeny, NFB. 41 min. b&w.
Memorandum (Pour mémoire). With John Spotton. Prod: John Kemeny, NFB. 58 min. b&w.

1967 **Never a Backward Step** (La Presse et son empire). With Arthur Hammond and John Spotton. Prod: Guy Glover, NFB. 57 min. b&w.

1968 **Saul Alinsky Went to War.** With Peter Pearson. Prod: John Kemeny, NFB. 57 min. b&w.

1970 **Tiger Child.** Prod: Roman Kroitor & Kiichi Ichikawa, Multi-Screen Corp. for Expo '70.

1971 **The Noblest of Callings, the Vilest of Trades.** With Cameron Graham. Prod: CBC "CBC White Paper". 90 min. col.

BIBLIOGRAPHY

Ici Radio-Canada, Vol. 5, No. 26, June 19, 1971, p. 3, "Bethune, héros de notre temps".

The Montreal Star, September 3, 1966, p. 27, "The Face on the Documentary Floor", by Stephen Franklin.

Film Quarterly (the English periodical), Winter 1966-67, a review of **Memorandum,** by Henry Breitrose.

Maclean's Magazine, November 1968, p. 111, "Q: Where's the Best Place to See Canada in '70? A: Osaka" (review of **Tiger Child**).

The Canadian Magazine, April 25, 1970, p. 16, "The Fuji Film—Good, Almost Great" (on **Tiger Child**).

The Montreal Star, July 11, 1970, "*Tiger Child* Packs 'em In at the Very Fat Caterpillar Called a Pavilion at Osaka", by Harry Reade.

American Cinematographer, July 1970. Most of this issue dedicated to "Film at Expo '70", with a discussion of **Tiger Child** by Brittain, Dufaux and Kroitor.

Le Cinéma canadien. (References.)

CARLE, GILLES

Born in Maniwaki, Quebec, in 1929, Gilles Carle began his career as a
graphic artist (his drawings grace *How To Make or Not to Make a Canadian
Film*) and critic, joining the National Film Board in 1960 as a researcher.
His first feature, **La Vie heureuse de Léopold Z**, a happy comedy about
a snow-plow driver, was also the first National Film Board feature to gain
popularity in Quebec movie houses. He has since been critically and
popularly received in France. Carle's charm is in part attributable to
his fast-moving action, watched over by an ironic eye. He is a partner in
the production company Carle-Lamy in Montreal.

FILMOGRAPHY

1961 **Manger**. With Louis Portugais. Prod: Fernand Dansereau and Victor
Jobin. NFB. 30 min. b&w.
Dimanche d'Amérique. Prod: Jacques Bobet, NFB. 28 min. b&w.

1962 **Patinoire** (The Rink). Prod: Jacques Bobet, NFB. 10 min. col.

1963 **Natation** (Olympic Swimmers) Prod: Jacques Bobet, NFB. 27 min.
b&w.
Patte mouillée (The Big Swim) Prod: Jacques Bobet, NFB. 10 min.
b&w.

1964 **Solange dans nos campagnes**. Prod: Jacques Bobet, NFB. 26 min.
b&w.
Un Air de famille. Prod: Fernand Dansereau and Victor Jobin, NFB.
28 min. b&w.
Percé on the Rocks (Percé on the Rocks). Prod: Jacques Bobet, NFB.
10 min. col.

1965 **La Vie heureuse de Léopold Z** (The Merry World of Leopold Z)
Prod: Jacques Bobet, NFB. 69 min. b&w.

1966 **Place à Olivier Guimond**. Prod: André Lamy, Onyx Films Inc. 60
min. col.

1967 **Place aux Jerolas**. Prod: André Lamy, Onyx Films Inc. 60 min. col.
Le Québec à l'heure de l'Expo. Prod: Raymond-Marie Léger, Office
du film du Québec for l'Office d'information et de publicité et le
ministère de l'industrie et du commerce. 20 min. col.

1968 **Le Viol d'une jeune fille douce** (The Rape of a Sweet Young Girl). Prod: Onyx-Fournier Ltée. 85 min. col.

1970 **Red.** Prod: Lamy, Onyx Films/S.M.A. 101 min. col.

Les Mâles. Prod: Fernand Rigard, Onyx Films/France Films. 113 min. col.

Stereo. Prod: Office du Film du Québec. 18 min. col.

1972 **La Vraie Nature de Bernadette.** Prod: Pierre Lamy, Les Productions Carle-Lamy. 97 min. col.

Les Chevaliers. Prod: C.O.F.C.I. for O.R.T.F. 55 min. col.

1973 **La Mort d'un bûcheron.** Prod. Pierre Lamy, Carle-Lamy Productions. 115 min. col.

Les Corps célestes (in preparation).

(l. to r.) Marcel Sabourin, Denyse Filiatrault and Carole Laure in Carle's la Mort d'un bûcheron.

BIBLIOGRAPHY

Cinéastes du Québec 2: Gilles Carle, CQDC, 1970. Criticism, an interview by Robert Daudelin and Roger Frappier, filmography and bibliography.

The Montreal Gazette, November 22, 1969, "Gilles Carle: from Percé Rocks to Indians", by Dane Lanken. (Interview.)

Montreal Star, November 27, 1971, p. C1, "Joys of Moviemaking", by Martin Malina, (Interview.)

Le Devoir, Montreal, December 28, 1968 (on **The Rape of a Sweet Young Girl**).

Québec-Presse, Montreal, November 2, 1969, an interview on **Red**.

Cinéma 69 (Paris) No. 140, November 2, 1969, interview on **Red**.

Séquences, No. 65, April 1971, pp. 4-15 (interview).

Dossiers de cinéma: 1, Fides, 1968, on **Percé on the Rocks**.

The Montreal Star, August 24, 1968, "Gilles Carle's Bouillabaisse of Visual Exuberance", by Stephen Franklin.

Le Soleil, Quebec, June 6, 1970, p. 42, "Gilles Carle, un réalisateur solitaire", by Paul Roux.

Le Magazine Maclean, March 1972, pp. 38, 41, 45-49, "Gilles Carle, la québécoise en tête", by Jacques Guay.

Reviews in: *Vingt Ans de cinéma au Canada français, Essais sur le cinéma québécois, Jeune Cinéma canadien, Le Cinéma québécois: tendances et prolongements,* and *Le Cinéma canadien.*

CARRIERE, MARCEL

Born in Bouchette, Quebec in 1935, Marcel Carrière studied electronic engineering, joining the National Film Board first as a summer student and later full-time as a sound engineer in 1956. In that capacity he has been involved with some of the most impressive films produced by the Board: **Lonely Boy, Stravinsky** (Kroitor and Koenig); **Le Chat dans le sac, Un Jeu si simple** (Groulx); **The Days of Whiskey Gap** (Low); **Les Raquetteurs** (Brault and Groulx); **Les Enfants du silence** (Brault and Jutra); **Rose et Landry** (Rouch and Godbout); **Le Festin des morts** (Dansereau); **60 Cycles** (Labrecque); **Pour la suite du monde** (Brault and Perrault). Carrière also did the sound for Jutra's independently produced **A tout prendre**. He has worked as a cameraman, shooting **Nassau** with Bob Drew Associates in New York, and recently Gosselin's **Capture**. Carrière teaches in the Department of Communications at the University of Quebec.

FILMOGRAPHY

1961 **La Lutte** (Wrestling). With Claude Jutra, Claude Fournier & Michel Brault. Prod: Jacques Bobet, NFB. 28 min. b&w.

1963 **Rencontres à Mitzic**. With Georges Dufaux. Prod: Fernand Dansereau, NFB. 27 min. b&w.

1965 **Villeneuve, peintre-barbier**. Prod: Fernand Dansereau, NFB. 16 min. col.

1966 **Bois-francs**. Prod: Michel Moreau, NFB. 26 min. col.

1967 **The Indian Speaks** (L'Indien parle). Prod: André Belleau, NFB. 40 min. col.

1968 **Les Zouaves** or **Avec tambours et trompettes**. Prod: Robert Forget, NFB. 28 min. col.

   Better Housing in B.C. Prod: André Belleau, NFB for Central Mortgage and Housing Corp. 16 min. col.

   Episode. Prod: Robert Forget, NFB. 59 min. col.

1969 **Saint-Denis dans le temps** . . . Prod: Robert Forget, NFB. 84 min. col.

1970 **Hotel-château**. Prod: Marc Beaudet, NFB. 59 min. b&w.

   10 Milles/heures. Prod: Marc Beaudet & Pierre Maheu, NFB for Osaka '70. 17 min. col.

1972 **Paul Laliberté** (feature work in progress).

BIBLIOGRAPHY

La Presse, April 28, 1970, "Comment passer un Québec", by Luc Perreault.

La Presse, April 25, 1970, on **Saint-Denis dans le temps** . . .

Image et Son, No. 252, 1971, pp. 243-244.

How to Make or Not to Make a Canadian Film, "Where's the Sound?", by Marcel Carrière on his work in sound.

Canadian Film — Past and Present, La Cinémathèque canadienne, 1967, article by Carrière on the filming of **Stravinsky**. Available for reference only at film study libraries and reprinted in *Eléments pour un nouveau cinéma,* by Louis Marcorelles, UNESCO, Paris, 1970.

Le Devoir, April 25, 1970, an interview.

Reviews in: *Vingt Ans de cinéma au Canada français, Le Cinéma canadien* and *Le Cinéma québécois: tendances et prolongements.*

CARTER, PETER

Born in England in 1933, Peter Carter joined Crawley Films in 1954 as an assistant editor and later as an assistant director. In the latter capacity, Carter worked closely with Paul Almond, Don Haldane, George Gorman and Fergus MacDonald — all of whom directed segments for the series "R.C.M.P." After four years in England, Carter returned to Canada as assistant director on Maxine Samuel's "Seaway" and "Forest Rangers", and CBC's "Hatch's Mill". As an associate producer he has been involved with Paul Almond's **Act of the Heart** and Eric Till's **A Fan's Notes**. His feature **The Rowdyman** was written by and stars actor Gordon Pinsent; executive producer was F. R. Crawley. Carter has directed many dramatic television shows in CBC's "Anthology" and "Theatre Canada".

FILMOGRAPHY

1969 **Does Anybody Here Know Denny?** Prod: CBC "Corwin". 90 min. col.

1970 **The Salient**. Prod: CBC "Theatre Canada". 30 min. col.
The Day They Killed the Snowman. Prod: CBC "Theatre Canada". 60 min. col.
God's Sparrows. Prod: CBC "Theatre Canada". 30 min. col.
In Exile. Prod: CBC "Theatre Canada". 30 min. col.
A Token Gesture. Prod: CBC "Theatre Canada". 30 min. col.
Rigmarole. Prod: CBC "Theatre Canada". 30 min. col.
The Mercenaries. Prod: CBC "Anthology". 90 min. col.

1972 **The Rowdyman**. Prod: Lawrence Dane, Canart Films. 96 min. col.

BIBLIOGRAPHY

The Ottawa Citizen, August 27, 1971, "Canadian Actor Turns to Playwriting".

Maclean's Magazine, June, 1972, by John Hofsess.

CHABOT, JEAN

Born in Saint-Jean-Baptiste in 1945, Jean Chabot received his BA and studied economics at the University of Montreal. He first made a number of short films and worked in Montreal at Cinéfilms as an assistant cameraman and editor. As a critic, Chabot has written for *Le Devoir, Sept-Jours,* and *Cinéma Québec* and his interviews feature prominently in the dossier *Cinéastes du Québec* published by Le Conseil québécois pour la diffusion du cinéma. Chabot's first feature film, **Mon Enfance à Montréal,** a surreal and poignant image of a family locked in poverty, was produced within the program "Premières Oeuvres" at the National Film Board under Jean-Pierre Lefebvre's direction.

Marc Hébert as the father and Nana de Varennes as the mother in Chabot's touching image of childhood, Mon Enfance à Montréal.

FILMOGRAPHY

1965 **Le Chapeau**. Prod: Independent. 30 min. col.
Dormez-vous. Prod: Independent. 30 min. b&w.

1966 **Porte Silence**. Prod: Independent. 15 min. b&w.

1967 **Des Pas dans l'univers**. Prod: Independent. 10 min. b&w.

1968 **Un Bicycle pour Pit**. With Clovis Durand. Prod: Independent. 20 min. col.

1970 **Mon Enfance à Montréal**. Prod: Jean-Pierre Lefebvre, NFB. 65 min. b&w.

1971 **Travelling Blues.** Prod: Les Ateliers audio-visuels du Québec for l'Office du film du Québec. 10 min. col.

Des Images travaillent. Prod: Les Ateliers audio-visuels du Québec for OFQ. 3 min. col.

1972 **Une Nuit en Amérique** (feature work in progress).

BIBLIOGRAPHY

L'Action Québec, July 24, 1969, a review of **Un Bicycle pour Pit,** by Jean-Pierre Guay.

Québec-Presse, February 14, 1972, *"Mon Enfance à Montréal,* l'histoire d'une enfance déracinée et brisée", an interview.

La Presse, February 13, 1971, "Jean Chabot".

Le Devoir, January 20, 1971, "Un témoignage de Jean Chabot et une précision de Jacques Parent", by Jean-Pierre Tadros.

Québec-Presse, February 15, 1970, "Les points sur les 'i' ", by Jean Chabot.

Le Devoir, February 13, 1971, "Deux jeunes cinéastes face à la réalité", by Jean-Pierre Tadros.

La Presse, March 7, 1970, "Cinéma québécois: la relève", by Luc Perreault.

CHAMBERS, JACK

Painter, sculptor, poet Jack Chambers was born in London, Ontario in 1931 and continues to live and work there. He founded the London Filmmakers' Coop in order to distribute films made by a number of artists living in the area — Greg Curnoe, Keewatin Dewdney, Fraser Boa and John Boyle; all are involved in making "personal films". Chambers' films are investigative in nature, not only in the subject matter but in the possibilities of the medium itself.

FILMOGRAPHY

1966 **Mosaic.** Prod: Independent. 9 min. b&w.

1967 **Hybrid.** Prod: Independent. 14 min. col.
  Little Red Ridinghood. Prod: Independent. 25 min. col.
  R34. Prod: Independent. 30 min. col.

1968 **Circle.** Prod: Independent. 35 min. col.
 -69

1970 **Heart of London.** Prod: Independent. 80 min. col.

1971 **C.C.C.I.** Prod: Independent. 20 min. col.

Chambers' films are distributed by the London Filmmakers' Coop and the Canadian Film-Makers' Distribution Centre.

BIBLIOGRAPHY

Artscanada, June 1968, "Artists as Filmmakers", by Ross Woodman, on the London group, in particular Chambers.

Artscanada, December 1968, "Let there be darkness", by Barry Lord.

Artscanada, April 1970, "The New Canadian Cinema: Images from the Age of Paradox", by Gene Youngblood, on the work of Greg Curnoe, Keewatin Dewdney and Chambers.

Toronto Daily Star, July 10, 1969, "Portrait of the Artist as a Winner".

CHAPMAN, CHRISTOPHER

Born in Toronto in 1927, Christopher Chapman is well-known as a director of poetic films on nature. Working first as a designer, Chapman began his film career by working alone with a Bolex camera, joining Crawley Films for eight months after making his first independent film, **The Seasons**. The multiple-dynamic image technique was pioneered by Chapman for **A Place to Stand** (Ontario Pavilion, Expo '67) and later used in Ontario's contribution to Osaka '70; as many as fifteen images work together on a 70mm image with a twelve-track sound system. In 1968, Chapman worked with Gower Champion on his mixed-media Broadway show, *The Happy Time,* creating a 70mm film sequence.

FILMOGRAPHY

1953 **The Seasons.** Prod: C. Chapman. 18 min. col.

1958 **Quetico.** Prod: C. Chapman for Quetico Foundation. 20 min. col.

1960 **Essay in Film.** Prod: C. Chapman, CBC. 10 min. b&w.

1961 **Village in the Dust.** Prod: C. Chapman for Imperial Oil. 20 min. col.

1962 **Saguenay.** Prod: Crawley Films for Aluminum Co. of Canada. 20 min. col.

1963 **The Persistent Seed** (Le Vert vivace). Prod: Hugh O'Connor, NFB. 14 min. col.

1964 **Enduring Wilderness** (Jardins sauvages). Prod: Ernest Reid, NFB. 28 min. col.

    Loring and Wyle. Prod: C. Chapman, CBC "Telescope". 30 min. b&w.

    Magic Molecule (La Molecule magique). With Hugh O'Conner. Prod: Nicholas Balla, NFB. 9 min. col.

    Expedition Bluenose. Prod: Maurice Taylor & John Trent, Taylor Television Productions for CBC. 60 min. col.

1967 **A Place to Stand.** Prod: C. Chapman, Exec. Prod: David Mackay, TDF Artists Limited for the Ontario Government. 17½ min. col.

1970 **Impressions 1670-1970.** Prod: Christopher Chapman Ltd. for the Hudson Bay Co. 34 min. col.

    Ontario. Prod: Christopher Chapman Ltd. for the Ontario Government and Osaka '70. 24 min. col.

    Festival. Prod: Christopher Chapman Ltd. 20 min. col. (a shortened, six-track version of **Ontario** for Ontario Place, Toronto).

BIBLIOGRAPHY

How to Make or Not to Make a Canadian Film, "The Birth of *A Place to Stand*", by Chapman.

Canadian Cinematography, January-February 1965, pp. 3, 6, 7, "Shooting *Expedition Bluenose",* by Chapman.

Toronto Daily Star, October 30, 1970, p. 7, a letter by Chapman headed "Is Call of the Wilderness Getting Too Dim to Hear?".

Food for Thought, Canadian Association for Adult Education, April 1958, pp. 319-325, "An interview with Christopher Chapman".

The Globe Magazine, May 9, 1959, pp. 16-17, "He Believes He Can Make His Kind of Film and Make a Living", by Dean Walker (an interview).

The Globe and Mail, July 12, 1969, "Chris Chapman Has two Places to Stand," by Melinda McCracken.

Weekend Magazine, No. 45, 1968, "Christopher Chapman is Collecting the Magic", by James Quig.

The Globe and Mail, June 3, 1970, "Ontario at Expo '70: More of the Same".

Le Cinéma canadien (references).

COTE, GUY L.

Born in Ottawa in 1925, Guy Côté (aided and assisted by his wife Nancy) has made a profound contribution in all areas of Canadian cinema; his work at the National Film Board has involved both the production and distribution of films, his own directing career having begun in amateur film circles at Oxford with the abstract film-ballet, *Between Two Worlds.* As a critic, Côté has contributed to leading world film magazines and his private critical collection, one of the largest and most impressive in Canada, now resides in (indeed, forms the basis of) Le Centre de documentation cinématographique of the Bibliothèque Nationale in Montreal. In the area of film education, Côté founded the bulletin *Canadian Newsreel* in 1952 as a liaison between film societies, and later organized (with Dorothy

Burritt), the Canadian Federation of Film Societies. This organization, in collaboration with the Canadian Film Institute, encouraged thousands of people in societies across the country to become literate in film. One of the first film archivists in Canada, Côté's personal collection is now owned by La Cinémathèque québécoise; this organization grew out of Connaissance du cinéma which Côté founded in 1962. Another large film archive which exists at the Canadian Film Institute was also co-founded by Côté. Director of the former Montreal International Film Festival, founder and first director of l'Association professionnelle des cinéastes, Côté is a pioneer without equal. Côté has produced numerous films. Among his recent ones are Jacques Leduc's **Chantal en vrac, Nominingue . . . depuis qu'il existe** and **Là ou ailleurs,** a number of Pierre Perrault's films and Anne Claire Poirier's **De mère en fille**.

FILMOGRAPHY (incomplete)

1957 **Industrial Canada** (Le Canada industriel). Prod: Nicholas Balla, NFB. 18 min. b&w.

1958 **Railroaders** (Les Cheminots) Prod: Tom Daly, NFB. 21 min. b&w.

1959 **Fishermen** (Les Pêcheurs) Prod: Tom Daly, NFB. 22 min. b&w.

1960 **Roughnecks** (Les Maîtres-sondeurs) Prod: Tom Daly, NFB. 21 min. b&w.

1961 **Cattle Ranch** (Têtes blanches) Prod: Tom Daly, NFB. 20 min. col.

1962 **Kindergarten**. Prod: Tom Daly, NFB. 22 min. b&w.
   An Essay on Science (Cité savante) Prod: Tom Daly, NFB. 20 min. col.

1965 **Regards sur l'occultisme**, parts 1 & 2. Prod: André Belleau, NFB. 58 min. each. b&w.

1972 **Tranquillement, pas vite**, parts 1 and 2. Prod: Normand Cloutier, NFB. 88 min. and 66 min. b&w.
   Mauricio-Cooperation. Prod: NFB (in preparation).

BIBLIOGRAPHY

Dossiers de cinéma: 1, Nos. 11 & 15, Edition Fides, 1968, on **Roughnecks** and **Cattle Ranch**.

Cahiers du cinéma, No. 53, December 1955, "Canada: un cinema pratique", by Côté.

The Quarterly of Film, Radio and Television, Vol. 7, No. 4, pp. 335-340, "Cinéma sans sense", by Côté.

Artscanada, April 1970, pp. 35-38, "Anybody Making Shorts These Days?", also by Côté.

Le Devoir, February 12, 1972, "Une partialité qui devient vite heurtante", on **Tranquillement, pas vite.**

Le Devoir, February 3, 1972, "Masse et petits groupes dans l'église", by Edmond Robillard, on **Tranquillement, pas vite.**

Cinéma Québec, Vol. 1, No. 8, March-April, 1972, pp. 21-26, a section by Richard Gay.

Reviews in: *Le Cinéma québécois: tendances et prolongements, Vingt Ans de cinéma au Canada français* (has an article by Pierre Pagneau), and *Jeune Cinéma canadien.*

Articles on Côté's work as an archivist:
The Montrealer, August 1966, p. 19, "Film Keeper, Guy L. Côté", by Martin Bronstein.

Objectif, April-May 1965, pp. 3-16, "Procès d'une collection", by Pierre Hébert.

Canadian Cinematography, May-June 1964, pp. 10-11, "Selling Job Must Be Done on Feature Films Says Guy Côté".

Le Magazine de la Presse, February 13, 1965, pp. 6, 8-9, "Les Mordus du cinéma ont enfin leur musée", by Lysiane Gagnon.

Objectif 62, August 1962, pp. 3-7, "Tous les mémoires du monde", by Côté.

Séquences, No. 26, pp. 4-5, "Cinéma, art et industrie".

CRONENBERG, DAVID

Born in Toronto in 1943, David Cronenberg studied literature at the University of Toronto. Severely structured, his two features **Stereo** and **Crimes of the Future** are philosophically witty comments on the relationship of the technological to the human world. Virtually a one-man unit, Cronenberg has acted as director, producer, writer and cameraman on all his independently-produced films.

FILMOGRAPHY

1966 **Transfer.** Prod: Independent. 7 min. col.
 From the Drain. Prod: Independent. 14 min. col.

1969 **Stereo.** Prod: D. Cronenberg, Emergent Films. 65 min. b&w.

1970 **Crimes of the Future.** Prod: D. Cronenberg, Emergent Films. 63 min. col.

1972 **Secret Weapons.** Prod: CBC "Program X". 22 min. col.

 Satyr's Tongue (feature work in progress).

BIBLIOGRAPHY

Take One, Vol. 2, Nos. 3 and 6.

Monthly Film Bulletin, British Film Institute, Vol. 38, No. 453, October 1971; and Vol. 38, No. 454, November 1971, both articles written by Tony Rayns.

The Montreal Gazette, June 23, 1969, *"Stereo* – an Interesting First", by Jacob Siskind.

The Montreal Star, June 23, 1969, "New Movies: Canadian Film Fresh, Unconventional", by Martin Malina.

Le Droit, Ottawa, June 24, 1969, *Stereo* de David Cronenberg", by Murray Maltais.

The Globe and Mail, October 18, 1969, "Happy Film Images and Money

to Boot", an interview by K.D.; and August 9, 1969, "New York Firm
Buys Toronto Man's Film", also an interview.

Film (England), No. 58, Spring 1970, pp. 27-28, "Filmmaking in Canada",
an interview.

DALY, THOMAS

Born in Toronto in 1918, Tom Daly came to the National Film Board in
1940 directly from university to work with Stuart Legg on the war propaganda film series, "The World in Action"; **Churchill's Island, The Gates
of Italy** and **The War for Men's Minds** used stockshots and newsreel footage in hard-hitting war documents. **The War for Men's Minds** used footage
from Leni Riefenstahl's **Triumph of the Will**, a film commissioned by
Hitler. From 1950 to 1964 Daly was executive producer of Unit B at
the National Film Board; consisting of about forty persons, Unit B made
all manner of films — animated, live action, educational and experimental—
and enclosed the Candid Eye Unit which was making films for television.
A producer and editor of wide experience, Daly was the editor-in-chief on
Labyrinth, a multi-screen film produced by the National Film Board for
Expo '67. Among his directed films are those in "The World in Action"
series — **Our Northern Neighbour** (1943), **Inside France** (1944), **Atlantic
Crossroads, Gateway to Asia, Ordeal by Ice, Road to Reich** (1945) and
Guilty Men (1946). Films he has produced include the following:
Universe (Low and Kroitor), **Circle of the Sun** and **The Days of the
Whiskey Gap** (Low), **Paul Tomkowicz, Street-Railway Switchman** (Kroi-
tor), **Runner** and **Cowboy and Indian** (Owen), **Satan's Choice** (Shebib)
and **Prologue** (Spry). Tom Daly is presently an executive producer at the
National Film Board.

BIBLIOGRAPHY

Objectif, October 1961, pp. 21-22, "Dix-sept artisans du cinéma canadien",
a critical article with a filmography up-to-date at publication.

Objectif, No. 9-10.

How to Make or Not to Make a Canadian Film, "From 'World in Action'
to 'Man in His World' ", by Daly.

DANSEREAU, FERNAND

Born in Montreal in 1928, Fernand Dansereau worked as a journalist before joining the NFB in 1956. One of the founding members of the NFB's French Unit, he helped to produce the French television series, "Temps présent", and later was involved in films dealing with social change for the Société Nouvelle Unit. Whether Dansereau is concerned with fictional stories, such as **La Canne à pêche** (from a story by Anne Hebert) and **Ca n'est pas le temps des romans**, or films as tools of change (**Saint-Jérome** and **Tout l'temps, tout l'temps, tout l'temps . . .?**) his character studies are heightened by a transforming perception. Dansereau is co-founder and president of a Montreal organization, In-Media, which produces visual documents for social change as well as providing services for social animation.

FILMOGRAPHY

1957 **La Communauté juive de Montréal**. Prod: Guy Glover, NFB. 29 min. b&w.

1958 **Le Maître du Pérou**. Prod: Léonard Forest, NFB "Panoramique". 49 min. b&w.

Pays neuf. Prod: Guy Glover and Léonard Forest, NFB. 45 min. b&w.

1959 **John Lyman, peintre**. Prod: Léonard Forest, NFB. 28 min. b&w.

La Canne à pêche. Prod: Léonard Forest, NFB "Temps présent". 30 min. b&w.

Pierre Beaulieu. Prod: Léonard Forest, NFB. Two parts of 30 min. each. b&w.

1960 **Les Administrateurs**. With Jacques Godbout. Prod: Léonard Forest, NFB. 60 min. b&w.

Congrès. With Jean Dansereau and Georges Dufaux. Prod: NFB. 28 min. b&w.

1965 **Le Festin des morts** (Mission of Fear). Prod: André Belleau, NFB. 79 min. b&w.

1967 **Ca n'est pas le temps des romans** (This is no Time for Romance). Prod: NFB. 28 min. col.

1968 **Saint-Jérome**. Prod: Robert Forget, NFB. 114 min. b&w (plus the original footage in a series of satellite films).

1969 **Tout l'temps, tout l'temps, tout l'temps . . . ?** Prod: Robert Forget, NFB. 115 min. b&w.

   Jonquière. Prod: F. Dansereau, S.M.A. Incorp. 28 min. b&w.

1970 **Le Ski!** (Ski!). Prod: Jean Dansereau, Les Cinéastes associés. 14 min. col.

1971 **Faut aller parmi l'monde pour le savoir . . .** Prod: In-Media for SSJB and SNQ. 84 min. col.

1972 **Rencontre.** Prod: Paul Larose, NFB. 88 min. b&w.

BIBLIOGRAPHY

Cinéma Québec, Vol. 1, No. 4, pp. 12-21. Criticism, interview and bio-filmography.

La Presse, Montreal, April 10, 1971, p. D9, "J'ai opté pour la libération"; and March 6, 1970 (interviews).

Le Devoir, Montreal, March 21, 1970 (interview).

Liberté, Vol. 8, No. 2/3, March-June 1966, pp. 73-77, an article by Dansereau.

La Presse, February 28, 1970, p. 41, "Le triomphe du vécu sur la fiction", by Luc Perrault.

La Presse, April 10, 1971, p. D9, "La clé du spectateur", by Luc Perrault.

Le Soleil, Québec, April 10, 1971, "A propos de libération".

La Presse, March 14, 1970, p. 23, "Un secteur de pointe".

Le Cinéma québecois: tendances et prolongements has a critique by Pierre Pageau.

Objectif 65, No. 32, August 1965, by Jean-Pierre Lefebvre, on **Le Festin des morts.**

Séquences, No. 51, December 1967, pp. 23-24, "Dialogue avec des cinéastes canadiens, le travail", by Maryse Grandbois.

Dossier du cinéastes No. 10: Fernand Dansereau, CQDC, 1972. A complete filmography, bibliography, reviews and an interview.

Challenge for Change Newsletter, Vol. 1, No. 2, Fall 1968, "Channelling Change in Quebec: Fernand Dansereau's *Saint-Jérome";* and Vol. 1, No. 3, Winter 1968-69, *"Saint-Jérome:* the Experience of a Filmmaker as Social Animator", by Fernand Dansereau.

DANSEREAU, MIREILLE

Born in Montreal in 1943, Mireille Dansereau studied film at the University of Montreal and the Royal College of Art in London. It was in London that she won first prize in the 1969 National Student Film Festival for her film, **Compromise.** Dansereau has worked in various capacities — as editor, script-assistant, soundwoman, producer, researcher and interviewer — for the CBC, National Film Board and ORTF in Paris. Aside from her film work, Dansereau has videotaped a number of programs for the Board's Challenge for Change Unit on women exploring themselves in work, and for a community group on immigrant women entitled **Les Immigrants.** Her film **Forum** was originally shot on video and she has since directed a video session with students at Sir George Williams University in Montreal. A member of a cooperative production unit, Dansereau is working with Anne-Claire Poirier on a series of films by and about women, produced by the National Film Board.

FILMOGRAPHY

1967 **Moi, un jour.** Prod: Independent. 10 min. b&w.

1968 **Compromise.** Prod: Independent. 28 min. b&w.

1969 **Forum.** Prod: Independent. 60 min. b&w.

1970 **Coccinelle.** Prod: Independent. 3 min. col.

1972 **La Vie rêvée.** Prod: Guy Bergeron at l'Association coopérative des productions audiovisuelles. 90 min. col.

   A propos d'une réflexion sur le mariage. Prod: NFB (in preparation).

Ms. Dansereau's independent films are distributed by Coopérative cinéastes independants, Montreal.

BIBLIOGRAPHY

La Patrie, October 13, 1968, "Une cinéaste québécoise à Londres."

Québec-Presse, January 18, 1970, *"Forum* ou comment se parler d'amour en se crachant à la figure".

The Montreal Star, November 14, 1970, *"Forum:* a Nifty Melodrama", by Juan Rodriquez.

Montréal-Matin, August 29, 1971, *"La Vie rêvée*: dont revait Mireille Dansereau", an interview by François Piazza.

Montreal Flash, September 27, 1971, "Le sexe faible a enfin son premier réalisateur cinématographique". (Interview.)

Chatelaine (French language), February 1972, "Tout sur tout". (Interview.)

Québec-Presse, August 1, 1971, p. 24, by Carol Faucher, "Une trentaine de jeunes cinéastes fondent une coopérative de production", on the founding and operation of the Association coopérative des productions audiovisuelles.

DEVLIN, BERNARD

Born in Quebec City in 1923, Bernard Devlin entered the National Film Board in 1946 as an editor, writer and director. He has been particularly involved in a number of series for television — among them, "On the Spot", which began in 1953 and was a series of documentary reports. Moving from English to French television production in 1954, Devlin produced the French version of "On the Spot" (Sur le vif) and collaborated with Léonard Forest, Fernand Dansereau and Louis Portugais on the series "Passe-partout" and "Panoramique". Devlin was the producer of the eighteen films of the series "Les Artisans de notre histoire" (produced in English by Julian Biggs). Devlin was director of the French section of production and head of English production at the National Film Board before returning recently to active film direction.

FILMOGRAPHY (incomplete)

1952 **L'Homme aux oiseaux** (The Bird Fancier). Prod: Guy Glover, NFB. 30 min. b&w.

1953 **L'Abatis** (The Settler). With Raymond Garceau. Prod: Guy Glover, NFB. 16 min. b&w.
Strongman. Prod: B. Devlin, NFB "On the Spot". 15 min. b&w.

1954 **Survival in the Bush.** Prod: Robert Anderson, NFB. 30 min. b&w.

1955 **L'Abbé Pierre.** Prod: B. Devlin, NFB "Sur le vif". 15 min. b&w.

1956 **Night Children.** Prod: Julian Biggs, NFB "On the Spot". 29 min. b&w.

1957 **Les Suspects.** Prod: Guy Glover, NFB "Passe-partout". 30 min. b&w.

1958 **Les Brûlés** (The Promised Land). Prod: Léonard Forest and Guy Glover, NFB "Panoramique". 114 min. b&w.

1960 **La Misère des autres** (Walk Down Any Street). Prod: Léonard Forest, NFB. 28 min. b&w.

1961 **Dubois et fils.** With Raymond Le Boursier. Prod: Léonard Forest, NFB. 59 min. b&w.

1962 **La Soif de l'or** (The Gold Seekers). With Raymond Garceau. Prod: R. Garceau and B. Devlin, NFB. 28 min. b&w.

1964 **David Thompson, the Great Mapmaker.** (David Thompson, cartographe). Prod: Guy Glover, NFB. 28 min. b&w.
The Voyageurs (Les Voyageurs). Prod: Nicolas Balla, NFB. 20 min. col.

1970 **The End of Nancy J.** Prod: B. Devlin, NFB for the Department of Fisheries and Forestry. 22 min. col.

BIBLIOGRAPHY

Séquences, October 1962, pp. 13-21, a review and interview by Pierre Théberge on **Louis-Hippolyte Lafontaine** (from the series, "Les Artisans de notre histoire").

References in: *Jeune Cinéma canadien, Le Cinéma canadien, Le Cinéma québécois: tendances et prolongements,* and *Vingt Ans de cinéma au Canada français.*

DUFAUX, GEORGES

Born in France in 1927, Georges Dufaux studied at the Ecole nationale de cinématographie before joining the National Film Board in 1956. As a cameraman he worked on two early drama series, "Passe-partout" and "Panoramique", being made weekly by the NFB for French television. In 1958 he shot Colin Low's **City Out of Time** and the following year joined Koenig, Kroitor and Filgate in the Candid Eye Unit, shooting the French section of **The Days Before Christmas**, Filgate's **Blood and Fire** and **I Was a Ninety Pound Weakling**. Since then, Dufaux has co-directed a number of films, among them **C'est pas la faute à Jacques Cartier**, a musical comedy. As a cinematographer, he shot **Rose et Landry** with Jean Rouch, **Tiger Child** for the Osaka exhibition and one of the first features for the French unit of the NFB, **le Festin des morts**. Harvey Hart's **Fortune and Men's Eyes**, Paul Almond's **Isabel**, Jacques Godbout's **Yul 871** and Clément Perron's **Taureau** were all shot by Dufaux.

FILMOGRAPHY

1959 **Bientôt Noël**. With T. Macartney-Filgate, W. Koenig and Stanley Jackson. Prod: Koenig and Kroitor, NFB. 30 min. b&w.

1960 **I Was a Ninety Pound Weakling**. With Wolf Koenig. Prod: R. Kroitor and W. Koenig, NFB. 24 min. b&w.

1961 **Les Dieux**. With Jacques Godbout. Prod: Fernand Dansereau, NFB. 29 min. b&w.

Pour quelques arpents de neige (Strangers for the Day). With Jacques Godbout. Prod: F. Dansereau, NFB. 28 min. b&w.

1962 **36,000 Brasses**. Prod: F. Dansereau, NFB. 28 min. b&w.

1963 **Rencontres à Mitzic**. With Marcel Carrière. Prod: F. Dansereau, NFB. 27 min. b&w.

1964 **Caroline**. With Clément Perron. Prod: F. Dansereau, NFB. 27 min. b&w.

A propos d'une plage. Prod: Claude Nedjar and André Belleau, NFB & ORTF. 26 min. b&w.

1965 **Les Départs nécessaires** (Sudden Departure) Prod: Marcel Martin, NFB. 35 min. b&w.

1966 **Precision** (Précision) Prod: Jacques Bobet, NFB. 10 min. col.

Michèle Chicoine in Clément Perron and George Dufaux's C'est pas la faute à Jacques Cartier.

1967 **Cinéma et Réalité.** With Clément Perron. Prod: C. Perron and
G. Dufaux, NFB. 58 min. b&w.

C'est pas la faute à Jacques Cartier. With Clément Perron. Prod:
C. Perron and G. Dufaux, NFB. 72 min. col.

1969 **L'Homme multiplié.** With Claude Godbout. Prod: Clément Perron,
NFB for split screen cinema, Terre des Homes.

1972 **A Cris perdus.** With Marc Beaudet. Prod: François Séguillon, NFB.
45 min. col.

BIBLIOGRAPHY

Liberté, Vol. 8, No. 2-3, March-June 1966, pp. 84-90, "Le fameux cinéma
candide", an interview by Jean-Claude Labrecque on the Candid Eye Unit.

How to Make or Not to Make a Canadian Film, "Picture and Film", by
Dufaux.

American Cinematographer, July 1970, pp. 671, 680-681, "Filming *Tiger
Child* in the World's Largest Film Format", by Dufaux. (The entire issue
is devoted to "Film at Expo '70".)

Dossiers du cinéma: 1, Fides, 1968, has a review of **Caroline**.

L'Action, July 25, 1969, a review of **C'est pas la faute à Jacques Cartier**.

The Globe and Mail, June 10, 1964, "A Cinematic Poem", by Dennis
Braithwaite (also a review of **C'est pas la faute à Jacques Cartier**).

References in: *Le Cinéma canadien, Vingt Ans de cinéma au Canada
français* and *Jeune Cinéma canadien.*

DUKE, DARYL

Born in Vancouver, Daryl Duke graduated in English and philosophy from the University of British Columbia. In 1950 he joined the National Film Board as a writer, film editor and assistant director. In 1953 he returned to Vancouver and to CBUT as supervising producer of the Vancouver Film Unit, working with Ron Kelly, Gene Lawrence and Allan King, among others. In Toronto in 1958 to 1964, Duke produced "Close-Up", "Explorations" and "Quest", leaving for the United States in 1964 to produce the Steve Allen Show and later the Les Crane Show for ABC. Since 1965 Duke has worked mainly in film and the following television series: "Telescope", "Document", "Sunday", and "Quentin Durgens" in Canada, and "The Senators", "The Psychiatrist" and "The Bold Ones" in the United States. Duke received an Emmy Award in 1970 as best director for **The Day the Lion Died** made in the series, "The Senators". Duke joined Norman Klenman and Edward Cowan in 1968 to form a production company, Galanty Productions in Vancouver.

FILMOGRAPHY (incomplete)

1965 **The Saskatchewan.** Prod: D. Duke, CBC. 60 min. col.

1968 **Thy Brother's Keeper.** Prod: CBC, "Quentin Durgens". 60 min. col.
Chocolate Fudge with Walnuts. Prod: CBC, "Quentin Durgens". 60 min. col.
The Road to Chaldaea. Prod: CBC, "Quentin Durgens". 120 min. col.

1969 **Hollywood: the Canadians.** Prod: Galanty Productions for CTV. 58 min. col.
The Spike in the Wall. Prod: Philip Keatly, CBC, "Manipulations". 60 min. col.

1970 **West Coast on my Mind.** Prod: D. Duke, Galanty Productions for CBC. 58 min. col.
God Bless the Children. Prod: Edgar Small, Universal Studios. 120 min. col.

1971 **The Cradle of Hercules.** Prod: Jack Laird, Universal Studios. 120 min. col.

The President's Plane is Missing. Prod: Mark Carliner, ABC Circle Films. 120 min. col.

1972 **Payday.** Prod: Marty Fink, Don Charpenter, Independent. 107 min. col.

BIBLIOGRAPHY

Toronto Daily Star, December 28, 1963, pp. 13, 20, "Star of the Year, TV Producer Daryl Duke", by Bob Reguly.

Toronto Daily Star, October 20, 1966, "Daryl Duke Shatters Momentary CBC Calm", by Roy Shields.

EWING, IAIN

Novelist, actor, songwriter, Iain Ewing was born in Ottawa in 1945; he attended the University of Toronto, studying history and philosophy. Ewing's film work has involved many of Toronto's young filmmakers in a kind of repertory cinema: Clarke Mackey photographed Ewing's **Picaro, Kill** and **Eat Anything** while Ewing worked on David Sector's **The Offering,** starred in David Cronenberg's **Stereo** and **Crimes of the Future,** was assistant editor on Don Shebib's **Goin' Down the Road** and acted, sang and wrote music for Mackey's **The Only Thing You Know.** Ewing travelled to India in 1971-72.

FILMOGRAPHY

1967 **Picaro.** Prod: Independent. 27 min. col.

1969 **A Short Film.** Prod: Independent. 3 min. b&w.
      Kill. Prod: Independent. 85 min. b&w.

1970 **Eat Anything.** Prod: Hallelujah Productions. 84 min. col.

All of Iain Ewing's films are distributed by the Canadian Film-makers' Distribution Centre.

BIBLIOGRAPHY

The Globe and Mail, November 19, 1966, p. 17, "Shoestring Productions Ltd.", by Bruce Lawson.

The Gazette, Montreal, October 21, 1966, "Young Filmmaker Repelled by Plastic People", by Marilyn Argue.

Take One, Vol. 2, No. 3, in which Ewing co-interviewed Peter Fonda.

Saturday Night, February 1970, a review by Marshall Delaney.

Toronto Daily Star, December 13, 1968, "5 'Shot' at T-D Centre — That's Show Biz".

FERGUSON, GRAHAME

Born in Toronto in 1929, Grahame Ferguson attended the University of Toronto where he was actively involved in the film society. He was a summer student at the National Film Board in 1950 and with the Swedish film director, Arne Sucksdorff on **The Flute and the Arrow,** filmed in India. Ferguson has lived, and made the majority of his films, in the United States. In 1970 he returned to Canada to set up Grahame Ferguson Films Ltd. and recently, Multi-Screen Corporation with Roman Kroitor and Robert Kerr, in Montreal and Galt, Ontario. This unit developed the revolutionary Imax system used at Ontario Place. Ferguson has also made numerous documentaries and commercials in the United States and Canada.

FILMOGRAPHY

1961 **The Legend of Rudolph Valentino.** Prod: Saul J. Turell and Paul Killiam for Wolper-Sterling. 60 min. b&w.

1964 **The Love Goddesses.** Prod: G. Ferguson and Saul J. Turell for Walter Reade-Sterling Inc. 83 min. b&w. & col.

1965 **The Days of Dylan Thomas.** Prod: Rollie McKenna, Grahame Ferguson Films Ltd. 25 min. b&w.

1967 **Man and the Polar Regions.** Prod: G. Ferguson and Robert Kerr, Ferguson-Kerr Multi-Screen Ltd. for Expo '67. 18 min. col.

1968 **The Virgin President.** Prod: G. Ferguson, Severn Darden and James Hubbard, Grahame Ferguson Films Ltd. 85 min. b&w.

IBM Close-Up. With Roman Kroitor. Prod: R. Kroitor, Multi-Screen Corp. for IBM.

1971 **North of Superior.** Prod: G. Ferguson, Multi-Screen Corp. for Ontario Place. 18 min. col.

1972 **The Question of Television Violence.** Prod: Colin Low, NFB for "Challenge for Change" (work in progress).

BIBLIOGRAPHY

The Montreal Star, January 22, 1966, "Questions and Answers from Film-maker Ferguson", by Martin Malina (interview).

The Montreal Star, December 24, 1966, "Eighteen Months for Eighteen Minutes", by Dusty Vineberg (interview).

The Globe and Mail, October 5, 1965, "Lack of Funds Curbs Filming in Canada", by Frank Morriss (interview).

La Presse, July 16, 1966, "Une galerie des grandes déesses du septième art", by Michèle Favreau (interview).

The Toronto Daily Star, October 16, 1965, p. 20, "Fifty Years of Love Goddesses: Did Bara's Charms Pale Bardot's?", by David Cobb.

The Telegram, Toronto, October 23, 1965, "The Lovely Love Goddesses", by Clyde Gilmour.

Films and Filming, July 1, 1965, a review of **The Love Goddesses.**

Maclean's Magazine, January 1972, "Your Friendly Neighbourhood Cinéastes", by John Hofsess.

The Ottawa Journal, November 2, 1968, "What's new at the movies, you ask? Multivision, that's what! With a screen seven storeys high and half again as wide", by Jeff Carruthers.

FOREST, LEONARD

Born in Chelsea, Massachusetts in 1928 of Acadian parents, Léonard Forest grew up in Moncton, New Brunswick. He worked as a broadcaster and journalist before joining the National Film Board in 1953. As a director and producer, Forest has been involved in a number of television series — "Passe-partout", "Temps present", "Panoramique" and "Profils et Paysages"; the latter series, with direction by Bernard Devlin, Fernand Dansereau, Louis Portuguais and Claude Jutra, marks the significant steps of the social and political evolution of French Canada. A published poet, Forest has written the scenarios for many films — among them, **Pêcheurs de Pomcoup, La Vie est courte, Amitiés haïtiennes, Mémoire en fête** and **les Acadiens de la dispersion**. Forest has recently been involved in "Société nouvelle", the French Unit's "Challenge for Change"; his innovative work there includes **La noce n'est pas finie**, a fictional feature with historical dimensions, collectively written and acted by citizens in north-east New Brunswick.

FILMOGRAPHY

1954 **La Femme de ménage.** Prod: Roger Blais, NFB. 11 min. b&w.

1955 **Les Aboiteaux** (The Dikes). With Roger Blais. Prod: Roger Blais, NFB. 29 min. b&w.

    Midinette (Needles and Pins). With Roger Blais. Prod: Roger Blais, NFB. 19 min. b&w.

1956 **Pêcheurs de Pomcoup** (Fishermen of Pubnico). With Victor Jobin. Prod: Roger Blais, NFB. 25 min. b&w.

    Le Monde des femmes. Prod: NFB. 30 min.

1957 **The Whole World Over — Mexican Episode.** Prod: Julian Biggs, NFB. 30 min. b&w.

1958 **Amitiés haïtiennes**. Prod: Guy Glover, NFB "Passe-partout". 30 min. b&w.

1964 **Mémoire en fête** (Walls of Memory). Prod: Marcel Martin, NFB. 27 min. b&w.

A la recherche de l'innocence (In Search of Innocence) Prod: Jacques Bobet and Victor Jobin, NFB. 28 min. col.

1968 **Les Acadiens de la dispersion**. Prod: Clément Perron, NFB. 118 min. b&w.

1969 **Acadie libre**. Prod: Francois Seguillon, NFB. 22 min. b&w. A satellite film of **les Acadiens de la dispersion**.

1971 **La noce n'est pas finie**. Prod: François Séquillon, NFB. 84 min. b&w.

1972 **Out of Silence**. Prod: Robert Verrall and Dorothy Courtois, NFB. 38 min. col.

Nord-est 2000. Prod: NFB. (A videotape production currently in the works.)

BIBLIOGRAPHY

Objectif, No. 31, February-March 1965, "Travelling arrière", by Christian Rasselet — a review of **Mémoire en fête**.

La Presse, January 7, 1967, an article by Forest on **Les Acadiens de la dispersion**; and August 31, 1968, an interview with him concerning the same film.

(Press clippings re: **Les Acadiens de la dispersion**, September 10, 1968, have been collected by the National Film Board and are available at their offices or at film study centres.)

Le Soleil, Quebec, October 2, 1971, "Société nouvelle veut déranger", by G. Rheault on **La noce n'est pas finie**.

Medium Media, No. 1, Autumn 1971, "Un film c'est une question", an interview with Forest on **La noce n'est pas finie**.

Challenge for Change Newsletter, No. 7, Winter 1972, "Fiction Film as Social Animator". (Interview.)

Liberté, January-February, 1969 #9, pp. 69-70, "Un cinéaste à la recherche d'un film", by Forest.

A number of reviews in: *Jeune Cinéma canadien, Le Cinéma québécois: tendances et prolongements* and *Vingt Ans de cinéma au Canada français.*

Léonard Forest with members of the cast of La noce n'est pas finie.

FOURNIER, CLAUDE

Born in Waterloo, Quebec in 1931, Claude Fournier has been a journalist,
a publicist, poet and photographer as well as a filmmaker. As a cameraman,
Fournier shot many films that he directed or co-directed at the National
Film Board, and in the U.S. films directed by Leacock, Drew and Penne-
baker whom he joined for eighteen months in 1962; among the latter
are **Susan Star** and **Playboy Bunnies** by D. A. Pennebaker, **Nehru** by
Richard Leacock and **Eddie Sachs at Indianapolis** by Robert Drew and
Leacock. In 1963 he formed his own company in Montreal producing for
a number of ORTF and Radio-Canada television series; among these are
"Vingt ans express", "Cent Millions de jeunes" and "Villes du Canada".
The latter series was directed by Claude Sylvestre and shot by Fournier
and Michel Brault. In 1966 he worked with Omega Productions and
Crawley Films to produce a triple-screen production for the fifth theatre
of the Canadian Pavillion at Expo '67. Fournier's talent as a humorist has
made his features widely appealing to Quebec audiences.

FILMOGRAPHY

1959 **Télesphore Legaré, garde-pêche.** Prod: Léonard Forest, NFB. 29 min.
b&w.

1960 **La France sur un caillou.** With Gilles Groulx. Prod: Jacques Bobet,
NFB. 28 min. b&w.

Alfred Desrochers, poète. Prod: Léonard Forest, Jean Roy and Victor
Jobin, NFB. 28 min. b&w.

1961 **La Lutte** (Wrestling). With Claude Jutra, Michel Brault and Marcel
Carrière. Prod: Jacques Bobet, NFB. 28 min. b&w.

1962 **Midwestern Floods.** Prod: Filmakers/Drew Associates. 20 min. b&w.

1963 "Vingt ans express". Prod: Les Films Claude Fournier for Radio-
-64 Canada. 20-28 min. each. b&w. The following were directed by
Fournier: **Témoins de Jehova, Maliotenam, Les Jeunes Romanciers,
Bohèmes '64, Les Allelluyahs, Serge et Réal, Armageddon.**

1965 **Deux Femmes.** Prod: Les Films Claude Fournier for Radio-Canada,
"Cent Millions de jeunes". 28 min. b&w.

1966 **Londres.** Prod: Les Films Claude Fournier. 28 min. b&w.

Ti-Jean. Prod: Les Films Claude Fournier for Radio-Canada, "Cent Millions de jeunes". 28 min. b&w.

Tony Roman. Prod: Les Films Claude Fournier for Radio-Canada. 54 min. b&w.

Columbium. Prod: Office du Film du Quebec for Expo '67. 8 min. col.

Québec an 2000. Prod: Office du Film du Québec for Quebec Pavilion, Expo '67. 5 min. col.

On sait où entrer Tony, mais c'est les notes. Prod: Les Films Claude Fournier. 30 min. b&w.

Sebring, la cinquième heure. Prod: Les Films Claude Fournier. 20 min. col.

1968 **Le Dossier Nelligan**. Prod: Onyx-Fournier for Office du Film du Québec (OFQ). 80 min. col.

Hearts (Coeurs neufs). Prod: Les Films Claude Fournier for OFQ. 19 min. col.

Trente-mille employés de l'état du Québec. Prod: Les Films Claude Fournier for Le Conseil des syndicats nationaux. Six half-hour films.

Du général au particulier. Prod: Les Films Claude Fournier for OFQ. 28 min. col.

1970 **Deux Femmes en or**. Prod: Onyx-Fournier and France Films. 108 min. col.

1971 **Les Chats bottés** (The Master Cats). With Marie-Josée Raymond. Prod: Onyx-Fournier and France Films. 100 min. col.

1972 **Alien Thunder**. Prod: Onyx-Fournier (feature work in progress).

BIBLIOGRAPHY

Soirée Claude Fournier, The Cinématheque canadienne, 1966, a pamphlet with a filmography, critiques and an article by Fournier. Available only in film study libraries.

Séquences, April 1969, "Procès à Nelligan", by Léo Bonneville, on **le Dossier Nelligan**.

La Presse, March 15, 1969, "Protestation contre *le Dossier Nelligan*".

La Presse, March 1, 1969, *"Le Dossier Nelligan:* un procès jugé d'avance", by Luc Perreault.

Le Devoir, February 22, 1969, "Fallait-il nous tuer ce mythe?", by Claude Nadon and André Major, on **le Dossier Nelligan**.

The Montreal Star, May 23, 1970, "A Film *d'auteur*? No", by Martin Malina, on **Deux Femmes en or**.

The Montreal Gazette, June 13, 1970, on **Deux Femmes en or**.

Le Devoir, June 9, 1971, "Divertir en faisant 'miauler' de rire", by Jean-Pierre Tadros, on **les Chats bottés**.

La Presse, June 12, 1971, "Claude Fournier a le succès amer".

Québec-Presse, June 13, 1971, *"Les Chats bottés:* des vedettes connues des grosses farces, un film commercial", by Carol Faucher.

Le Devoir, May 23, 1970, "Claude Fournier par lui-même (ou presque)", by Christian Allegre — interview.

La Presse, May 23, 1970, "Claude Fournier, un gars qui ne se prend pas pour un autre", by Luc Perreault — interview.

A number of reviews in: *Vingt Ans de cinéma au Canada français, Le Cinéma québécois: tendances et prolongements* and *Jeune Cinéma canadien.*

FOX, BERYL

Born in Flin Flon, Manitoba in 1931, Beryl Fox studied history at the University of Toronto and joined the CBC in 1961, working on a number of public affairs series — "The Critical Years", "Document" and "This Hour Has Seven Days". Fox received the Wilderness Award given for the best television documentary and the Woman of the Year Award in 1966 for her coverage of the Viet Nam war, **Mills of the Gods: Viet Nam**; she and Douglas Leiterman received their first Wilderness Award for **One More River**. After the demise of "Seven Days", Fox worked with CBS and is presently a director/producer with Hobel-Leiterman Productions Ltd. in Toronto, co-producing "Here Come the Seventies (Towards the Year 2000)".

FILMOGRAPHY

1962 **Balance of Terror.** With D. Leiterman. Prod: D. Leiterman, Talent Associates-Paramount. 60 min.

   Servant of All. With D. Leiterman. Prod: D. Leiterman, CBC, "Document". 60 min.

1963 **Three on a Match.** With D. Leiterman. Prod: D. Leiterman, CBC, "Document".

   The Single Woman and the Double Standard. Prod: B. Fox, CBC.

   The Chief. With D. Leiterman. Prod: D. Leiterman, CBC. "Document". 60 min.

1964 **One More River.** With D. Leiterman. Prod: D. Leiterman, CBC, "Intertel". 50 min. b&w.

   Summer in Mississippi. Prod: B. Fox, CBC, "Seven Days". 27 min. b&w.

   The Honorable René Levesque. Prod: D. Leiterman, CBC.

1965 **Youth: In Search of Morality.** Prod: D. Leiterman, CBC, "Seven Days".

   Mills of the Gods: Viet Nam. Prod: B. Fox, CBC, "Seven Days". 56 min. b&w.

1968 **Last Reflections on a War.** Prod: B. Fox, CBS.

1969 **Be a Man — Sell Out.** Prod: CTV, "The Fabulous Sixties".

   North With the Spring. Prod: Hobel-Leiterman Prod. for CTV.

1971 **The Family: Life Styles of the Future.** Prod: Philip Hobel, for Hobel-Leiterman Productions, for "Here Come the Seventies".

1972 **Cinema: The Living Camera.** Prod: D. Leiterman for Hobel-Leiterman Productions, for "Here Come the Seventies".

   Human Potential (in progress).

BIBLIOGRAPHY

CBC Times, October 1964, an article by Fox on **Summer in Mississippi**.

Maclean's Magazine, February 1966, "One Woman's War", by Fox.

Star Weekly, February 12, 1966, "Front Line Filmmaker", by Margaret Steen.

Toronto Daily Star, May 22, 1965, "TV's Ash-blonde Paradox from Out of the West", by Marilyn Dunlop.

Star TV Week (Toronto), March 9, 1967, pp. 12, 34-35, "Beryl Fox", by H.R.W. Morrison.

Maclean's Magazine, July 23, 1966.

GAGNON, CHARLES

Painter and experimental filmmaker, Charles Gagnon was born in Montreal in 1934. He designed the Christian Pavilion at Expo '67, as well as creating the film for that exhibition, **The Eighth Day**. As a painter, Gagnon has had wide exhibition in Canada, the United States and Europe. He continues to work in Montreal, acting as artist-in-residence in the Department of Communication Arts, Loyola College.

FILMOGRAPHY

1967 **The Eighth Day** (Le Huitième Jour). Prod: C. Gagnon for the Christian Pavilion, Expo '67. 13 min. b&w.

1968 **The Sound of Space** (Le Son d'un espace). Prod: Independent. 27 min. b&w. Silent.

1966 **Pierre Mercure 1927-1966**. Prod: Independent. 33 min. col.
-70

1972 **R-69-Two Years Later.** Prod: Independent. 75 min. col. (work in progress).

All Gagnon's films are distributed by the *Coopérative cinéastes indépendants* and the *Canadian Film-makers' Distribution Centre.*

BIBLIOGRAPHY

Artscanada, April, 1970, pp. 39-42, "Charles Gagnon, Painter, Filmmaker, 35 Years Old, Lives in Montreal", by Danielle Corbeil.

The Montreal Star, October 2, 1971, "Zooming In . . . to Reach Out", by Denis O'Brien, on the Communication Arts Department at Loyola College.

La Presse, March 8, 1969, "Le tableau est aussi le monde", by Normand Theriault, on Gagnon's work as a painter.

GARCEAU, RAYMOND

Born near Trois-Rivières in 1919, Raymond Garceau entered the National Film Board in 1945 after studying agriculture at Laval University. His work there included a series of pre-"Challenge for Change" films made for ARDA (Aménagement rural et développement agricole); under the production of Garceau and André Belleau, the people of the lower St. Lawrence and the Gaspé were encouraged to express their problems and awareness of rural development. One of the classical poets of Canadian cinema, Garceau has produced many dramatic portraits in his investigation of life in a rural setting. His first feature, **le Grand Rock**, expresses the loss of innocence when faced with urban values.

FILMOGRAPHY (incomplete)

1952 **Le Bedeau.** Prod: Bernard Devlin, NFB. 6 min. b&w.
   L'Abatis (The Settler). With Bernard Devlin. Prod: Guy Glover, NFB. 16 min. b&w.

1953 **Monsieur le maire** (Mister Mayor). Prod: Roger Blais, NFB. 11 min. b&w.

Referendum (Tempest in Town). Prod: Bernard Devlin, NFB. 13 min. b&w.

1956 **La Drave** (Log Drive). Prod: David Bairstow, NFB. 29 min. b&w.

1957 **Ti-Jean s'en va dans l'ouest** (Ti-Jean Goes West). Prod: Léonard Forest, NFB. 25 min. col.

1958 **Une Ile du St. Laurent** (Crane Island). Prod: Léonard Forest, NFB. 11 min. b&w.

1961 **Rivière-la-paix**. Prod: Léonard Forest, NFB. 29 min. b&w.

La Chaudière (Wayward River). Prod: Léonard Forest, NFB. 28 min. b&w.

1962 **L'Homme du lac** (Alexis Ladouceur, métis) (The Lake Man). Prod: Victor Jobin and Bernard Devlin, NFB. 28 min. b&w.

La Soif de l'or (The Gold Seekers). With Bernard Devlin. Prod: R. Garceau and B. Devlin, NFB. 28 min. b&w.

1963 **Les Petits Arpents** (The Little Acres). Prod: Fernand Dansereau and Victor Jobin, NFB. 24 min. b&w.

1964 **Une Année à Vaucluse**. Prod: R. Garceau, NFB, "Temps présent". 28 min. b&w.

1965 **Travailleur forestier**. Prod: André Belleau, NFB, "ARDA No. 16", 22 min. b&w.

1966 **Diableries d'un sourcier** (The Water Devil). Prod: Guy L. Côté, NFB. 21 min. col.

1967 **Le Grand Rock**. Prod: Guy L. Côté, NFB. 73 min. col.

1969 **Vive la France**. Prod: Laurence Paré, NFB. 80 min. b&w.

1971 **Et du fils**. Prod: Pierre Gauvreau, NFB. 90 min. col.

1972 **Guérissez-nous du mal**. Prod: Paul Larose, NFB. 27 min. col.

BIBLIOGRAPHY

Objectif, November-December 1966, pp. 36-38, "Bandes à part".

Québec-Presse, December 21, 1968, "Congédier au moins 300 autres parasites à l'ONF", by A.B.

La Presse, April 8, 1967, pp. 21 and 39, "Le premier long metrage en couleur de l'ONF: *Le Grand Rock".*

La Presse, August 8, 1967, *"Le Grand Rock:* un film de Raymond Garceau sur la déchéance d'une génération sacrifiée", by Luc Perreault.

Press clippings collected by the NFB on **le Grand Rock**, March 28, 1969, available only at film study libraries.

Soirée Raymond Garceau, La Cinémathèque canadienne, January 1966, a pamphlet including a filmography, interview and criticism. Available only at film study libraries.

Séquences, April 1969, pp. 44-45, an interview.

La Presse, March 1, 1969, p. 29, "Un film qui accroche le gros public", interview by Luc Perreault.

La Patrie, Montreal, October 5, 1969, an interview.

Objectif published a series, "Les carnets d'un p'tit Garceau", by Garceau, in the following issues: No. 1, May-June 1966; No. 2, August 1966; No. 3, November-December 1966; No. 4, May 1967; and No. 5, August-September 1967.

Short reviews in: *Jeune Cinéma canadien; Essais sur le cinéma québécois Le Cinéma québécois; tendances et prolongements, Vingt ans de cinéma au Canada français* and *le Cinéma canadien.*

GODBOUT, JACQUES

Jacques Godbout has distinguished himself as a man of letters, publishing numerous collections of poetry and novels, and founding and editing the literary review, *Liberté*. After his studies at the University of Montreal Godbout taught in Ethiopia. He joined the National Film Board as a scriptwriter in 1958 becoming a director and later, in 1970, director of French production. His acclaimed musical-comedy **IXE-13** tells of the exploits of the Canadian espionage agent IXE-13, popular in serial novels by Pierre Saurel during the 1950s. François Dompierre and Godbout collaborated on the music and lyrics

FILMOGRAPHY

1961 **Les Dieux**. With Georges Dufaux. Prod: Fernand Dansereau and Victor Jobin, NFB. 28 min. b&w.

1962 **Pour quelques arpents de neige** (Strangers for a Day). With Georges Dufaux. Prod: Fernand Dansereau, NFB. 28 min. b&w.

A Saint Henri, le 5 septembre (September Five at Saint Henri). Prod: Fernand Dansereau, NFB. 42 min. b&w.

1963 **Rose et Landry**. With Jean Rouch. Prod: Fernand Dansereau, NFB. 28 min. b&w.

Paul Emile Borduas. Prod: Fernand Dansereau, NFB. 21 min. col.

1964 **Le monde va nous prendre pour des sauvages** (People Might Laugh at Us). With Françoise Bujold. Prod: André Belleau, NFB. 9 min. col.

Fabienne sans son Jules (Fabienne). Prod: Jacques Bobet, NFB. 27 min. b&w.

1965 **Huit Témoins**. Prod: André Belleau, NFB. 58 min. b&w.

1966 **Yul 871**. Prod: André Belleau, NFB. 71 min. b&w.

1968 **Kid Sentiment**. Prod: Clément Perron, NFB. 88 min. b&w.

1970 **Les Vrais Cousins**. Prod: Paul Larose, ORTF and NFB. 53 min. b&w.

1971 **IXE-13**. Prod: Pierre Gauvreau, NFB. 113 min. col.

Marc Laurendeau in an intriguing scene from Godbout's musical comedy, IXE-13.

BIBLIOGRAPHY

Cinéastes du Quebec No. 9: Jacques Godbout, CQDC, 1972, has interviews, criticism and a complete filmography.

Essais sur le cinéma québécois, has a review of **Kid Sentiment**.

La Presse, March 24, 1968, "Godbout nous dit comment est né son film *Kid Sentiment";* March 30, 1968, "Les jeunes évoluent-ils vers la confusion des sexes?"; and March 30, 1968, "Un film vrai sur la jeunesse d'aujour-d'hui".

Séquences #52, February 1968, pp. 22-23, "Le récit cinématographique: dialogue avec Jacques Godbout". (Interview.)

Objectif, May 1967, pp. 35-42, re: the production of **Yul-871**.

How to Make or Not to Make a Canadian Film, "A Trap: the Script", by Godbout.

Liberté, Vol. 8, No. 2-3, March-June 1966, an article by Godbout.

Le Soleil, September 7, 1968, "Jacques Godbout: Il est impensable d'établir une industrie du cinéma dans le schème capitaliste du Québec actuel", by Claude Daigneault.

Canadian Literature, No. 46, Autumn 1970, "Le Temps: la poésie du cinéma", part of a collection of articles under the title, " 'Write Me a Film': A Symposium by Canadian Filmmakers".

Le Devoir, Montreal, June 1, 1968, an interview on **Kid Sentiment**.

Parti-pris, No. 7, April 1964, an interview on the series, "Temps présent".

The Montreal Gazette, February 19, 1972, "Move Over James Bond, IXE-13 est arrivé", by Dane Lanken.

Short reviews in: *Le Cinéma québécois: tendances et prolongements, Le Cinéma canadien, Vingt ans de cinéma au Canada français* and *Jeune Cinéma canadien.*

Fifteen Songs from **IXE–13** have been recorded by Louise Forestier and Les Cyniques (Gamma Records, GS-148).

GOSSELIN, BERNARD

Born in Drummondville in 1934, Bernard Gosselin studied printing at the École des arts graphique and worked as a printer before joining the title department at the National Film Board in 1956. Gosselin worked as an assistant editor, location manager and assistant cameraman; he assisted Brault in shooting **Pour la suite du monde** and Labrecque in his **60 Cycles**. Perrault's **Un Pays sans bon sens**, **Le Règne du jour** and **Les Voitures d'eau**, Godout's **Huit Témoins**, Brault's **Entre la mer et l'eau douce**, Lamothe's **Les Bûcherons de la Manouane** and Groulx's **Voir Miami** were all shot by Gosselin. He is presently shooting a series of films with Perrault on the communities around James Bay. Gosselin's feature **Le Martien de Noël** is a children's Christmas story.

FILMOGRAPHY

1962 **Le Jeu de l'hiver** (The Joy of Winter). With Jean Dansereau. Prod: Tom Daly, NFB. 15 min. b&w.

1968 **Le Beau Plaisir** (Beluga Days).With Pierre Perrault. Prod: Jacques Bobet and Guy L. Côté, NFB. 15 min. col.

1969 **Capture**. Prod: Marc Beaudet, NFB. 17 min. col.

1970 **Passage au nord-ouest**. Prod: François Séguillon, NFB. 27 min. col.
Odyssée du Manhattan (Manhattan Odyssey) Prod: François Séguillon, NFB. 8 min. col.

1971 **Le Martien de Noël** (The Christmas Martian). Prod: Faroun and Les Cinéastes associés Inc. 66 min. col.

1972 **César et son canot d'écorce** (Cesar's Bark Canoe). Prod: Paul Larose, NFB. 50 min. col.
Raquette (Working title).

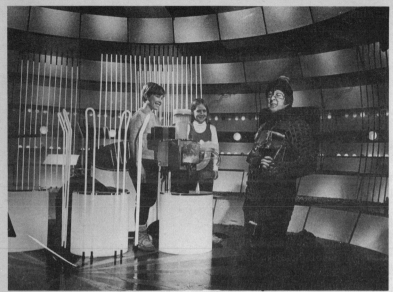

Scene from Gosselin's le Martien de Noël

BIBLIOGRAPHY

Le Cinéma québécois: tendances et prolongements, has a short critique by Yvan Patry.

La Presse, March 14, 1970; and October 7, 1971, "Bernard Gosselin estime que les films pour enfants sont malhonnêtes" – both interviews.

All the following are reviews of **le Martien de Noël:**

La Presse, August 7, 1971, P. B4, "Un rêve de jeunesse réalisé", by Luc Perreault.

Le Soleil, Quebec, August 6, 1971, *"Le Martien de Noël:* cinéma", by Paul Roux.

Point de mire, Vol. 2, No. 28, August 14, 1971, p. 25.

GROULX, GILLES

Born in Montreal, 1931, Gilles Groulx started his cinematic career as a newsreel editor and director for Radio-Canada before joining the NFB in 1956 to work with Michel Brault, Marcel Carrière, Claude Fournier and Louis Portugais; his first film, **Les Raquetteurs** was co-directed with Michel Brault. Wolf Koenig and Roman Kroitor of the Candid Eye Unit introduced **Les Raquetteurs** to Mrs. Robert Flaherty on her search for material for the 1958 Flaherty Seminar. This critical recognition given to the film marks the beginning of the French Unit at the National Film Board. Groulx's first feature, **Le Chat dans le sac**, reflected and gave coherence to Quebec's political and cultural awakening. Today that film stands as a watershed in Quebec cinema.

FILMOGRAPHY

1958 **Les Raquetteurs**. With Michel Brault. Prod: Louis Portugais. NFB. 28 min. b&w.

1959 **Normetal**. Prod: Louis Portugais. NFB. 17 min. b&w. Unsigned.

1960 **La France sur un caillou**. With Claude Fournier. Prod: Jacques Bobet, NFB. 28 min. b&w.

1961 **Golden Gloves**. Prod: Fernand Dansereau and Victor Jobin, NFB. 28 min. b&w.

1962 **Voir Miami**. Prod: Fernand Dansereau, NFB. 28 min. b&w.

1963 **Un Jeu si simple**. Prod: Jacques Bobet, NFB. 30 min. col. & b&w.

1964 **Le Chat dans le sac** (The Cat in the Bag). Prod: Jacques Bobet. NFB. 80 min. b&w.

1966 **Québec . . . .?** With Michel Brault. Prod: Les Cinéastes associés Inc. for Office du Film du Québec. 30 min.

1969 **Où êtes-vous donc?** Prod: Guy L. Côté, NFB. 95 min. col.

Entre tu et vous. Prod: Jean-Pierre Lefebvre, NFB. 65 min. b&w.

1972 **1461 Jours**. Prod: Paul Larose, NFB. (Feature in progress.)

BIBLIOGRAPHY

Cinéastes du Québec 1: Gilles Groulx, CQDC, 1969, has criticism, an interview, a filmography and bibliography. Includes an article by Robert Daudelin (translated into English in *Second Wave,* edited by Robin Woods, pp. 120-123, Praeger, N.Y., 1970).

Cahiers du cinéma in English, No. 4, "10 Questions to 5 Canadian Filmmakers". Interview.

Montreal Star, November 22, 1969, "Gilles Groulx — an Interview with M. Paskall".

Dossiers de cinéma: 1, Editions Fides, Ottawa 1968, has a review of **un Jeu si simple**.

Gilles Cinéma Groulx: le lynx inquiet, edited by Patrick Straram and Jean-Marc Piotte, published by Cinémathèque québécoise/éditions québécoises, 1971. Available from Diffusion-Québec, 3611 St. Denis, Montreal, 845-2535, and from the Cinémathèque québécoise, 360 McGill Street, Montreal.

Several reviews in: *Le Cinéma québécois: tendances et prolongements, Vingt Ans de cinéma au Canada français, Essais sur le cinéma québécois,* and *Jeune Cinéma canadien.*

Barbara Ulrich in Groulx's le Chat dans le sac.

HALDANE, DONALD

Born in Edmonton, Alberta in 1914, Don Haldane studied drama at Yale University and later directed in theatres in the United States and western Canada. He became involved in industrial filmmaking before joining the NFB as a free-lance director in 1954 to work on the television series, "Perspective". Subsequently, Haldane directed shows for a number of television series — among them "Forest Ranger" and "RCMP" — which produced highly trained film crews. The first English feature produced by the NFB, **The Drylanders**, was directed by Haldane, with a script by M. Charles Cohen that dramatized Prairie settlement. In 1961, Haldane formed Westminster Films in Toronto, producing largely industrial documentaries.

FILMOGRAPHY (incomplete)

1956 **Who Is Sylvia?** Prod: Julian Biggs, NFB. 29 min. b&w.
   Crossroads. Prod: Julian Biggs, NFB. 29 min. b&w.

1957 **Joe and Roxy**. Prod: Julian Biggs, NFB. 30 min. b&w.

1959 **The Gifted Ones**. Prod: David Bairstow. 30 min. b&w.

1960 **Eternal Children**. Prod: David Bairstow. 30 min. b&w.

1961 **Nikki, Wild Dog of the North**. (With Jack Couffer.) Prod: Lee Gordon, Disney Productions. 100 min. col.

1963 **The Drylanders** (Un Autre Pays). Prod: Peter Jones, NFB. 70 min. b&w.

1965 "Forest Ranger" (13 of the series). Prod: Maxine Samuels, CBC. 30 min. each.

1969 **Rye on the Rocks**. Prod: Westminster Films for International Nickel. 14 min. col.

1971 **The Reincarnate**. Prod: Nat Taylor, Meridian Films. 101 min. col.

BIBLIOGRAPHY

The Telegram, Toronto, October 5, 1963, "A Drama of the Canadian West", by Clyde Gilmour.

The Telegram, January 14, 1964, "Honest Dust-bowl Drama", by Clyde Gilmour.

The Star Weekly, August 31, 1963, pp. 2-4, 6-7, *"Drylanders:* Wide Screen Saga of the West", by Bill Stephenson.

Canadian Cinematography, May-June 1962, pp. 3-4, "Special Effects Ease Problems on *Drylanders",* by John Gunn.

La Presse, Montreal, May 9, 1964, p. 17, *"Un Autre Pays:* les aléas du blé gras et ingrat", by Alain Pontaut.

HART, HARVEY

Born in Toronto in 1928, Harvey Hart helped to form one of the first production units of the CBC along with Norman Jewison, Sydney Newman, Arthur Hiller, Paul Almond and Robert Allen. He also originated "Front Page Challenge" and "Fighting Words". Having done his television apprenticeship in New York, Hart directed and produced drama for CBC's "Folio", "Quest" and "Festival" as well as working in live drama; both the Crest and the Civic Square Theatre in Toronto (the latter co-founded by Hart) presented plays directed by Hart. Returning to the United States in 1963, Hart directed episodes for a number of television series — "The Young Lawyers", "Peyton Place", "Channing", "Alfred Hitchcock Presents", "Ben Casey" and "Mannix"; many of his television pilots were later released as commercial features. Hart has also directed single dramas for American television, notably Miller's **The Crucible** for "Startime" and Andreyev's **He Who Gets Slapped** for "Play of the Week". Hart returned to Canada in 1971 to direct John Herbert's script of prison life, **Fortune and Men's Eyes,** which was photographed by Georges Dufaux.

FILMOGRAPHY

1960 **Enemy of the People.** Prod: CBC, "Startime". 90 min. b&w.

1961 **The Luck of Ginger Coffey**. Prod: CBC, "Festival". 90 min. b&w.
Ondine. Prod: CBC, "Festival". 90 min. b&w.
The Quare Fellow. Prod: CBC, "Festival". 90 min. b&w.

1963 **David Chapter 2**. Prod: CBC, "Festival". 90 min. b&w.
The Wild Duck. Prod: CBC, "Festival". 90 min. b&w.

1964 **Eli the Fanatic**. Prod: CBC, "Quest". 30 min. b&w.
A Very Close Family. Prod: CBC, "Festival". 90 min. b&w.
Bus Riley's Back in Town. Prod: Elliott Kastner, Universal. 92 min.

1965 **The Dark Intruder**. Prod: Jack Laird, Universal. 59 min.

1968 **The Sweet Ride**. Prod: Joe Pasternak, 20th Century Fox. 110 min.
col.

1969 **David Chapter 3**. Prod: CBC, "Festival". 90 min.

1971 **Fortune and Men's Eyes** (Aux yeux des hommes) Prod: Lester
Persky, Lewis Allen and Donald Ginsberg, MGM and Cinemex.
100 min. col.

1972 **Mahoney's Estate**. Prod: Alexis Kanner, Topaz Productions. 105 min.
col.

BIBLIOGRAPHY

Toronto Daily Star, February 28, 1959, "An Open Letter to Nathan
Cohen from Harvey Hart".

Weekend Magazine, Vol. 2, No. 22, pp. 22-23, "Ginger Coffey is Brought
to the TV Screen", by Frank Lowe and Louis Jaques.

The Globe and Mail, February 3, 1965, "Hart Leaves CBC", by Frank
Morriss.

The Telegram Showcase, Toronto, April 30, 1966, "How Hollywood Re-
built Ann-Margaret".

La Presse, Montreal, October 21, 1967, "Harvey Hart se pose des questions sur la jeunesse", by Axel Madsen.

The Toronto Telegram, April 17, 1971, "CBC-TV's Golden Boy of
Drama Returns After a 5-Year Absence".

The Globe and Mail, January 9, 1971, "Herbert's Fortune in Quebec Jail", by Martin Knelman.

Maclean's Magazine, December, 1970, *"Fortune and Men's Eyes* – a Report from the Set in a Quebec City Prison", by John Hofsess.

Québec-Presse, Montreal, October 17, 1971, *"Fortune and Men's Eyes:* un film à la Hollywood . . . ".

The Montreal Star, February 13, 1971, "The Wheel of Fortune", by Martin Malina.

The Montreal Gazette, February 6, 1971, "A Fortune for an Apostle", by Dane Lanken.

Séquences, No. 67, December 1971, pp. 34-35, a review of **Bus Riley's Back in Town.**

HEROUX, DENIS

Born in Montreal, 1940, Denis Héroux studied history at the University of Montreal where he directed his first film with Denys Arcand and Stephane Venne; **Seul ou avec d'autres** was the first feature film to be made on the university circuit. (Larry Kent's **Bitter Ash** and David Secter's **Winter Kept Us Warm** soon followed.) A writer and director for Radio-Canada, Héroux has since directed a number of features which have had popular appeal. One of these, **Sept Fois par jour**, is an Israeli-Canadian co-production written by the Canadian, Ted Allan.

FILMOGRAPHY

1962 **Seul ou avec d'autres.** With Denys Arcand and Stephane Venne. Prod: Denis Héroux, Association générale des étudiants de l'Université de Montréal. 65 min. b&w.

1964 **Jusqu'au cou.** Prod: AGEUM. 90 min. b&w.

1965 **Pas de vacances pour les idoles**. Prod: Claude Héroux, Onyx Films and Latino Films Ltd. 80 min. b&w.

1967 **Mais où sont les anglais d'antan?** Prod: Radio-Canada. 30 min. b&w.
Cent Ans déjà. Prod: Radio-Canada. 30 min. b&w.
Une Ville à vivre. Prod: Radio-Canada. 60 min. b&w.

1968 **Valérie**. Prod: André Link and John Dunning, Cinepix Inc. 95 min. b&w.

1969 **L'Initiation** (The Initiation). Prod: John Dunning and André Link, Cinepix Inc. 91 min. col.

1970 **L'Amour humain** (The Awakening). Prod: John Dunning, André Link and Claude Héroux, Cinepix Inc. and Les Productions Héroux. 90 min. col.

1971 **Sept Fois par jour** (Seven Times a Day). Prod: John Kemeny and Claude Héroux, Les Productions Héroux, Minotaur Film Productions, France Film and Steiner Films. 98 min. col.
La Fille du roi and **Les Acadiens**. Prod: Onyx Films for the series "La feuille d'érable" which was co-produced by Radio-Canada and the national television networks of France, Belgium, Switzerland and Germany. Both 60 min. and col.

1972 **Un Enfant comme les autres**. Prod: Cinévidéo, Bellevue-Pathé and Famous Players. 88 min. col.
Quelques Arpents de neige. Prod: Cinévidéo. 120 min. col.
J'ai mon voyage (feature in progress).

BIBLIOGRAPHY

Objectif, No. 36, August 1966, "Les 101 questions sur le cinéma canadien". Interview.

Rélations, No. 342, October 1969, p. 281, *"Valérie,* film antiquébécois", by Yves Lever.

La Presse, January 31, 1970, "L'indépendance pour quoi faire?", by Luc Perreault. Interview.

La Presse, May 3, 1969, "Denis Héroux: jouer le jeu de la mythologie", by Luc Perreault. Interview.

Actualité, November 1970, "Denis Héroux et le déculottage des défroqués", by Jean-Louis Morgan. Interview.

Le Devoir, October 16, 1970, p. 10, "Comment atteindre tous les publics ... et ne rien dire", by Jean-Pierre Tadros.

The Montreal Gazette, October 17, 1970, p. 43, "Denis Héroux Plans his Films to Generate Family Discussion".

La Presse, January 31, 1970, p. 35, "L'ambition de Cinépix", by Luc Perreault.

JUTRA, CLAUDE

Born in Montreal, 1930, Claude Jutra graduated from medical school, making his first short films as a student with the collaboration of Michel Brault. As an actor, Jutra worked with Norman McLaren on **A Chairy Tale** and starred in his own **A tout prendre** and **Mon Oncle Antoine.** He has worked extensively within the National Film Board, joining Claude Sylvestre and Brault on the television series "Images en boîte" and involving himself in many of the seminal films produced by the French Unit. In his collaboration with the French filmmaker-anthropologist Jean Rouch in documenting the Niger Republic, Jutra has been instrumental in the cross-fertilization of documentary/*cinéma-vérité* techniques. Jutra's fictional work is marked by a warm attentiveness to his characters; he has been assisted in his efforts by Clément Perron and Anne Hébert who wrote **Mon Oncle Antoine** and **Kamouraska** respectively. Jutra was the founding president of L'Association professionnelle des cinéastes.

FILMOGRAPHY

1947 **Le Dément du Lac Jean Jeune.**

1949 **Mouvement perpétuel.** Prod: Independent. 15 min. b&w.

1956 **Pierrot des bois**, 11 min. b&w.

Les Jeunesses musicales. Prod: Roger Blais, NFB. 44 min. b&w.

1957 **A Chairy Tale** (Il était une chaise). With Norman McLaren. Prod: Tom Daly, NFB. 10 min. b&w.

1958 **Les Mains nettes.** Prod: Guy Glover and Léonard Forest, NFB. 75 min. b&w.

Fred Barry, comédien. Prod: Léonard Forest, NFB. 30 min. b&w.

1959 **Anna la bonne.** Prod: François Truffaut, Films du Carosse, Paris. 10 min. b&w.

Félix Leclerc, troubadour. Prod: Léonard Forest, NFB. 30 min. b&w.

1961 **Le Niger — jeune république.** Prod: Bernard Devlin. NFB. 58 min. b&w.

La Lutte (Wrestling) with Michel Brault, Claude Fournier, Marcel Carrière. Prod: Jacques Bobet. NFB. 28 min. b&w.

1962 **Québec-USA** or **L'Invasion pacifique** (Visit to a Foreign Country). With Michel Brault. Prod: Fernand Dansereau, NFB. 28 min. b&w.

1963 **Les Enfants du silence.** With Michel Brault. Prod: Fernand Dansereau and Victor Jobin. NFB. 24 min. b&w.

Petit Discours de la méthode. With Pierre Patry. Prod: Fernand Dansereau and Victor Jobin, NFB. 27 min. b&w.

A tout prendre (Take It All). Prod: Les Films Cassiopée and Orion Films. 110 min. b&w.

1966 **Comment savoir** (Knowing to Learn). Prod: Marcel Martin, NFB. 70 min. b&w.

Rouli-Roulant (The Devil's Toy). Prod: Les Films Cassiopée for NFB. 14 min. b&w.

1969 **Wow.** Prod: Robert Forget, NFB. 95 min. col.
Au coeur de la ville. Prod: OFQ. 5 min. col.

1970 **Marie-Christine.** Prod: OFQ. 10 min. col.
Mon Oncle Antoine. Prod: Marc Beaudet, NFB and Gendon Films Ltd. 100 min. col.

1972 **Kamouraska.** Prod: Les Films Carle-Lamy and France Film. (Feature work in progress.)

BIBLIOGRAPHY

Cinéastes du Québec 4: Claude Jutra, CQDC, 1970. Critique by Jean Chabot, interview, filmography and bibliography.

Cahiers du cinéma in English, No. 4, p. 45, "10 Questions to 5 Canadian Filmmakers".

McGill Medical Journal, Vol. 38, December 1969, "Dr. Claude Jutra: Film-maker", by Ronald Blumer.

Le Devoir, October 11, 1971, p. 13, "A la découverte de Claude Jutra, acteur", by Jean-Pierre Tadros.

The Montreal Star, November 13, 1971, p. C11, "Jutra's Stock Goes Up", by Martin Malina.

Jean Duceppe as Antoine and young Jacques Gagnon in Jutra's Mon Oncle Antoine.

La Presse, July 16, 1966, p. 6, "Claude Jutra ou les confidences d'un professeur de cinéma", by Michèle Favreau.

How to Make or Not to Make a Canadian Film, "How Not to Make a Canadian Film", an amusing article by Jutra.

Cahiers du cinéma, No. 113, November 1960, pp. 32-43; No. 115, January 1961, pp. 23-33; and No. 116, February 1961, pp. 39-44.

Objectif, No. 3, December 1960, pp. 3-16, "Michel Brault et Claude Jutra racontent Jean Rouch", an interview with Robert Daudelin and Michel Patenaude.

L'Ecran, Montreal, No. 2, pp. 7-15, "Entretien de deux cinéastes", in which Brault and Jutra talk about Jean Rouch and Norman McLaren.

Reviews in: *Le Cinéma québécois: tendances et prolongements, Le Cinéma canadien, Jeune Cinéma canadien* and *Essais sur le cinéma québécois.*

KACZENDER, GEORGE

George Kaczender was born in Budapest, Hungary in 1933 and came to the National Film Board in 1957 having worked as an assistant-director in his homeland. While at the Board he worked as an editor on numerous films, including **Nahanni** and his own **Phoebe** and **You're No Good**; he also authored these films and co-authored with Timothy Findlay his feature, **Don't Let the Angels Fall.** Kaczender left the Board in 1969 to co-found International Cinemedia Center Ltd. and Minotaur Film Productions Inc. He now free-lances as a director-producer out of Montreal.

FILMOGRAPHY

1963 **Ballerina** (Margaret Mercier, ballerine). Prod: Nicholas Balla, NFB. 28 min. b&w.

City Scene. Prod: Gordon Burwash, NFB. 28 min. b&w.

1966 **The Game**. Prod: John Kemeny, NFB. 28 min. b&w.

1967 **Little White Crimes**. Prod: John Kemeny, NFB. 28 min. b&w.

1964 **Phoebe** (Sylvie). Prod: Julian Biggs, NFB. 28 min. b&w.

1965 **You're No Good** (Eddie). Prod: John Kemeny, NFB. 28 min. b&w.

1966 **The World of Three**. Prod: Nicholas Balla, NFB. 28 min. b&w.

1967 **Sabre and Foil** (Sabre et Fleuret) Prod: John Kemeny, NFB. 7 min. b&w.

1968 **Don't Let the Angels Fall** (Seul les enfants étaient présents) Prod: John Kemeny, NFB. 99 min. b&w.

1969 **Freud: The Hidden Nature of Man**. Prod: International Cinemedia Center Ltd. 27 min. col.
Marxism. Prod: International Cinemedia Center Ltd. 27 min. col.

1970 **Newton: The Mind that Found the Future**. Prod: International Cinemedia Center Ltd. 20 min. col.

1971 **The Story of a Peanut Butter Sandwich**. Prod: G. Kaczender, International Cinemedia Center Ltd. 13 min.
Brown Wolf. Prod: International Cinemedia Center Ltd. 28 min.

1972 **U-Turn** (Feature in progress).

BIBLIOGRAPHY

The Montreal Star, October 24, 1964, "National Film Board Presents New Television Series", by Don Newnham, an interview.

The Montreal Star, February 21, 1970, "Rita, Say Hi to George", by Carol Pascoe.

The Saturday Gazette, May 3, 1969, p. 29, "Kaczender on Tape on Kaczender on Film or *Don't Let the Angels Fall* and Other Filmic Events", by Jacob Siskind.

La Presse, November 1, 1969, "What do the Angels Want?", by Luc Perreault.

Jeune Cinéma canadien — a short reference.

On **Don't Let the Angels Fall**:

Photo-Journal, Montreal, November 12, 1969, p. 66.

The Globe and Mail, October 25, 1969, by Kaspars Dzeguze.

Variety, May 14, 1969.

Cinema Canada, September-October 1969, pp. 18 and 24, "NFB Feature Wins Accolades at Cannes", by Gerald Pratley.

KELLY, RON

Born in Vancouver in 1929, Ron Kelly was a painter before joining the CBC in 1954 to become part of the famed Vancouver Film Unit; his **A Bit of Bark** inaugurated the production of dramatic films in the CBC. Kelly also pioneered the dramatic use of the handheld camera for the modern retelling of the Easter story in **Open Grave**. Winner of the Wilderness Award for **The Thirties: A Glimpse of a Decade**, Kelly captured his second for **The Last Man in the World**. Kelly's most impressive work has evolved out of his dramatic insight into historical events; he wrote the scripts for both **Springhill** and **Megantic Outlaw**. His feature, **Waiting for Caroline**, was co-produced by the CBC and the National Film Board.

FILMOGRAPHY (incomplete)

1957 **Spanish Village**. Prod: Ron Kelly, CBC. 29 min. b&w.

1958 **Dark Gods**. Prod: Ron Kelly, CBC. 28 min. b&w.
   The Lacondonnes. Prod: Ron Kelly, CBC. 29 min. b&w.

1959 **A Bit of Bark**. Prod: CBC. 30 min. b&w.
   Object Matrimony. Prod: CBC. 30 min. b&w.
   The Seeds. Prod: CBC. 45 min. b&w.

1960 **Back of the Sun**. Prod: BBC. 30 min.

1961 **The Tearaways.** Prod: BBC. 30 min.

1962 **Montreal.** Prod: CBC. 60 min. b&w.

1963 **So This is Life.** Prod: CBC. 60 min.
   Caio Maria. Prod: CBC. 60 min.

1964 **The Thirties: A Glimpse of a Decade.** Prod: Thom Benson, CBC. 50 min. b&w.
   Open Grave. Prod: Ron Kelly, CBC for "Horizon" series. 50 min. b&w.

1965 **The Gift.** Prod: Ron Kelly, CBC. 60 min.
   Quo Vadis Mrs. Lum. Prod: Peter Jones, NFB. 28 min. b&w.

1966 **The Last Man in the World.** Prod: Ronald Weyman, CBC. 50 min. b&w.
   Such is Life. Prod: Winston Hibbler, CBC. 60 min. b&w.

1967 **Waiting for Caroline.** Prod: Walford Hewitson, NFB and CBC. 84 min. col.

1969 **King of the Grizzlies.** Prod: Disney Studios. 90 min. col.

1970 **Megantic Outlaw.** Prod: Ron Kelly, CBC. 90 min. col.

1971 **Springhill.** Prod: Ron Kelly, CBC. 90 min. col.

BIBLIOGRAPHY

The Film and Ron Kelly, from the Canadian Filmography Series, No. 102, Canadian Film Institute, 1965. It has an interview with Kelly by Charlotte Gobeil and a filmography up to publication date. (Out of print. Available at film study centres.)

Canadian Cinematography, November-December 1965, pp. 11-14, "Conversations on Film with Ron Kelly"; and March-April 1964, pp. 11-14, "Film Features Hand-held Camera", on **Open Grave.**

The Toronto Telegram, August 22, 1964, p. 7, "The Revolution-maker", an interview by Jon Ruddy.

The Montreal Star, January 14, 1967, pp. 2-3, " 'Caroline' Seems to be Worth Waiting For", by Dusty Vineberg.

Star Weekly Magazine, September 23, 1967, pp. 18-23, "One Girl's Struggle with the Eternal Triangle, Canadian Style".

How to Make or Not to Make a Canadian Film, "Hello 'Caroline', Good-bye", an article by George Robertson, who wrote **Waiting for Caroline**.

References in: *Le Cinéma canadien* and *Hommage to the Vancouver Film Unit,* the latter published by La Cinémathèque canadienne.

Alexandra Stewart as Caroline in Kelly's Waiting for Caroline.

KENT, LAWRENCE

Born in South Africa in 1938, Larry Kent emigrated to Vancouver in
1957 where he worked as a printer and studied theatre and psychology
at the University of British Columbia; it was there that he wrote a play,
The Africaaner, and directed his first film. **Bitter Ash** was one of the first
films to be shot and distributed on the university circuit (a year earlier,
students at the University of Montreal had produced **Seul ou avec d'autres**).
Kent presently lives in Montreal where he has starred in Lefebvre's **Q-bec
My Love** and directed a number of features. He has recently worked on
a film for children and taught at a CEGEP in Montreal.

FILMOGRAPHY

1963 **Bitter Ash**. Prod: Lawrence L. Kent Prod. 83 min. b&w.

1964 **Sweet Substitute** or **Caressed**. Prod: Lawrence L. Kent Prod. 81 min.
b&w.

1965 **When Tomorrow Dies**. Prod: Lawrence L. Kent Prod. 91 min. b&w.

1967 **High**. Prod: Lawrence L. Kent Prod. 84 min. b&w. & col.

1968 **Facade**. Prod: Lawrence L. Kent Prod. 80 min. col.

1969 **Saskatchewan – 45° Below**. Prod: Tom Daly, NFB. 14 min. col.

1971 **The Apprentice** (Fleur-bleue). Prod: Donald Brittain, Potterton
Productions. 85 min. col.

1972 **Cold Pizza**. Prod: Mike Rubbo, NFB. 30 min. col. ·

Keep It in the Family. Prod: Kit Films. (Feature in progress.)

All Kent's films, other than those produced by the National Film Board,
are distributed by the Cooperative cinéastes indépendants in Montreal.

BIBLIOGRAPHY

Objectif, No. 37, November-December 1966, "101 questions sur le cinéma
canadien", an interview.

Take One, Vol. 1, No. 4, "The Triumph and Trials of Larry Kent".
Interview.

The Telegram, Toronto, January 13, 1968, "If I'm Going to Show Nudity", an interview with Noah James.

The Georgian, Sir George Williams University, Montreal, November 5, 1968, "Larry Kent Talks with Peter Bors".

Touchstone, No. 2, September 1965, p. 7-14, "Larry Kent: on Film in Canada". Interview.

The Telegram, Toronto, August 9, 1967, by Gordon Sheppard on **High**.

La Presse, November 2, 1968, "Un film canadien qui risque d'être fort contesté", by Luc Perreault, on **High**.

The Telegram, November 27, 1965, by Gerald Pratley on **When Tomorrow Dies**.

La Presse, September 10, 1971, "Une fleur déjà fanée", by Luc Perreault.

Québec-Presse, September 19, 1971, *"Fleur-bleue:* un film politique raté", by Carol Faucher.

KING, ALLAN

Born in Vancouver in 1930, Allan King began his career with the CBC Vancouver Film Unit which had been founded in 1953 by Stan Fox, Jack Long and Arla Saare. King's early documentary style was influenced by, and in turn influenced, the "Candid Eye" productions at the NFB. The fictional-documentary style which King has since evolved in **Warrendale** and **A Married Couple** has opened up an innovative structure for feature films. In 1962 King established his own production company with offices in England and Toronto with associates Richard Leiterman, William Brayne, Chris Wangler and Peter Moseley. The company has recently ceased operations in Canada.

FILMOGRAPHY (incomplete)

1956 **Skid Row**. Prod: A. King, CBC. 38 min. b&w.

1957 **Pemberton Valley**. Prod: A. King, CBC. 59 min. b&w.

1960 **Rickshaw** (Rickshaw Boy). Prod: A. King, CBC "Closeup". 28 min. b&w.

1961 **A Matter of Pride**. A. King, CBC. 57 min. b&w.
     Dreams. Prod. A. King. CBC "Quest". 28 min. b&w.

1964 **Bjorn's Inferno**. Prod: A. King, CBC "Document". 53 min. b&w.
     Running Away Backwards or **Coming of Age in Ibiza**. Prod: A. King, CBC "Document". 60 min. b&w.

1967 **Warrendale**. Prod: A. King, Allan King Associates for CBC "Document". 100 min. b&w.

1969 **A Married Couple**. Prod: A. King, Allan King Associates for Aquarius Films Ltd. 112 min. col.

1972 **Come On Children**. Prod: A. King, Allan King Associates. 92 min. col.

BIBLIOGRAPHY

Allan King, Canadian Filmography Series No. 105, The Canadian Film Institute. Has an interview with Bruce Martin and a complete filmography. Revised edition, 1971.

An Allan King Retrospective, La Cinémathèque canadienne, April 1966. A 30-page brochure.

Warrendale, a booklet on the making of the film, available from Warrendale's successor, Browndale, in Oakridges, Ontario.

Canadian Cinematography, Vol. 4, No. 4, May-June 1965, pp. 11-14, "Conversations on Film with Allan King". Interview.

The Reel Thing, Vol. 1, No. 1, The Ontario Film Association, "An Interview with Allan King", by Wayne Cunningham.

Film Quarterly, Summer 1970, pp. 9-23, "The Fictional Documentary:

Interview with the Makers of *A Married Couple"*, by Alan Rosenthal. (Also published in Rosenthal's *The New Documentary in Action,* University of California Press, Berkeley, 1971.)

How to Make or Not to Make a Canadian Film, "Canadian-Cinema-Vancouver", an article by King on his early work.

Saturday Night, September 1971, pp. 30-32, "A Director Hoping for a Miracle", by Morris Wolfe.

Take One, Vol. 1, No. 5, "The Director as Pilgrim".

The Globe and Mail, Nov. 1, 1969, p. 23, "A Moviemaker Gets Personal", by Martin Knelman.

Positif, No. 100, December/68-January/69, pp. 83-37, "Les journées de 'Positif' ",

Objectif 61, October 1961, pp. 21-22, "Dix-sept artisans du cinéma canadien".

References in: *Le Cinéma canadien* and *Jeune Cinéma canadien.*

KOHANYI, JULIUS

Born in 1936 in Kelowna, British Columbia, Julius Kohanyi spent his early years in Hungary before returning to Canada. Largely self-taught, Kohanyi first began to film people and events around his Toronto home — and all his films retain this sense of community. Much of Kohanyi's work has evolved out of his interest in art — he made **Little Monday** from John Gould's drawings, **Tevye** from Saul Field's work and directed a short on the sculpture of Henry Moore. An independent filmmaker, Kohanyi also teaches his craft in Toronto.

FILMOGRAPHY

1960 **Requiem for a City Block**. Prod: Independent. 30 min. b&w.

1961 **The Softness of Concrete**. Prod: Independent. 30 min. b&w.

1963 **The Herring Belt**. Prod: Independent. 23 min. b&w.

1964 **The Artists' Workshop**. Prod: Independent. 26 min. b&w.

1965 **Little Monday**. Prod: Independent. 17 min. b&w.

1967 **Teddy**. Prod: Victor Solnick, Group Film Productions. 30 min. b&w.

1968 **Henry Moore**. Prod: Independent. 26 min. col.

1969 **Tevye**. Prod: Haida Films. 17 min. col.

1970 **Images**. Prod: Harold Levy, Empire Films Ltd. 10 min. col.

1971 **Eight Short Films on Art**. Prod: J. Kohanyi, CBC. 3-8 min. each. col.

1972 **Rodin**. Prod: Independent. 30 min. col.

Gates of Hell. Prod: Independent. 10 min. col.

Mr. Kohanyi's films are distributed by the Canadian Film Distribution Centre, Toronto.

BIBLIOGRAPHY

Performing Arts in Canada, Vol. 5, No. 3-4, 1968, pp. 26-31, *"Henry Moore",* by Jean Bruce.

The Globe and Mail, December 16, 1965, "Auto Repair Shop Keeps Film Rolling", by Frank Morriss.

The Montreal Star, April 22, 1967, "The customers' cars will have to wait until he's finished the movie".

The Globe and Mail, December 6, 1967, "Kohanyi Makes Film of Moore".

The Gazette, Montreal, April 17, 1967, p. 18, "A Look at a Promising Young Film Director".

KOENIG, WOLF

Animator, cameraman, editor, scriptwriter, director and producer, Wolf Koenig has proven himself to be a most inventive, creative and influential filmmaker. Born in Germany in 1927, he joined the National Film Board in 1948. From Koenig's original idea, based on the spirit of Cartier-Bresson's photography, the Candid Eye Unit created many remarkable documentary portraits for television between 1957 and 1960; produced by Roman Kroitor and Wolf Koenig, the Unit operated within Tom Daly's Unit B. In recent years, Koenig has been producing live action and animated material in Studio A; with Bob Verrall, Koenig has been involved in **The House that Jack Built, Hot Stuff, Tilt, Man the Polluter, Hard Rider** and **Exeter**.

FILMOGRAPHY

1952 **The Romance of Transportation in Canada** (Sports et Transports). With Colin Low and Robert Verrall. Prod: Tom Daly, NFB. 11 min. col.

1955 **Structure of Unions.** Prod: Tom Daly, NFB. 11 min. col.

1957 **It's a Crime** (C'est criminel). With Gerald Potterton. Prod: Tom Daly, NFB for the Department of Labour. 13 min. col.

   City of Gold (Capitale de l'or). With Colin Low. Prod: Tom Daly, NFB. 22 min. b&w.

1958 **The Days Before Christmas** (Bientôt Noël). With Terence Macartney-Filgate, Stanley Jackson and Georges Dufaux. Prod: R. Kroitor and W. Koenig, NFB. 30 min. b&w.

1959 **Glenn Gould – Off the Record** (Glenn Gould). With Roman Kroitor. Prod: R. Kroitor and W. Koenig, NFB. 29 min. b&w.

   Glenn Gould – On the Record (Glenn Gould). With Roman Kroitor. Prod: R. Kroitor and W. Koenig, NFB. 29 min. b&w.

1960 **I Was a Ninety Pound Weakling.** With Georges Dufaux. Prod: R. Kroitor and W. Koenig, NFB. 24 min. b&w.

1961 **Festival in Puerto Rico.** With Roman Kroitor. Prod: R. Kroitor and W. Koenig, NFB. 28 min. b&w.

1962 **Lonely Boy.** (Paul Anka). With Roman Kroitor. Prod: R. Kroitor, NFB. 27 min. b&w.

1965 **Stravinsky**. With Roman Kroitor. Prod: R. Kroitor, NFB. 49 min. b&w.

1967 **Steeltown**. With Rex Tasker. Prod: Walford Hewitson, NFB. 56 min. col.

BIBLIOGRAPHY

Dossiers de cinéma: 1, Fides, 1968, revues of **Lonely Boy** and **City of Gold**.

Séquences, February 1963, pp. 38-40, on **Lonely Boy**.

Numerous references in *Jeune Cinéma canadien* and *Le Cinéma canadien.*

Objectif 61, pp. 21-22, "Dix-sept artisans du cinéma canadien", criticism and a filmography.

How to Make or Not to Make a Canadian Film, "A Note on 'Candid Eye' ", by Koenig.

Canadian Film – Past and Present, La Cinémathèque canadienne, 1967, an article by Marcel Carrière on the filming of **Stravinsky**. Available for reference at film study libraries and reprinted in *Eléments pour un nouveau cinéma,* by Louis Marcorelles, UNESCO, Paris, 1970.

Objectif, Vol. 2, No. 5-6, 1962, an interview by Michel Patenaude re: **Lonely Boy**, **The Days Before Christmas** and the Candid Eye Unit.

KROITOR, ROMAN

Born in Yorkton, Saskatchewan in 1926, Roman Kroitor joined the National Film Board in 1949. As a director-producer in the Candid Eye Unit, Kroitor has worked closely with Wolf Koenig, Stanley Jackson, Terence Macartney-Filgate, Colin Low and Georges Dufaux. With Koenig, Kroitor went on to make two fascinating portraits of public figures, Stravinsky and Paul Anka, using the "Candid Eye" technique. The National Film Board's **Labyrinth** project at Expo '67 was headed up by Kroitor and in 1967 he joined Robert Kerr and Grahame Ferguson in founding Multi-Screen Corporation; this company produced **Tiger Child** (directed by Donald Brittain) for the Fuji Group Pavilion at Expo '70 in Osaka.

FILMOGRAPHY

1954 **Paul Tomkowicz, Street-Railway Switchman** (Paul Tomkowicz, nettoyeur d'aiguillages). Prod: Tom Daly, NFB. 9 min. b&w.

1955 **Farm Calendar** (L'Année à la ferme). Prod: Tom Daly, NFB. 44 min. b&w.

1956 **The Great Plains** (Les Grandes Plaines). Prod: Tom Daly, NFB. 24 min. b&w.

1959 **Glenn Gould — Off the Record** (Glenn Gould). With Wolf Koenig. Prod: R. Kroitor and W. Koenig, NFB. 29 min. b&w.

Glenn Gould — On the Record (Glenn Gould). With Wolf Koenig. Prod: R. Kroitor and W. Koenig, NFB. 29 min. b&w.

1960 **Universe** (Notre univers). With Colin Low. Prod: C. Low, R. Kroitor and Tom Daly, NFB. 26 min. col.

1961 **The Living Machine** (La Machine à penser). Prod: R. Kroitor, NFB. Parts 1 & 2, 28 min. each. b&w.

Festival in Puerto Rico. With W. Koenig. Prod: R. Kroitor and W. Koenig, NFB. 28 min. b&w.

1962 **Lonely Boy** (Paul Anka). With Wolf Koenig. Prod: R. Kroitor, NFB. 27 min. b&w.

1965 **Stravinsky**. With Wolf Koenig. Prod: R. Kroitor and W. Koenig, NFB. 49 min. b&w.

1967 **Labyrinth.** With Colin Low and Hugh O'Connor. Prod: NFB for Expo '67.

1968 **IBM Close-up.** With Grahame Ferguson. Prod: R. Kroitor, Multi-Screen Corp. for IBM.

1972 **Code Name Running Jump.** Prod: R. Kroitor, Multi-Screen Corp. for Department of National Defence. 17 min. col.

BIBLIOGRAPHY

Jeune Cinéma canadien, has a short biography and criticism.

Le Cinéma canadien — numerous references.

Dossiers de cinéma: 1, Fides, 1968, on **Lonely Boy**.

La Presse, July 1, 1967, "Le Labyrinthe de l'Expo, cinéma de l'avenir", an interview. Reprinted in *Dossiers de Cinéma: 1.*

Terence Macartney-Filgate, Canadian Filmography Series #104, The Canadian Film Institute, "On Terence Macartney-Filgate, the Candid Eye and Filmmaking", by Kroitor. (Out of print. Available at film study centres.)

Objectif 61, "Dix-sept artisans du cinéma canadien", an interview.

The Montreal Gazette, February 8, 1969, "From Labyrinth to Multiscreen", by Dane Lanken.

American Cinematography, July 1970, on "Film at Expo '70", has a discussion with Kroitor, Brittain and Dufaux on the production of **Tiger Child**.

For further information on the Candid Eye Unit, see WOLF KOENIG (p.97), and INTRODUCTION TO CANADIAN FILM (p.1).

LABRECQUE, JEAN-CLAUDE

As a cameraman, Jean-Claude Labrecque has been involved with many of Canada's most important films; he worked with Claude Jutra on **A tout prendre**, with Groulx on **Le Chat dans le sac**, with Macartney-Filgate on **The Hundredth Summer**, on Eric Till's **A Great Big Thing**, Don Owen's **Notes For a Film About Donna and Gail** and **The Ernie Game**, Carle's **La Vie heureuse de Léopold Z** and Lefebvre's **Les Maudits Sauvages**. Since 1964, Labrecque has been directing films which are documents of Quebec life. He was born in Quebec City in 1938.

FILMOGRAPHY

1964 **60 Cycles**. Prod: Jacques Bobet, NFB. 17 min. col.

1965 **Intermède** (Feux follets). Prod: Jacques Bobet, NFB. 10 min. col.
La Guerre des pianos. With Jean Dansereau. Prod: Jacques Bobet, NFB. 35 min. b&w.

1967 **La Visite du Général De Gaulle au Québec**. Prod: Les Films Jean-Claude Labrecque Inc. for Office du film du Québec. 28 min. col.

1968 **Canada — pays vaste** (Canada — The Land). With Rex Tasker. Prod: John Kemeny and Robert Baylis, NFB for Expo '70, Osaka. 8 min. col.
La Vie. Prod: Les Films Jean-Claude Labrecque Inc. 60 min. b&w.

1969 **Les Canots de glace**. Prod: Les Films Jean-Claude Labrecque Inc. for Office du film du Québec. 15 min. col.

1970 **Essai à la mille**. Prod: Les Films Jean-Claude Labrecque. 7 min. col.
La Nuit de la poésie. With Jean-Pierre Masse. Prod: Marc Beaudet, NFB. 111 min. col.

1972 **Hochelaga**. Prod: Jacques Parent, Les Films Jean-Claude Labreque Inc. for Office du film du Quebec. 9 min. col.
Les Smattes. Prod: Les Films Jean-Claude Labrecque Inc./Les Productions Carle-Lamy/Cinak. 90 min. col.
Images de la Gaspésie. Prod: Les Films Jean-Claude Labrecque for l'Office du Film du Québec. 10 min. col.

BIBLIOGRAPHY

Cinéastes du Québec No. 7: Jean-Claude Labrecque, CQDC, 1971, a collection of criticism, an interview, editing plan for **60 Cycles,** a filmography and a bibliography.

Dossiers de cinéma: 1, Fides, 1968, on **60 Cycles.**

Take One, Vol. 1, No. 2, pp. 13-16, an interview.

Cinema Canada, September 1968, p. 11, an interview by Gerald Pratley.

Point de mire, December 18, 1971, Vol. 3, No. 10, "Autour de Jean-Claude Labrecque et des smattes", interview.

La Presse, January 23, 1971, "Une Trêve avant la guerilla", by Luc Perreault. Interview.

Québec-Presse, August 16, 1970, interview and review of **La Nuit de la poésie.**

References in: *Vingt Ans de cinéma au Canada français, Jeune Cinéma canadien, Essais sur le cinéma québécois, Le Cinéma canadien* and *Le Cinéma québécois: tendances et prolongements.*

LAMOTHE, ARTHUR

Born in France in 1928, Arthur Lamothe joined the National Film Board
in 1961 working on Gilles Carle's **Manger** and **Dimanche d'Amérique** and
as researcher and writer on Godbout and Dufaux's **Pour quelques arpents
de neige**. Although Lamothe has worked in fiction cinema (notably
Poussière sur la ville, from a story by André Langevin) most of his work
has involved the reality of labour and its social and political meaning.
Lamothe has been active as a writer and critic of cinema; one of the
founding members of Connaissance du cinéma (now La Cinémathèque
québécoise) and of L'Association professionnelle de cinéastes, he created
his own production house, La Société générale cinématographique (SGC)
in 1965, and in 1972 Les Ateliers audio-visuels du Québec.

FILMOGRAPHY

1962 **Les Bûcherons de la Manouane** (Manouane River Lumberjacks).
Prod: Fernand Dansereau and Victor Jobin, NFB. 28 min. b&w.

1963 **De Montréal à Manicouagan** (Montreal-Manicouagan). Prod:
Fernand Dansereau, NFB. 28 min. b&w.

1965 **La neige a fondu sur la Manicouagan**. Prod: Marcel Martin, NFB.
58 min. b&w.
Poussière sur la ville. Prod: Pierre Patry and Jean Roy, Cooperatio
Inc. and SGC. 95 min. b&w.

1966 **La Moisson** (Harvesting). Prod: Guy L. Côté and Marcel Martin,
NFB. 10 min. col.

1967 **Le Train du Labrador**. Prod: Société nouvelle des établissements
Gaumont. 28 min. b&w.
Ce Soir-là, Gilles Vigneault . . . . Prod: SGC and Omniart. 70 min.
col.

1969 **Pour une éducation de qualité**. Prod: SGC for La Corporation des
enseignants du Québec. Series of six films of 30 min. each.
Au-delà des murs. Prod: SGC for OFQ. 28 min. col.

1970 **Le mépris n'aura qu'un temps**. Prod: SGC for le Conseil des Syndicats nationaux (CSN). 95 min. b&w & col.

1971 **Conflit scolaire St-Léonard**. Prod: SGC. 12 min. b&w.
Un Homme et son boss. Prod: SGC. 7 min. b&w.

1972 **La Route de fer**. Prod: Les Ateliers audio-visuels du Québec. 10 min.
Les Gars de Lapalme. With Francois Dupuis. Prod: Les Ateliers
audio-visuels du Québec for CSN.
Special Delivery. With Francois Dupuis. Prod: Les Ateliers audio-
visuels du Québec.

BIBLIOGRAPHY

Cinéastes du Québec 6: Arthur Lamothe, CQDC, 1971, has an analysis of
Le mépris n'aura,qu'un temps, an interview, criticism, bibliography and a
filmography.

Dossiers de Cinéma: 1, Fides, 1968, on **Les Bûcherons de la Manouane**.

La Patrie, Montreal, January 7, 1968, an interview on **Ce Soir-là, Gilles
Vigneault** . . .

Cinéma Québec, Vol. 1, No. 1, May 1971, pp. 10-18, on **Le mépris
n'aura qu'un temps.**

Take One, Vol. 1, No. 2, pp. 13-16, "Canadian Filmmakers: Arthur
Lamothe and Jean-Claude Labrecque". Interview.

Cahiers du cinéma in English, No. 4, "10 Questions to 5 Canadian
Filmmakers", an interview.

Le Soleil, Quebec, June 8, 1968, p. 41, an interview by Claude Daigneault.

Séquences #53, pp. 19-24, interview by Léo Bonneville.

How to Make or Not to Make a Canadian Film, "The Actor and Film",
by Lamothe.

References in: *Jeune Cinéma canadien, Essais sur la cinéma québécois,
Vingt Ans de cinéma au Canada français* and *Le Cinéma québécois:
tendances et prolongements.*

LAVOIE, RICHARD

Born in 1937, Richard Lavoie studied first the trumpet and then the flute before following his father's footsteps into film (his father, Herménégilde Lavoie, had been making tourism films since 1936). Living quietly in Tewksbury (outside Quebec City), Richard Lavoie has concentrated his efforts on short and sponsored films, primarily having to do with the Quebec City area and with New Quebec. In 1956, Lavoie visited Cuba, and — four years later — Russia. He has since travelled to New York, Czechoslovakia, Japan, and Cyprus, among other places. In 1971, a projected feature, **Yogine**, which was to have starred the Japanese actor Tatsuya Nakadai, fell through at the last minute.

FILMOGRAPHY (incomplete)

1956 **One Heart and One Soul** (religious). 30 min. col.

1957 **Stop** (road safety). 25 min. col.

1958 **Produits de santé** (industrial). 32 min. col.

1958 "Cézar", a series of 90-minute TV shows for children
-59

1959 **Old Quebec, Gateway to Canada's New Wealth** (industrial and tourism promotion). 25 min. col.

1960 **Itarnitak** (Eskimo sculpture). 19 min. b&w.

1961 **Franciscaines Missionnaires** (religious). 30 min. col.

1962 **Dialogue avec la terre** (geology). 26 min. col.

1963 **L'Exposition provinciale de Québec**. 20 min. col.
-64

1964 **Noël à l'Ile aux Grues** (a Christmas story). 27 min. b&w.

1965 **Champs d'action** (for Hydro-Quebec). 15 min. col.
Les Cobayes (on Cyprus). 20 min. b&w.

1966 **L'Ile aux Oies**. 20 min. col.

1967 **Les Neo-québécois** (for the Quebec Pavilion at Expo). 3 min. b&w.

1971 **Vieux Koniak** (anthropology). 22 min. col.
Pathologie et linguistique. 9 min. col.
L'Avale-mot (medical). 9 min. col.

BIBLIOGRAPHY

"L'Avenir du cinéma canadien repose sur les jeunes", by Christiane Brunelle-Garon, *Le Soleil* (Quebec), February 4, 1962.

LAVUT, MARTIN

Actor, screenwriter and director, Martin Lavut was born in Toronto where he is now free-lancing. His work as an actor includes the role of Duddy in the CBC's adaptation of *The Apprenticeship of Duddy Kravitz* by Mordecai Richler, and touring with the satirical troupe, *Second City*. His screenplay for **Jenny** was filmed by George Bloomfield in 1970. Lavut has directed numerous television commercials and segments for variety programs, and has been filmmaker in residence at Washington University. In 1970 he produced radio movies for the blind in the program "Ideas", consisting largely of archival sounds from both television and radio.

FILMOGRAPHY

1965 **Leni Riefenstahl**. Prod: CBC "Tuesday Night". 30 min. b&w.
      Marshall McLuhan. Prod: CBC "Other Voices". 30 min. b&w.

1968 **At Home**. Prod: M. Lavut, CBC. 14 min. b&w.

1970 **The Life Game**. Prod: Jesse Nishihata, CBC. 57 min. b&w.

BIBLIOGRAPHY

The Globe and Mail, September 22, 1970, by Blaik Kirby, on **The Life Game**.

The Toronto Star, October 10, 1969, by Martin Knelman, on **At Home**.

The Telegram, Toronto, May 23, 1970, an interview by Pat Annesley.

Miss Chatelaine, August 10, 1971, Vol. 8, No. 4, "Let's Hear It for Don & Morley & Martin & Ivan & Sylvia & Eric . . .", by Kay Armatage.

LEDUC, JACQUES

Born in Montreal in 1941, Jacques Leduc entered the National Film Board in 1962 as an assistant-cameraman; in this capacity he worked on Jutra's **Comment savoir**, Fernand Dansereau's **le Festin des morts**, Labrecque's **60 Cycles** and Owen's **Nobody Waved Goodbye.** Leduc has shot three of Lefebvre's films — **Il ne faut pas mourir pour ça**, **Mon Amie Pierrette** and **Ultimatum** — and acted as assistant-director on Godbout's **Yul 871**. His feature, **On est loin du soleil,** is a delicate tale revolving around the social and religious spirit of Brother André, founder of Montreal's St. Joseph Oratory.

FILMOGRAPHY

1967 **Chantal: en vrac.** Prod: Guy L. Côté, NFB. 50 min. col.

1968 **Nominingue . . . depuis qu'il existe.** Prod: Guy L. Côté, NFB. 73 min. col and b&w.

1969 **Là ou ailleurs.** With Pierre Bernier. Prod: Guy L. Côté, NFB. 10 min. col.

1970 **Ca marche.** With Arnie Gelbart. Prod: NFB for the Minister of Labour and the Minister of Immigration. 16 min. col.
Cap d'Espoir. Prod: Pierre Maheu, NFB. 60 min. col. Not released.

1971 **On est loin du soleil.** Prod: Paul Larose, NFB. 79 min. b&w.

1972 **Je chante à cheval avec Willie Lamothe.** With Pierre Bernier, Lucien Menard, Alain Dostie, Suzanne Demers. Prod: Paul Larose, NFB. 57 min. col.
La Tendresse ordinaire. Prod: Paul Larose, NFB. 90 min. col.
La Guitare. Prod: Paul Larose, NFB. (Short in progress.)

BIBLIOGRAPHY

Objectif, August 1967, by Pierre Hébert on **Chantal: en vrac.**

The following are reviews of **On est loin du soleil**:

Cinéma Québec, November 1971, pp. 6-8, "L'évidence mise à nue", by André Leroux.

Point de mire, Vol. 2, No. 33, September 17, 1971, pp. 40-41.

Séquences, No. 68, February 1972, pp. 38-39.

Montréal-Matin, September 26, 1971, pp. 6-7, by François Piazza.

Québec-Presse, December 26, 1971, "Nous sommes tous des frères André", by Robert Lévesque, an interview.

Québec-Presse, November 21, 1971, "Quand je fais une tournée au Québec avec un film québécois, j'ai l'impression de faire du cinéma clandestin", by Carol Faucher. Interview.

Reviews of Leduc's early work in: *Essais sur le cinéma québécois* and *Le Cinéma canadien.*

LEFEBVRE, JEAN-PIERRE

Born in Montreal in 1941, Lefebvre is Quebec's most prolific filmmaker. Poet and critic (Lefebvre was a staff writer on the now-defunct cinema review, *Objectif*), he creates visual poems with his films; his sense of humour and irony give his work warmth and poignancy. He has worked largely as an independent, forming his own company, Cinak, which has co-produced Arcand's **La Maudite Galette** and Labrecque's **Les Smattes**. While head of the Fiction Studio at the National Film Board, Lefebvre produced a series, "Premières Oeuvres" which include the first feature films of Jean Chabot, André Théberge, Michel Audy, Yvan Patry and Fernand Bélanger.

FILMOGRAPHY

1964 **L'Homoman**. Prod: Les Films Jean-Pierre Lefebvre. 24 min. b&w.

1965 **Le Révolutionnaire**. Prod: Les Films Jean-Pierre Lefebvre. 74 min. b&w.

Patricia et Jean Baptiste. Prod: Les Films Jean-Pierre Lefebvre. 83 min. b&w.

Mon Oeil (My Eye). Prod: Les Films Jean-Pierre Lefebvre. 90 min. b&w.

1967 **Il ne faut pas mourir pour ça** (Don't Let It Kill You). Prod: Les Films Jean-Pierre Lefebvre. 75 min. b&w.

Mon Amie Pierrette. Prod: Clément Perron, NFB. 68 min. col.

1968 **Jusqu'au coeur**. Prod: Clément Perron, NFB. 93 min. col. and b&w.

1969 **La Chambre blanche** (House of Light). Prod: Cinak. 80 min. b&w.

1970 **Un Succès commercial** or **Q-bec My Love**. Prod: Cinak. 83 min. b&w.

1971 **Les Maudits Sauvages** (Those Damned Savages). Prod. Cinak. 90 min. col.

1972 **Ultimatum**. Prod: Cinak. (Feature in progress.)

All of Lefebvre's films, except those produced by the National Film Board, are distributed by Faroun Films, Montreal.

BIBLIOGRAPHY

Cinéastes du Québec 3: Jean-Pierre Lefebvre, CQDC, 1970. A collection of criticisms, an interview, extracts of dialogue from **Q-bec My Love**, a filmography and a complete bibliography.

Jean-Pierre Lefebvre, Renald Bérubé and Yvan Patry, eds., Les Presses de l'université du Québec, 1971 (C.P. 250, Station N, Montreal 129, Canada), has critiques, interviews, documents and a filmography.

Objectif has several of Lefebvre's own critical articles.

Cahiers du cinéma in English, No. 4, "10 Questions to 5 Canadian Film-makers", an article by and an interview with Lefebvre.

How to Make or Not to Make a Canadian Film, "Technique is Absurd", by Lefebvre.

Second Wave, Robin Wood, ed., Praeger, N.Y. 1970, "Jean-Pierre Lefebvre", by Jean Chabot.

Take One, Vol. 1, No. 7, pp. 10-13, "The Gentle Revolutionary", by Graham Fraser.

Toronto Telegram, August 2, 1967, "How to Resist the Yanks", a talk with Lefebvre and Clyde Gilmour.

The Montreal Gazette, March 29, 1969, p. 15, "Jean-Pierre Lefebvre: Movies for Culture", by Dane Lanken.

Le Devoir, Montreal, April 16, 1969, an interview on **La Chambre blanche**.

Le Devoir, February 1, 1969, "Jean-Pierre Lefebvre: 'Il faut faire des témoignages' ", by Claude Nadon.

Le Devoir, February 8, 1969, p. 17, "Godard et Lefebvre, quand le cinéma devient des fables-témoignáges", by Claude Nadon.

Articles in: *Essais sur le cinéma québécois,* by Dominique Noguez; *Jeune Cinéma canadien,* by Rene Predal; *Vingt Ans de cinéma au Canada français,* by Robert Daudelin; *Le Cinéma canadien,* by Gilles Marsolais; and *Le Cinéma québécois: tendances et prolongements,* in the chapter entitled, "Le sens de la contestation et Jean-Pierre Lefebvre", by André Larsen.

Scene from Lefebvre's la Chambre blanche.

LEITERMAN, DOUGLAS

Born in South Porcupine, Ontario in 1927, Douglas Leiterman worked as a newspaper journalist after studying economics and law at the University of British Columbia and Harvard. His work in television began when he joined the CBC in 1958. Leiterman is best known for his founding and producing of CBC's "Document" and "This Hour Has Seven Days" (the latter with Patrick Watson). Leiterman left Canada in 1966 to work with CBS News but has since returned to set up his own company, Hobel-Leiterman Productions Ltd. of Toronto, which produces television documentaries. In recent years, Leiterman has been producing for "The Fabulous Sixties", "Here Come the Seventies" and "Face to Face to Face".

FILMOGRAPHY (incomplete)

1958 **The Doukhobors**. Prod: D. Leiterman, CBC, Toronto.

1959 **The Age of Mackenzie King**. Prod: D. Leiterman, CBC, Toronto. 120 min.

1960 **U.N. in Peril**. Prod: CBC "The Critical Years". 90 min.

1961 **Forty Million Shoes**. Prod: D. Leiterman, CBC "Intertel", 60 min.

1962 **Balance of Terror**. With Beryl Fox. Prod: D. Leiterman, Talent Associates — Paramount. 60 min.
Servant of All. With B. Fox. Prod: D. Leiterman, CBC "Document". 60 min.
Don't Label Me. Prod: D. Leiterman, CBC "Intertel". 60 min.

1963 **Three on a Match**. With B. Fox. Prod: D. Leiterman, CBC "Document".
The Chief. With B. Fox. Prod: D. Leiterman, CBC "Document". 60 min.

1964 **One More River**. With B. Fox. Prod: D. Leiterman, CBC "Intertel". 50 min. b&w.

1964 "This Hour has Seven Days". Prod./Dir./Writers: D. Leiterman and
-65 Patrick Watson. Ex-Prod: Reeves Hagan.

1965 "This Hour has Seven Days". Ex-Prod./Dir./Writers: D. Leiterman
-66 and P. Watson. Prod: Robert E. Hoyt and Ken Lefoli.

1966 **The Democrats in '66**. Prod: D. Leiterman, CBS, 60 min.
1969 **Fasten Your Seatbelts**. Prod. D. Leiterman, NET/CBC. 60 min.

BIBLIOGRAPHY

Hommage à "This Hour has Seven Days", La Cinémathèque canadienne.

Maclean's Magazine, July 23, 1966.

The Globe and Mail, January 11, 1969, "Return of the Seven Days' Wonder".

Toronto Daily Star, May 6, 1967, "Leiterman Says: 'I Was Banished From My Homeland' ", by Antony Ferry.

Take One, Vol. 1, No. 1, pp. 11-12, "Notes of a Man Preparing to Leave His Country", by D. Leiterman.

Time, Canadian edition, May 22, 1964, p. 14.

Maclean's Magazine, February 6, 1965, p. 12, "How to Survive in the CBC Jungle — and Other TV Tribal Secrets".

Maclean's Magazine, March 5, 1966, p. 8, "The Show that Survives by Success Alone".

Creativity in Communication, a speech by Leiterman, available on cassette for $3.50 from the Edmonton A/V Association, c/o Educational Media Division, Department of Extension, University of Alberta.

LEITERMAN, RICHARD

Leiterman was born in northern Ontario in 1935. After studying with
Stan Fox of the Vancouver Film Unit, he began his career as a cameraman,
shooting news for the CBC in Vancouver. Later he went to London,
England where he was involved in news and documentary filming. In
1961, he joined Allan King in his London office to form Allan King
Associates. The stylistic freedom and facility he has developed through
his experience in *cinéma-vérité* style television documentaries also marks
his recent work on a number of feature films. Leiterman was associate
director (with Allan King) as well as cinematographer of **A Married Couple**.

FILMOGRAPHY (Incomplete)

Richard Leiterman's major cinematographic credits are as follows (directors
included):

Allan King:	**Running Away Backwards** or **Coming of Age in Ibiza** (1964)
	The New Woman (1968)
	A Married Couple (1969)
Don Shebib:	**Goin' Down the Road** (1970)
	Rip-Off (1971)
	Paul Bradley (1972)
Douglas Leiterman and Beryl Fox:	**One More River** (1964)
Beryl Fox:	**Summer In Mississippi** (1964)
	Cinema: The Living Camera (1972)
Terence Macartney-Filgate:	**Christopher Plummer** (1967)
René Bonnière:	**Hamlet** (1972)
William Fruet:	**Wedding in White** (1972)

BIBLIOGRAPHY

Toronto Daily Star, November 8, 1969, "It's Said This Man Was Born With a Camera in His Hands", by Dorothy Mikos.

Film Quarterly, Summer 1970, pp. 9-23, "The Fictional Documentary: Interviews with the Makers of *A Married Couple",* by Alan Rosenthal. (Reprinted in Rosenthal's *The New Documentary in Action,* University of California Press, Berkely, 1971.)

Armies of the Night, Part IV, "Saturday Night and All of Sunday", by Norman Mailer, General Publishing Company Ltd., Canada, 1968 — has a portrait of Leiterman in action.

Cinema Canada, Second Edition, No. 1, March 1972, an interview by George Koller.

LORD, JEAN-CLAUDE

Born in Montreal in 1943, Jean-Claude Lord obtained his B.A. in 1963, and that year began a long apprenticeship in the cinema. During the year he co-authored and acted as assistant-director on Pierre Patry's **Trouble-fête** (the Canadian entry at Cannes in 1964). He later assisted Patry in the direction of two other features, **La Corde au cou** and **Cain**, and a short, **Il y eut un soir, il y eut un matin**. Since then Lord has been assistant director on a number of features, including Arthur Lamothe's **Poussière sur la ville**, Michel Brault's **Entre la mer et l'eau douce**, and Eric Till's **A Great Big Thing**, and was production manager on Roger Fournier's **Pile ou face**. Between 1967 and 1969 Lord was part-time director of the audio-visual department at the Vaudreuil (Quebec) Cultural Centre;

between 1969 and 1972, he regularly reviewed new films on the weekly show, "Bon Dimanche" (CFTM-TV, Montreal); and in 1971 he was film columnist for the Montreal weekly, *Petit Journal.*

FILMOGRAPHY

1965 **Délivrez-nous du mal**. Prod: Pierre Patry, Coopératio. 82 min. b&w.

1972 **Les Colombes**. Prod. Jean-Claude Lord, Les Films Jean-Claude Lord Inc. 116 min. col.

BIBLIOGRAPHY

Le Devoir, 7 July, 1969, review of **Délivrez-nous du mal** by Jean Chabot.

Reviews of **Les Colombes** in:
    Le Devoir, 16 Sept., 1972 (by Robert Guy Scully).
    La Presse, 16 Sept., 1972 (by Luc Perreault; along with an interview).
    Variety, 27 Sept., 1972 (by Jean-Pierre Tadros).

LOW, COLIN

Colin Low was born in Cardston, Alberta in 1926 and joined the National Film Board as an animator in 1945 at Norman McLaren's request. Later, as director of animation, Low produced Derek Lamb's **I Know an Old Lady Who Swallowed a Fly** and Gerald Potterton's **My Financial Career** and **The Ride**. Highly poetic, Low's films are investigations of our relationship with the past, and although his work in the Challenge for Change Unit was innovative in structure, it, too, was concerned with traditions. As film director for the Fogo Island project, Low was involved in the process of solving problems within a community (undertaken in conjunction with Newfoundland's Memorial University Extension Service, the project produced twenty-eight short films which were used as tools for community discussion). Low was guest producer with the Office of Economic Opportunity in the United States; he has also directed a film on hunger for the White House, and co-produced and co-directed **Labyrinth** with Roman Kroitor for Expo '67. Now head of the NFB's Challenge for Change Unit, Low has had an important and far-reaching effect on Canadian cinema. He was the winner of the Grierson Award at the 1972 Canadian Film Awards.

Colin Low with props for Universe, *the most popular film ever made at the National Film Board.*

FILMOGRAPHY

1951 **Age of the Beaver** (L'Age du castor). Prod: Tom Daly, NFB. 17 min. b&w.

1952 **The Romance of Transportation in Canada** (Sports et Transports). With Wolf Koenig and Robert Verrall. Prod: Tom Daly, NFB. 11 min. col.

1953 **Corral.** Prod: Tom Daly, NFB. 12 min. b&w.

1954 **The Jolifou Inn** (L'Auberge Jolifou). Prod: Tom Daly, NFB. 10 min. col.

1955 **Gold** (L'Or). Prod: Tom Daly, NFB. 11 min. b&w.

1957 **City of Gold** (Capitale de l'or). With Wolf Koenig. Prod: Tom Daly, NFB. 22 min. b&w.

1959 **City Out of Time** (Ville intemporelle). Prod: Tom Daly, NFB. 16 min. col.

1960 **Universe** (Notre Univers). With Roman Kroitor. Prod: C. Low, R. Kroitor and Tom Daly, NFB. 26 min. col.

   Circle of the Sun (Le Soleil perdu). Prod: Tom Daly, NFB. 29 min. col.

1961 **The Days of Whiskey Gap**. Prod: Roman Kroitor and Wolf Koenig, NFB. 28 min. b&w.

1963 **The Hutterites** (Les Hutterites). Prod: Tom Daly and Roman Kroitor, NFB. 28 min. b&w.

1967 **Labyrinth**. With Roman Kroitor and Hugh O'Connor. Prod: NFB for Expo '67.

1970 **The Winds of Fogo**. Prod: Tom Daly, NFB. 20 min. col.

BIBLIOGRAPHY

Dossiers de cinéma: 1, Fides, 1968, has reviews of **Corral** and **City of Gold**.

No. 174 of editions published by the Institut des hautes études cinématographiques, Paris, extensively reviews **City of Gold**. (Put together by the Canadian filmmaker, Jean-Pierre Masse.)

Objectif 61, No. 4, January 1961, pp. 21-25, "A la recherche du soleil", by Michel Regnier.

Images, Vol. 1, No. 3, April 1956, an interview by Arthur Lamothe.

Objectif 63, No. 23/24, October-November 1963, pp. 24-38, "Colin Low, poète de la survivance", by Jean-Pierre Lefebvre. Interview.

Séquences, No. 24, February 1961, pp. 29-30, "Un cinéaste canadien: Colin Low". Interview.

Séquences, No. 50, October 1967, pp. 22-23, "La création cinématographique: dialogue avec Colin Low". Interview.

How to Make or Not to Make a Canadian Film, "Will Story Film Use Multi-Screen?", by Low.

References in: *Jeune Cinéma canadien,* and *Le Cinéma canadien.*

MACARTNEY-FILGATE, TERENCE

Born in England in 1924, Terence Macartney-Filgate joined the NFB as a scriptwriter in 1954 and became a key member of the Candid Eye Unit between 1957-1960. The sense of actuality and ability to adapt readily to ongoing situations which were developed in the Unit have had reverberating effects, not only within the NFB but in *cinéma-vérité* everywhere. Since leaving the NFB, Filgate has spent time in the United States working with Leacock and the Maysles on "Primary". He has produced film in Lebanon, taught at UCLA, and most recently has been free-lancing out of the CBC, Toronto. He shot the live-action section of Gerald Potterton's **Pinter People** and has made a number of campaign films.

FILMOGRAPHY (incomplete)

1958 **The Days Before Christmas** (Bientôt Noël). With Wolf Koenig, George Dufaux and Stanley Jackson. Prod: R. Kroitor and W. Koenig, NFB. 30 min. b&w.

Blood and Fire. Prod: Roman Kroitor and Wolf Koenig, NFB. 30 min. b&w.

Police. Prod: Wolf Koenig and Roman Kroitor, NFB. 29 min. b&w.

Pilgrimage. Prod: Wolf Koenig, NFB. 29 min. b&w.

1959 **The Back-breaking Leaf** (La Feuille qui brise les reins). Prod: Roman Kroitor and Wolf Koenig, NFB. 29 min. b&w.

End of the Line. Prod: Roman Kroitor and Wolf Koenig, NFB. 30 min. b&w.

The Cars in Your Life. Prod: Roman Kroitor and Wolf Koenig, NFB. 29 min. b&w.

1960 **Emergency in Morocco**. Prod: United Nations and NFB. 16 min. b&w.

Pilot X-15. Prod: Time Broadcasting Inc. 30 min. b&w.

1962 **Robert Frost: A Lover's Quarrel**. (Director and cameraman for Vermont sequences.) Prod: WGBH and NET. 60 min. b&w.

1963 **Inside the Movie Kingdom**. Prod: NBC. 60 min. b&w.

1964 **South African Essays**. Prod: NET. 60 min.

The Hundredth Summer (Le Centième Eté). Prod: T. Macartney-Filgate, NFB. 52 min. col.

1965 **Vladimir Nabokov** with Robert Hughes. Prod: NET "Creative Persons". 30 min. b&w.

1966 **Composers U.S.A.: The Avant-Garde**. Prod: NET "Creative Persons". 30 min. b&w.

Portrait of Karsh. Prod: CBC "Telescope". 30 min. col.

1967 **Marshall McLuhan**. Prod: CBC "Telescope". 30 min. col.

Christopher Plummer. Prod: CBC for "TBA". 30 min. b&w.

Woody Allan. Prod: CBC. 20 min. b&w.

1969 **Up Against the System**. Prod. George C. Stoney, NFB "Challenge for Change". 20 min. b&w.

1970 **A. Y. Jackson: A Portrait**. Prod: CBC "Man at the Centre". 30 min. col.

1972 **Henry David Thoreau: The Beat of a Different Drummer**. Prod: T. Macartney-Filgate, CBC. 60 min. col.

BIBLIOGRAPHY

Terence Macartney-Filgate: The Candid Eye, Canadian Filmography Series #104, Canadian Film Institute, Ottawa, 1966. Has an interview by Sarah Jennings, comments by Gilles Gascon and Georges Dufaux, discussions with Roman Kroitor and Jean-Claude Labrecque on Filgate and the Candid Eye Unit, and a filmography. (Now out of print. Available at film study centres.)

Image et Son, April 1965, by Louis Marcorelles.

The Montreal Star, June 26, 1965, "Apartheid Documentary Shot Cloak-and-Dagger Style", by Raymond Heard.

MACKEY, CLARKE

Born in Port Colbourne, Ontario, 1950, Clarke Mackey made his first 8mm film after working with filmmakers Julius Kohanyi and David Secter. As well as editing film at the CBC, Toronto, Mackey has been cameraman on three of Iain Ewing's films —**Picaro**, **Kill** and **Eat Anything**; he also worked as an assistant sound man on David Secter's **The Offering** and edited a number of films by Dick Ballantine. Mackey's feature, **The Only Thing You Know**, won two Etrogs in the 1971 Canadian Film Awards, in the catagories "Best First Feature" and "Best Actress".

FILMOGRAPHY

1967 **On Nothing Days**. Prod: Independent. 25 min. b&w.
     Ruins. Prod: Independent. 10 min. col.

1968 **Grass**. Prod: Independent. 45 min. col.

1969 **Mihi P**. Prod: Independent. 28 min. b&w.

1971 **The Only Thing You Know**. Prod: Clarke Mackey Films. 82 min. col.

Clarke Mackey's films are distributed by the Canadian Film-Makers' Distribution Centre.

BIBLIOGRAPHY

Pot Pourri, December 1971, an interview by Pat Thorvaldson.

Maclean's Magazine, November 1971 and January 1972 — both articles by John Hofsess.

The Telegram, Toronto, October 9, 1971, "Fame's Reward Selling Books", by Sid Adilman; and August 14, 1971, "The Young Canadian Filmmaker's First Feature Tonight", also by Adilman.

Toronto Citizen, Vol. 2, No. 16, August 16, 1971, by Bruce Leaux.

Take One, Vol. 2, No. 12, pp. 20-21, by Bob Fothergill.

MARKSON, MORLEY

Designer, photographer, inventor and teacher, Morley Markson created the Kaleidoscope pavilion at Expo '67; as well as designing the three-chambered pavilion, Markson directed the films and produced the color, movement and sound interior within a mirror projection system. Intensely personal in feeling, Markson's films deal with the convolutions of individual and social expression when passing through different media. His two feature films, **The Tragic Diary of Zero the Fool** and **Breathing Together: Revolution of the Electric Family**, won first prizes at the Ann Arbor Film Festival in 1970 and 1971. Markson was born in Toronto and continues to work there.

FILMOGRAPHY

1967 **Man and Color.** Prod: M. Markson for Kaleidoscope Pavilion, Expo '67. 12 min. col.

1968 **Zero.** Prod: Independent. 12 min. b&w.
America Simultaneous: The Electric Family. Prod: Independent. A multi-screen sound spectacle.
Electrocution of the Word. Prod: Independent. 4 min. col.

1970 **The Tragic Diary of Zero the Fool** (Zéro le fou). Prod: Morley Markson and Associates Ltd. 72 min. b&w.

1971 **Breathing Together: Revolution of the Electric Family** (Vivre ensemble: la famille électrique). Prod: Morley Markson and Associates Ltd. 84 min. b&w.

Markson's films are distributed by the Canadian Film-Makers' Distribution Centre and Coopérative cinéastes indépendants.

BIBLIOGRAPHY

Toronto Daily Star, January 17, 1969, "Are You Beginning to See the Light?", by Martin Knelman.

Architecture Canada, October 1967, "Psychedelic Experience Without LSD".

Saturday Night, February 1970, "Movie Review", by Marshall Delaney.

CIL Oval, Vol. 35, No. 4, Winter 1966, "Expo's Potent Color Show — Kaleidoscope", by Joy Carroll.

Reviews of **Breathing Together** in:

Filmmakers Newsletter, N.Y., Vol. 4, No. 7, p. 49.

Jeune Cinéma, No. 56, June-July 1971, p. 34.

Positif, No. 130, September 1971, pp. 14-15.

Image et Son, No. 252, 1971, p. 30.

Le Soleil, October 30, 1971, "On ne connait pas l'issue du combat".

MASON, BILL

Bill Mason was born in Winnipeg, Manitoba in 1929. He was a painter and commercial artist before moving into animation. While working with Crawley Films, he portrayed the canoeist in Christopher Chapman's **Quetico** and shot a variety of films, among them **On the Top of a Continent** and **The Voyageurs**. Mason's love of the bush encouraged him to bring a storyline to his still photography, and as a conservationist, he has touched the popular imagination. Mason works out of the National Film Board.

FILMOGRAPHY

1965 **Wilderness Treasure**. Prod: Wilber Sutherland, Intervarsity Christian Fellowship. 20 min. col.

1966 **Paddle to the Sea** (Vogue-à-la-mer). Prod: Julian Biggs, NFB. 28 min. col.

1968 **The Rise and Fall of the Great Lakes**. Prod: Joseph Koenig, NFB. 17 min. col.

1969 **Blake**. Prod: Douglas Jackson, NFB. 19 min. col.

1971 **Death of a Legend** (La Fin d'un mythe). Prod: Barrie Howells, NFB. 51 min. col.

1972 **Cry of the Wild**. Prod: Bill Brind, NFB. 91 min. col.

BIBLIOGRAPHY

Pot Pourri, September 1971, an interview by Pat Thorvaldson. Reprinted in *Sight Lines,* November-December, 1971, pp. 4-8.

Reviews of **Death of a Legend**:

Québec-Presse, October 3, 1971, "Les loups ne sont pas si méchants qu'on le dit. . .", by Carol Faucher.

Le Grand Journal illustré, October 11-17, 1971, p. 24, *"La fin d'un myth . . .* les loups rendus sympathiques", by Benoit L'Herbier.

Ottawa Citizen, September 25, 1971, "Film Probes 'Bad Guy' Reputation of Wolves", by Gordon Stoneham.

MAY, DEREK

Painter and filmmaker, Derek May was born in London, England in 1932. He joined the National Film Board as an assistant editor in 1965, and acted in Don Owen's **Notes For a Film About Donna and Gail** and **The Ernie Game**; he was also art director for the latter production. May's own films can be described as "personal", very much in the tradition of the London, Ontario artist-filmmakers, Jack Chambers and Greg Curnoe, the kind of films which are generally found in the field of animation rather than live action. In 1971 May worked in video with the Challenge for Change Unit and the following year travelled and painted on a Canada Council grant.

FILMOGRAPHY

1967 **Angel**. Prod: Guy Glover, NFB. 7 min. col.

1968 **Niagara Falls**. Prod: Tom Daly, NFB. 28 min. col.

1969 **McBus**. Prod: Tom Daly, NFB. 15 min. col.

1971 **A Film for Max**. Prod: Tom Daly, NFB. 80 min. col. and b&w.
      Pandora. Prod: Tom Daly, NFB. 6 min. col.

BIBLIOGRAPHY

The Montreal Gazette, September 27, 1969, "Derek May: A Cosmic Weatherman", by Terry Ryan.

Artscanada, April 1970, p. 26, "Six Filmmakers in Search of an Alternative", by Terry Ryan.

Le Nouvelliste, Trois-Rivières, May 18, 1968, p. 173, on **Angel**.

Screen, Vol. 5, No. 2, pp. 15-17, on **Pandora**.

NOLD, WERNER

Born at St. Moritz, Switzerland in 1933, Werner Nold studied photography in his native land before coming to Canada in 1955. He worked first as a cameraman on two television series for the Quebec Film Board and later as cameraman and editor for Nova Films in Quebec City. In 1960 he joined the National Film Board as an editor, working on Gilles Carle's earliest films. One of the few editors of feature films in Canada, Nold received a Canada Council grant in 1972 in order to further study his craft in film centres. As well as his editing work, Nold has directed a short, **Préambule**, produced by Robert Forget and P. Maheu at the NFB, co-directed **Le Temps perdu** with Michel Brault and conceived as well as edited the 35mm split-screen production, **L'Eau**, for the Quebec Pavilion at Expo '67.

FILMOGRAPHY

The following is a partial list of Werner Nold's editing credits (directors included):

Gilles Carle:	**Dimanche d'Amérique** (1961)
	Patinoire (1962)
	Solange dans nos campagnes (1964)
	La Vie heureuse de Léopold Z (1965)
Michel Brault:	**Le Temps perdu** (1964)
	Entre la mer et l'eau douce (1967)
Pierre Perrault:	**Pour la suite du monde** (1963)
Denys Arcand:	**Champlain** (1963)
	La Route de l'ouest (1964)
Marcel Carrière:	**The Indian Speaks** (1967)
	Avec tambours et trompettes (1968)
	Episode (1968)
	Saint-Denis dans le temps . . . (1969)
Claude Jutra:	**A tout prendre** (1963)
	Comment savoir (1965)
	Rouli-roulant (1966)
	Marie-Christine (1970)
Jacques Godbout:	**IXE-13** (1972)
Jean-Claude Labrecque:	**60 Cycles** (1964)

BIBLIOGRAPHY

Le Cinéma québécois: tendances et prolongements, p. 122, article by Yvan Patry.

OWEN, DONALD

Born in Toronto in 1934, writer and poet Don Owen began his film career writing for Westminster Films and the National Film Board. His first directed work, **Runner**, shows the early promise of Owen's intimate portraiture and fluid style; with commentary by W. H. Auden, **Runner** is a poetic film, an interior drama of an ancient ritual. **Nobody Waved Goodbye**, which began as a short document, became an inspired feature receiving critical acclaim wherever it was shown. Recently Owen has been investigating a more formalized style as in **Gallery, A View of Time** and **Cowboy and Indian** which, nevertheless, retains the personal intimacy of his early work. Owen lives and works in Toronto.

FILMOGRAPHY

1962 **Runner** (Le Coureur) Prod: Tom Daly, NFB. 11 min. b&w.

1963 **Toronto Jazz**. Prod: Roman Kroitor, NFB. 27 min. b&w.

1964 **Nobody Waved Goodbye** (Départ sans adieux) Prod: Roman Kroitor and D. Owen, NFB. 80 min. b&w.

1965 **You Don't Back Down**. Prod: Joe Koenig, NFB. 28 min. b&w.

High Steel (Charpentier du ciel) Prod: Julian Biggs, NFB. 14 min. col.

1966 **Notes For a Film About Donna and Gail**. Prod: Julian Biggs, NFB. 49 min. b&w.

Ladies and Gentlemen: Mr. Leonard Cohen. With Donald Brittain Prod: John Kemeny, NFB. 41 min. b&w.

1967 **A Further Glimpse of Joey**. Prod: Ross McLean, NFB. 28 min. b&w.

The Ernie Game (Ernie). Prod: Gordon Burwash, CBC/NFB Co-production. 88 min. col.

1969 **Gallery, A View of Time**. Prod: Albright-Knox Gallery, Buffalo, N.Y. 14 min. col.

1970 **Snow in Venice**. Prod: Fletcher Markle, CBC "Telescope". 30 min. b&w.

1972 **Cowboy and Indian**. Prod: Tom Daly, NFB. 45 min. col.

BIBLIOGRAPHY

Image et Son, No. 230-231, September-October 1969, pp. 111-112, on **The Ernie Game**.

Dossiers de cinéma: 1, Fides, 1968, on **Runner** and **High Steel**.

The Montreal Star, December 14, 1968, "Tip-toe Through the Sculpture — on Film", by Denise Kalette, on **Gallery: A View of Time**.

The Globe and Mail, December 21, 1968, "Don Owen: Meditation With Film", by Martin Malina.

Objectif 63, Vol. 2, No. 10, pp. 31-32, "A pied ou en Bentley", by Jacques Leduc, on **Toronto Jazz**.

The Canadian, January 6, 1966, "Going Places by Staying in Canada", by Robert Miller.

Le Petit Journal, March 5, 1967, "Don Owen: il est très sûr de lui, et il a raison", by Danielle Sauvage.

Canadian Cinematography, May-June 1964, pp. 6, 7, & 16, "New Film Features Improvisation", by John Spotton, cameraman on **Nobody**

Waved Goodbye; and No. 30, January-February 1967, pp. 11-14, "Conversation on Film with Don Owen".

Various articles in: *Le Cinéma québécois: tendances et prolongements* (by L. and Y. Patry), *Jeune Cinéma canadien, Essais sur le cinéma québécois,* and *Le Cinéma canadien.*

Take One, Vol. 1, No. 2. Interview.

Séquences, no. 50, October 1967, pp. 24-26, "Dialogue avec des cinéastes canadiens, la création cinématographique". Interview.

Objectif, No. 37, November-December 1966, pp. 31-35, "101 questions à Don Owen sur *Nobody Waved Goodbye".* Interview.

Objectif, October-November 1964, pp. 47-49, "Bandes a part"; and Aug-ust-September 1965, pp. 30-33. Both Interviews.

Take One, Vol. 1, No. 6, 1967, pp. 4-6, "Adrift in a Sea of Mud", by Owen.

Don Owen with actors Julia Biggs and Peter Kastner during the shooting of Nobody Waved Goodbye.

PATRY, PIERRE

Born in Hull, Quebec in 1933, Pierre Patry joined the National Film Board in 1957 as a scriptwriter for the television series "Panoramique" after working in radio, television and the theatre as an actor and director; Patry also wrote two CBC television series, "Rue de l'Anse and "Le Grand Duc". In 1963 he founded Coopératio, a production company dedicated to feature films (no longer in existence). Operating as a framework for private industry, Coopératio was instrumental in the rapid growth of Quebec cinema. Patry also directed a number of features within this company. As a producer, Patry worked with Arthur Lamothe on **Poussière sur la ville**, on Michel Brault's **Entre la mer et l'eau douce**, Jean-Claude Lord's **Délivrez-nous du mal** and Eric Till's **A Great Big Thing**. More recently he worked as executive producer on Lord's **Les Colombes** (1972).

FILMOGRAPHY

1957 **La Roulotte**. Prod: NFB "Panoramique". 30 min. b&w.

1958 **Germain Guevremont, romancière**. Prod: Victor Jobin, NFB. 30 min. b&w.

1959 **Les Petites Soeurs** (The Little Sisters). Prod: Victor Jobin and Léonard Forest, NFB. 29 min. b&w.

   Le Chanoine Lionel Groulx, historien. Prod: Léonard Forest, NFB. Two episodes of 28 min. each. b&w.

1960 **Collège contemporain**. Prod: Léonard Forest, NFB. 20 min. b&w.

   Les Loisirs. With Clément Perron. Prod: Bernard Devlin, NFB. 28 min. b&w.

1962 **Louis-Hippolyte Lafontaine**. Prod: Bernard Devlin, NFB. 29 min. b&w.

1963 **Petit Discours de la méthode**. With Claude Jutra. Prod: Fernand Dansereau and Victor Jobin. NFB. 27 min. b&w.

   Il y eut un soir, il y eut un matin (Françoise). Prod: Fernand Dansereau, NFB. 34 min. b&w.

1964 **Trouble-fête**. Prod: Jean Roy, Roger Blais and P. Patry, Coopératio. 85 min. b&w.

1965 **La Corde au cou.** Prod: Jean Roy and P. Patry, Coopératio. 110 min.
b&w.

Caïn or **Les Marcheurs de la nuit**. Prod: P. Patry, Coopératio. 75 min.
b&w.

1966 **Trois Hommes au mille carré** (Ghosts of a River). With Jacques
Kasma. Prod: Michel Moreau, NFB. 20 min. col.

Candidat-gouverneur, Milton Shapp. With Morton Parker. Prod: P. Patry
and Morton Parker. 30 min. col.

BIBLIOGRAPHY

Séquences, No. 50, October 1967, pp. 15-21, "Une compagnie de cinéma
canadienne: Coopératio", an interview.

Objectif, August-September 1964, pp. 3-17, "Petit éloge des grandeurs
et des misères de la colonie française de l'Office national du film", by
Jean Pierre Lefebvre.

Séquences, No. 53, April 1968, pp. 25-28, "Dialogue avec des cinéastes
canadien — Le Couple — Pierre Patry", by Gisèle Tremblay and André
Leroux.

Séquences, No. 32, February 1963, pp. 11-14, "Entretien avec Pierre
Patry". Interview.

La Presse, January 18, 1964, "Pour faire naître notre cinéma on doit faire
tous les métiers", interview by Alain Pontaut.

Le Petit Journal, Montreal, December 12, 1965, "Pierre Patry: personne
ne me connaît", an interview by Michelle Gelinas.

Le Cinéma québécois: tendances et prolongements, a short critique by
Patry.

Numerous references in: *Le Cinéma canadien, Jeune Cinéma canadien*
and *Vingt Ans de cinéma au Canada français.*

Point de mire, Montreal, September 24, 1971, pp. 1-2, " 'Ferme ta
gueule, Patry, t'as rien à dire' par lui-meme", by André Lafrance.

PEARSON, PETER

Born in Toronto, 1938, Peter Pearson studied science and economics at the University of Toronto, advanced television production at Ryerson and graduated from the Centro Sperimentale di Cinematografia in Rome. Between 1964-66 Pearson directed and produced items for "Seven Days" and later for "Document", both for the CBC. His **Best Damn Fiddler from Calabogie to Kaladar**, made with the National Film Board, starring Kate Reid and Chris Wiggens was voted "Film of the Year" at the 1969 Canadian Film Awards. Pearson and Michael Milne launched their film company in Toronto in 1971.

FILMOGRAPHY

1965 **Sex in Advertising**. With Ron Mulholland. Prod: CBC "Seven Days", 4 min. b&w.

Mastroianni. Prod: CBC. 30 min. b&w.

1966 **This Blooming Business of Bilingualism.** Prod: CBC "Eight Stories Inside Quebec". 30 min. b&w.

What Ever Happened to Them All? Prod: CBC. 30 min. b&w.

"Northern Development Films". Co-dir. Prod: David Bairstow, NFB for the Dept. of Indian and Northern Affairs.

1967 **Inmate Training** (La Formation des détenus), Parts I & II. Prod: Douglas Jackson, NFB. 29 & 31 min. b&w.

1968 **Saul Alinsky Went to War**. With Donald Brittain. Prod: John Kemeny, NFB. 57 min. b&w.

The Best Damn Fiddler from Calabogie to Kaladar. Prod: John Kemeny, NFB. 49 min. b&w.

1969 **The Dowry**. Prod: William Canning, NFB. 20 min. col.

If I Don't Agree, Must I Go Away? Prod: P. Pearson, CBC & NET. 60 min. b&w.

Roar of the Hornet. Prod: Bill Davidson, Manitou Productions "Adventures in Rainbow Country". 30 min.

Long Tough Race. Prod: Bill Davidson, Manitou Productions "Adventures in Rainbow Country". 30 min.

1971 **Seasons in the Mind**. With Michael Milne. Prod: Milne-Pearson Productions Ltd., for Ontario Place. 22 min. col.

BIBLIOGRAPHY

The Telegram, Toronto, October 11, 1969, "Good Reasons for Being an Angry Young Man", by Sid Adilman.

Canadian Photography, June 1971, "How Milne-Pearson Productions Made Film for Ontario Cinesphere".

American Cinematographer, March, 1971, "Cinesphere at Ontario Place".

The Montreal Star, October 11, 1969, pp. 43-44, "Judgment on Film and Directors in Canada", by Marc Gervais.

The Village Voice, April 24, 1969, "Modest Quest", by Stephanie Harrington, on **If I Don't Agree, Must I Go Away?**

PERRAULT, PIERRE

Poet, dramatist and lawyer, Pierre Perrault added a visual dimension to his observations of the inhibitants of the north shore of the St. Lawrence. He wrote and produced a series of thirteen half-hour films, directed by René Bonnière, entitled "Au Pays de Neuve-France" and then extended his investigation with a film trilogy — **Pour la suite du monde, Le Règne du jour, Les Voitures d'eau** — which revolves around Marie and Alexis Tremblay, a couple strongly tied to their land. Through Perrault's poetic images we discover the source and strength of their roots. Extremely popular in France, these films have reinforced the French people's identification with the Québecois. Perrault's political awareness is expressed in **L'Acadie, l'Acadie** made with Michel Brault, and **Un Pays sans bon sens**: the latter film was made at the request of the English Unit to explain Quebec's attitudes. Perrault was born in Montreal in 1927.

FILMOGRAPHY

1963 **Pour la suite du monde** (Moontrap). With Michel Brault. Prod: Fernand Dansereau, NFB. 105 min. b&w.

1966 **Le Règne du jour**. Prod: Jacques Bobet and Guy L. Côté, NFB. 118 min. b&w.

1969 **Les Voitures d'eau** (River Schooners). Prod: Jacques Bobet and Guy L. Côté, NFB, 110 min. b&w.

Le Beau Plaisir (Beluga Days). With Bernard Gosselin. Prod: Jacques Bobet and Guy L. Côté, NFB. 15 min. col.

1970 **Un Pays sans bon sens, ou Wake Up, mes bons amis!!!** Prod: Tom Daly, Guy L. Côté and Paul Larose, NFB. 117 min. b&w.

1971 **L'Acadie, l'Acadie**. With Michel Brault. Prod: Guy L. Côté and Paul Larose, NFB. 117 min. b&w.

1972 **Chronique de la Baie James**. Prod: NFB. (Work in progress.)

BIBLIOGRAPHY

Cinéastes du Québec: Pierre Perrault, CQDC, 1970, has criticism, an interview, a filmography and a complete bibliography.

Image et Son, No. 256, almost entirely on Perreault's work, with an interview, and articles by Louis Marcorelles, Yves Lacroix and Guy Gauthier.

Téléciné (France), No. 168, March-April 1971, pp. 2-20, "Libre cours: Pierre Perrault", by Nicole Alson and Jean Aizac.

Le Cinéma québécois: tendances et prolongements, "Pierre Perrault et la découverte d'un langage", by Maximilien Laroche.

Take One, Vol. 1, No. 5, "The Director as Pilgrim".

Saturday Night, November 1968, pp. 24-28, "Marie and Alexis Tremblay, Movie Stars", by Graham Fraser.

How to Make or Not to Make a Canadian Film, "Film and Reality", by Perrault.

Un Pays sans bons sens, ou Wake Up, mes bons amis, by Pierre Perrault, Bernard Gosselin, Yves Leduc and Serge Beauchemin, Editions Lidec Inc., Montreal 1972. (Filmscript.)

Cinéma Québec, Vol. 1, No. 1, May 1971, "Se donner des outils de reflexion", by Perrault; much of this issue is on **Un Pays sans bon sens**.

Le Devoir, Montreal, November 28, 1970, on **Un Pays sans bon sens**.

Transcriptions of **Le Règne du jour** and **Les Voitures d'eau** published by Editions Lidec in 1968 and 1969 respectively.

PERRON, CLEMENT

Born in Quebec City in 1929, Clément Perron studied at the University of Laval and the Sorbonne before joining the National Film Board in 1957. As a scriptwriter, Perron has worked on Jean-Claude Labrecque's **Les Smattes**, Claude Jutra's **Mon Oncle Antoine** as well as his own **Taureau, Jour après jour** and **Caroline**, among others. As a producer, he has been involved with Godbout's **Kid Sentiment**, Lefebvre's **Jusqu'au coeur** and **Mon Amie Pierrette**, and Forest's **Les Acadiens de la dispersion**. Perron has worked closely with Georges Dufaux, directing with him the delightful comedy, **C'est pas la faute à Jacques Cartier**.

FILMOGRAPHY

1961 **Les Loisirs**. With Pierre Patry. Prod: Bernard Devlin, NFB. 28 min. b&w.

    Les Bacheliers de la cinquième. With François Séguillon. Prod: Bernard Devlin and Victor Jobin, NFB. 28 min. b&w.

1962 **Jour après jour** (Day After Day). Prod: Fernand Dansereau, Hubert Aquin and Victor Jobin, NFB. 28 min. b&w.

1963 **Marie-Victorin**. Prod: Victor Jobin and Fernand Dansereau, NFB. 25 min. col.

1964 **Caroline**. With Georges Dufaux. Prod: Fernand Dansereau, NFB. 27 min. b&w.

1965 **Salut Toronto!** (Bonjour Toronto!). With Marc Beaudet. Prod: Marcel Martin, NFB. 28 min. b&w.

1967 **Cinéma et Réalité**. With Georges Dufaux. Prod: G. Dufaux and C. Perron, NFB. 58 min. b&w.

C'est pas la faute à Jacques Cartier. With Georges Dufaux. Prod: G. Dufaux and C. Perron, NFB. 72 min. col.

1972 **Taureau**. Prod: Marc Beaudet, NFB. col. (Feature in progress.)

BIBLIOGRAPHY

Objectif, August-September 1964, pp. 3-17, "Petit éloge des grandeurs et des misères de la colonie française de l'Office national du film", by Jean-Pierre Lefebvre.

Séquences, No. 30, October 1962, pp. 49-52, "Rencontre avec Clément Perron", by Léo Bonneville. Interview.

Séquences, No. 31, December 1962, pp. 17-19, "Reflexion d'un scènartiste canadien", by Perron.

Parti-pris, No. 7, April 1964, pp. 16-18, "Un témoignage", by Perron.

Dossier de cinéma: 1, Fides, 1968, reviews of **Caroline** and **Jour après jour**.

La Tribune, Sherbrooke, December 31, 1971, "Du cinéma québecois en tant que . . . 'carte d'identité' ", by René Berthiaume.

Le Droit, Ottawa, December 24, 1971, "Avec Clément Perron, cinéaste qui n'a pas voulu devenir 'metaphysicien et niaiseaux' ", by Murray Maltais.

Séquences, No. 51, December 1967, "Dialogue avec des cinéastes canadiens, le travail", an interview by Maryse Grandbois.

La Presse, March 18, 1972, "La Beauce mise à nu", an interview by Luc
Perreault, on **Mon Oncle Antoine** and **Taureau**.

Québec-Presse, March 12, 1972, p. 26, *"Taureau* ou l'intolérance d'un
village de la Beauce."

Reviews in: *Jeune·Cinéma canadien, Le Cinéma québécois: tendances
et prolongements, Vingt Ans de cinéma au Canada français, Essais
sur le cinéma québécois* and *Le Cinéma canadien.*

POIRIER, ANNE-CLAIRE

Born in St. Hyacinthe, Quebec in 1932, Anne-Claire Poirier studied law
at the University of Montreal and later, theatre at the Conservatoire
d'art dramatique de la province de Québec. She free-lanced as a writer
and interviewer for Radio-Canada and in 1960 joined the NFB, assisting
on such productions as **Québec-USA** (Brault and Jutra), **Voir Miami**
(Groulx), and **Jour après jour** (Perron), which she edited. Her first
feature, **De mère en fille** (Mother To Be), with camera by François
Séguillon and Jean-Claude Labrecque, is based on diaries kept during
her own pregnancy. She is presently producing a series of six films for
television with a crew of women including Mireille Dansereau and Suzanne
Gibbard.

FILMOGRAPHY

1961 **Stampede** (Nomades de l'ouest). With Claude Fournier. Prod:
Jacques Bobet, NFB. 27 min. b&w.

1962 **30 Minutes, Mister Plummer.** Prod: Jacques Bobet, NFB. 28 min.
b&w.

1964 **La Fin des étés.** Prod: Jacques Bobet, NFB. 28 min. b&w.

1965 **Les Ludions.** Prod: Jacques Bobet, NFB. 23 min. b&w.

1968 **De mère en fille** (Mother To Be). Prod: Guy L. Côté. NFB. 75 min. b&w.

Impôt et tout . . . . et tout. Prod: Anne-Claire Poirier, NFB for the Department of National Revenue. Five films of 5 min. each. col.

1971 **Le savoir-faire s'impose**. Prod: Anne-Claire Poirier, NFB for the Department of National Revenue. Six films of 5 min. each. col.

1972 **En tant que femmes** (in progress).

BIBLIOGRAPHY

Chatelaine, November 1966, "Women in Canada", an interview.

Femmes d'Aujourd'hui (Belgium), No. 1283, December 3, 1969, pp. 64, 66-67, "Que fait-on pour les femmes au Canada?".

Press clippings on **De mère en fille**, collected by the NFB, March 31, 1969, are available at film study centres or any NFB office.

Liette Desjardins in Marie-Claire Poirier's De mère en fille.

RANSEN, MORT

Freelance actor, director and writer, Mort Ransen joined the National
Film Board in 1961, working on a number of films in conjunction with
other filmmakers. His dramatic documentaries include a film on and
by young people, **Christopher's Movie Matinée**, and on drug addiction,
The Circle, starring Don Francks. Ransen collaborated with the Indian
crew at the Board on the film **You Are on Indian Land** and has been
involved in the training of actors for film work. He has written a musical
comedy which he will also direct. Ransen was born in Montreal in 1933.

FILMOGRAPHY

1965 **John Hirsch: A Portrait of a Man and a Theater**. Prod: Julian Biggs,
NFB. 28 min. b&w.

1966 **No Reason to Stay** (Pour un bout de papier). Prod: John Kemeny,
NFB. 28 min. b&w.

1967 **The Circle**. Prod: John Kemeny, NFB. 57 min. b&w.

1968 **Christopher's Movie Matinée**. Prod: Joseph Koenig, NFB. 87 min.
col.

1969 **Falling From Ladders**. Prod: John Kemeny and Joseph Koenig,
NFB. 9 min. b&w.

1970 **Untouched and Pure**. With Christopher Cordeaux and Martin
Duckworth. Prod: Tom Daly and John Kemeny, NFB. 46 min. b&w.

BIBLIOGRAPHY

Ransen was interviewed on the CBC-TV series, "New Filmmakers" on
April 23, 1969; the executive producer of the program was Roslyn Farber,
CBC Toronto.

No Reason to Stay: A Study of the Film, by Paul A. Schreivogel, Geo. A.
Pflaum Publisher, Inc., Dayton, Ohio, 1969, 19 pp.

The following are reviews of **Christopher's Movie Matinée**:
Saturday Night, June 1969, pp. 44-45, "Once upon a time the flower
children said they were going to liberate us all. But that, alas, was in
the distant past: 1967", by Marshall Delaney.

The Globe and Mail, February 22, 1969, p. 22, *"Movie Matinée* Hidden from Movie Houses", by Melinda McCracken.

Toronto Daily Star, February 1, 1969, "A Movie about Kids only Kids are Seeing", by Martin Knelman.

Vie des arts, Summer 1969, No. 63, "A Cinema of Wandering", by Dominique Noguez, reviews **Matinée** with reference to other films on youth.

REITMAN, IVAN

Born in Ontario in 1947, Ivan Reitman made his first film while attending the National Film Board's Summer Institute. With Peter Rowe and John Hofsess, Reitman was involved in the McMaster Film Board where he directed, wrote, photographed, edited and wrote the music for **Orientation** which received nation-wide distribution; he later produced five short films and a feature, **Columbus of Sex**. A Bachelor of Music, Reitman scored all his films.

FILMOGRAPHY

1967 **Guitar Thing**. Prod: Independent. 7 min. col.

1968 **Orientation**. Prod: Ivan Reitman, McMaster Film Board. 25 min. col.
Freak Film. Prod: Ivan Reitman, McMaster Film Board. 7 min. b&w.

1971 **Foxy Lady**. Prod: Ivan Reitman, Ivan Reitman Productions. 88 min. col.

1972 **Cannibal Girls**. Prod: Dan Goldberg, Ivan Reitman Productions. 80 min. col.

BIBLIOGRAPHY

Saturday Night, August 1970, pp. 11-16, "The Witchcraft of Obscenity", by John Hofsess.

Maclean's Magazine, November 1970, p. 93, "The Magic and Decidedly 'Ungroovy' Garden of Filmmaker Ivan Reitman", by John Hofsess.

Toronto Telegram, September 1, 1971, "Moviemaker Must Hustle, Says Newcomer Reitman", by Sid Adilman.

Miss Chatelaine, August 10, 1971, Vol. 8, No. 4, "Let's Hear It for Don & Morely & Martin & Ivan & Sylvia & Eric . . .", by Kay Armatage.

RIMMER, DAVID

Born in 1943 in Vancouver, David Rimmer has worked there independently (and, with video, in 1971-72 in New York). An experimentalist, Rimmer explores the possibilities of the film medium. He has an uncanny ability to take a film cliché, often in the form of a stockshot, as in **Variations on a Cellophane Wrapper, The Dance** and **Surfacing on the Thames**, and discover — through spatial and temporal manipulation — a fresh and wonderful image. His work has a precision that is infused with a droll sense of humour. Rimmer won numerous awards at the 1969 Vancouver International Film Festival and has had showings at the Museum of Modern Art.

FILMOGRAPHY

1968 **Square Inch Field**. Prod: Independent. 13 min. col.

1969 **Migration**. Prod: Stan Fox, CBC "New World". 11 min. col.

1970 **Headend.** Prod: Independent. 2 min. col.

    Variations on a Cellophane Wrapper. Prod: Independent. 8 min. col.

    The Dance. Prod: Independent. 4 min. b&w.

    Surfacing on the Thames. Prod: Independent. 5 min. col.

    Blue Movie. Prod: Independent. 5 min. col.

    Landscape. Prod: Independent. 11 min. col.

1971 **Real Italian Pizza.** Prod: Independent. 12 min. col.

    Seashore. Prod: Independent. 12 min. col.

    Treefall. Prod: Independent. 5 min. b&w.

Mr. Rimmer's films are distributed by the Canadian Film-Makers' Distribution Centre, Pacific Cinémathèque Pacifique and the Coopérative cinéastes indépendants.

BIBLIOGRAPHY

The Vancouver Sun, September 12, 1969, p. 29, "And the Camera Betrays the Hand and Eye", by Charlotte Townsend.

Artscanada, April, 1970, pp. 7-13, "The New Canadian Cinema: Images from the Age of Paradox", by Gene Youngblood.

The Province, Vancouver, July 31, 1970, "Simple Genius", by Andreas Schroeder.

Take One, Vol. 2, No. 11, "Vancouver Letter", by Kirk Tougas.

The New York Times, October 8, 1972, p. 17 (Entertainment Section), "Quick — Who are David Rimmer and James Herbert?", by Roger Greenspun.

ROFFMAN, JULIAN

Born in Montreal in 1919, Julian Roffman attended McGill University, studied film at New York and Columbia Universities and then became an independent producer in the United States. Between 1934 and 1938 he directed for the "March of Time" series and produced a series of consumer films, "Getting Your Money's Worth". He returned to Canada and to the NFB in 1940 at John Grierson's request; Roffman was a producer in charge of the "Armed Service Production Program". In New York he was co-founder of Pioneer TV Films — now Screen Gems Inc. — producing television series, documentaries and commercials. Back in Canada, Roffman founded Meridian Productions with Ralph Foster (former Deputy Film Commissioner), and later Taylor-Roffman Productions Ltd., with Nathan Taylor. Roffman has directed hundreds of films, among them, **The Mask**, a 3-D horror story which comes equipped with 3-D glasses. In recent years, Roffman has been largely acting as a producer.

FILMOGRAPHY (incomplete)

1934 "March of Time" series: **Men of Medicine, The Father Devine Story,**
-38   **Bootleg Coal, The Huey Long Story, The Disinherited**.

1935 "Getting Your Money's Worth" series for Consumer Union Reports.
-36

1940 **And So They Live** (co-dir.) for the Sloan Foundation; **A Report to the People** for President Roosevelt.

1941 "Armed Services Production Program" — **Battle is Our Business,**
-45   **Up From the Ranks, Thirteen Platoon, The Proudest Girl in the World, So Proudly She Marches**. Prod: NFB.

1950 "United Nations" series — **United Nations Patrols, Israel, United**
-52   **Nations Magazine**.

1953 "Korean War Reports", "The Inner Sanctum", "The Big Story",
-54   "The Search", all series for American television. **Freedom to Read** for Columbia University Bi-centennial.

1954 **Canadian Grocer, Toronto Symphony** for NFB. **Here and There,**
-59   **Pour le sport** for CBC "Tips", a series for J. Arthur Rank Organization.

1959 **The Bloody Brood**. Prod: J. Roffman, Key Films Productions for Allied Artists Inc. 80 min.

1961 **The Mask** or **Eyes of Hell**. Prod: Nat Taylor, J. Roffman, Taylor-Roffman Productions. 83 min. col.

BIBLIOGRAPHY

Canadian Sponsor, October 19, 1959, "Blueprint for TV Expansion".

Toronto Daily Star, May 20, 1961, "Interview with Roffman", by Blaik Kirby.

Toronto Daily Star, October 26, 1961, "Canadian Film in N.Y. Premiere".

The Globe and Mail, December 27, 1969, "Launching the Canadian Feature Film into Orbit — with a U.S. Booster", by Kaspars Dzeguze.

ROWE, PETER

Peter Rowe started his film career in 1966 with the McMaster Film Board in Hamilton as cameraman on "Palace of Pleasure". In 1967 he became an assistant editor at the CBC and the following year joined Allan King Associates, where he worked as assistant editor on King's **The New Woman** and assistant cameraman and editor on Martin Lavut's **At Home**. In 1971 Rowe directed his first feature, **Neon Palace**, for ETV, a happy piece of nostalgia about the 50's and 60's. Born in Winnipeg in 1947, Rowe works out of Toronto.

FILMOGRAPHY

1967 **Buffalo Airport Visions**. Prod: McMaster Film Board. 19 min. b&w.

1968 **Golly Shit Sounds Like Something Andy Warhol Would Do.** Prod: Independent. 3 min. b&w.

144   *1. Filmmakers*

1970 **Neon Palace: A Fifties Trip, A Sixties Trip**. Prod: P. Rowe, Tony
     Hall and Jim Lewis, Acme Idea & Sale. 90 min. col.

1972 **Good Friday in Little Italy**. Prod: F. R. Crawley, Crawley Films.
     14 min. col.

BIBLIOGRAPHY

Toronto Daily Star, October 27, 1969, "Three Shoot on a Shoestring",
by Martin Knelman, on Cronenberg, Shebib and Rowe.

The Montreal Gazette, October 17, 1970, "Youth Looks Back to the
1950's with Nostalgic Eagerness", by Marilyn Becker, on **Neon Palace**.

Take One, Vol. 2, No. 10, pp. 32-34, by Bruce Pittman, on **Neon Palace**.

Maclean's Magazine, March 1971, p. 76, on **Neon Palace**.

The Hamilton Spectator, November 13, 1970, "Cinematic Scrapbook of
20 Years Basically Fun in the *Neon Palace*".

The Globe and Mail, January 9, 1971, "Rowe's got Promise — and an
Etrog to Prove it", by Betty Lee.

The Telegram Toronto, June 21, 1971, "Rowe Not a Putdowner", an
interview by Clyde Gilmour.

Miss Chatelaine, August 10, 1971, Vol. 8, No. 4, "Let's Hear it for Don
& Morely & Martin & Ivan & Sylvia & Eric . . . ", by Kay Armatage.

RUBBO, MICHAEL

Born in Melbourne, Australia in 1938, Michael Rubbo studied anthropology at Sydney University and travelled extensively in Asia. A painter and still photographer, Rubbo prepared an exhibition of photographs on village life in India for an Australian direct aid organization in 1962. He joined the National Film Board in 1965 after studying film at Stanford University. Rubbo has been stunningly successful in improvised work with young people and presently heads up a new department at the Board, Films for Children. **Sad Song of Yellow Skin**, a document of life in war-torn Saigon, won the 1971 Flaherty Award.

FILMOGRAPHY

1965 **True Source of Knowledge**. Prod: Independent. 30 min. b&w.

1966 **The Long Haul Men**. Prod: John Kemeny, NFB. 17 min. col.

1968 **Adventures**. Prod: Nicholas Balla, NFB. 10 min. col.
  That Mouse. Prod: Nicholas Balla, NFB. 14 min. col.

1969 **Mrs. Ryan's Drama Class**. Prod: Tom Daly and Cecily Burwash, NFB. 35 min. b&w.
  Sir! Sir! Prod: T. Daly and C. Burwash, NFB. 20 min. b&w.
  Here's to Harry's Grandfather. Prod: M. Rubbo, NFB. 58 min. col.

1970 **Summer's Nearly Over**. Prod: M. Rubbo, NFB. 30 min. col. (a shortened version of *Here's to Harry's Grandfather*).

1971 **Sad Song of Yellow Skin** (Le Jaune en péril). Prod: M. Rubbo, NFB. 58 min. col.
  Persistent and Finagling. Prod. M. Rubbo, NFB. 58 min. b&w.

1972 **Wet Earth and Warm People**. Prod: M. Rubbo, NFB. 59 min. col.

1973 **Quebec Film Industry**. Prod: Ian McLaren, NFB. 30 min. col.

BIBLIOGRAPHY

Screen, Vol. 5, No. 2, pp. 6-7, and pp. 23-27, on **Sad Song of Yellow Skin**.

Film News, N.Y., Vol. 28, No. 4, 1971, p. 10, on **Sad Song of Yellow Skin**.

The Montreal Star, March 24, 1971, p. 70, "*Sad Song* Showed an Absorbing View of Saigon Life", by Joan Irwin.

The New York Times, January 8, 1972, "Rubbo's *Sad Song of Yellow Skin"*, by Roger Greenspun.

Take One, Vol. 1, No. 7, "Love and Life in Children's Films", by Rubbo.

SAARE, ARLA

Born in Finland in 1915, Arla Saare came to Canada in 1924 and graduated from the Vancouver School of Art. In 1942 she joined the NFB where she began as a negative cutter and later headed the optical and special effects department. When television opened up in Toronto, Saare landed the single editing job available, and in 1953, moved to Vancouver to co-found, with Jack Long and Stan Fox, the Vancouver Film Unit. Since 1963, Saare has been a free-lance editor in Toronto.

FILMOGRAPHY

The Following is a partial list of Arla Saare's editing credits and the directors she has worked with:

Allan King:	**Skid Row** (1956)
	Pemberton Valley (1957)
	A Married Couple (1969)
	Come On Children (1972)
Ron Kelly:	**A Bit of Bark** (1959)
	The Thirties: A Glimpse of A Decade (1964)
	Open Grave (1964)
René Bonnière:	**Gratien Gélinas** (1967)
	Alex Colville (1967)
Douglas Leiterman:	**The North American Seasons** (1969)
Peter Pearson and Mike Milne:	**Seasons in the Mind** (1971)

Terence Macartney-Filgate:	**Portrait of Karsh** (1966)
	Marshall McLuhan (1967)
Jim Carney:	**At the Moment of Impact — Flight 831** (1965)

BIBLIOGRAPHY

Hommage to the Vancouver Film Unit, La Cinémathèque canadienne, on a series of showings in 1964. Available from film study libraries.

Film Quarterly, Summer, 1970, pp. 9-23, "The Fictional Documentary: Interviews with the Makers of *A Married Couple",* by Alan Rosenthal. Reprinted in Rosenthal's *The New Documentary in Action,* University of California Press, Berkeley, 1971.

SHANDEL, THOMAS

Born in St. Boniface, Manitoba in 1938, Tom Shandel studied theatre at the University of British Columbia and film at Stanford University. Actor, broadcaster and writer, Shandel wrote **Dr. Glass** for CBC'S "Festival", **Yukon**, a feature documentary produced by Alaska Safari Productions, and **The Activators**, a documentary produced by the National Film Board's Challenge for Change Unit. He has also scripted most of the films he has directed. In 1970 he represented Canada, along with Gerald Potterton and Michel Brault, in exchange film showings with The Russian Filmmakers' Institute (Moscow and Leningrad) and the Cinémathèque canadienne. Shandel's first feature, **Another Smith for Paradise**, was photographed on the west coast by Michael Lente.

FILMOGRAPHY

1968 **El Diablo**. Prod: CBC "The Enterprise". 4 min. col.
    Superfool. Prod: CBC "The Enterprise". 15 min. col.
    Nitobe. Prod: CBC. 12 min. col.
    Hum Central. Prod: CBC "New World Series". 25 min. b&w.

1969 **Generations**. Prod: CBC. 60 min. b&w.
    Community. Prod: CBC. 30 min. b&w.

1970 **Shall We Gather at the River**. Prod: Independent. 30 min. b&w.

1972 **Another Smith for Paradise**. Prod: Jim Margellos, Another Smith
    Productions Ltd. 101 min. col.

BIBLIOGRAPHY

La Presse, November 30, 1968, p. 30, "Un hippie-cinéaste qui aime vivre
à Vancouver", by Luc Perreault.

The Province, Vancouver, December 14, 1968, by Morrie Ruvinsky, on
Nitobi.

The Province, June 26, 1970, by Andreas Schroeder.

The Vancouver Sun, June 25, 1971, by Les Wedman, background information on **Another Smith for Paradise**.

Take One, Vol. 2, No. 4, "The Night *The Plastic Mile* Lost 500 Feet",
an article by Shandel on the censoring of Ruvinsky's **The Plastic Mile**
at the Vancouver Film Festival.

SHEBIB, DON

Born in Toronto in 1938, Don Shebib graduated in sociology from the University of Toronto before enrolling at UCLA as a student of cinematography. Shebib served a long apprenticeship in television and the National Film Board before making his first feature, **Goin' Down the Road**, a controlled fiction-documentary which touched the Canadian collective consciousness. Shebib has had a productive relationship with dramatist-scriptwriter Bill Fruet who wrote both **Goin' Down the Road** and **Rip-Off**.

FILMOGRAPHY

1961 **Train Ride**. Prod: UCLA. 13 min. b&w.

1962 **The Duel**. Prod: UCLA. 8 min. b&w.
   Joey. Prod. D. Shebib, UCLA. 18 min. b&w.

1963 **Surfin'**. Prod: Ross McLean, CBC. 25 min. b&w.

1964 **Revival**. Prod: UCLA. 10 min. b&w.

1966 **Satan's Choice**. Prod: Tom Daly, NFB. 28 min. b&w.
   Christalot Hanson. Prod: Dick Ballentine, CTV, "This Land is People". 14 min. b&w.
   The Everdale Place. Prod: Dick Ballentine, CTV, "This Land is People". 22 min. b&w.
   David Secter. Prod: Dick Ballentine, CTV, "This Land is People". 14 min. b&w.
   Alan. Prod: Ross McLean, CBC, "T.B.A."

1967 **Basketball**. Prod: Ross McLean, CBC, "T.B.A.", 21 min. b&w.

1968 **San Francisco Summer 1967**. Prod: CBC. col.
   Unknown Soldier. Prod: Ross McLean, CBC. 4 min. b&w.

1969 **Good Times, Bad Times**. Prod: Ross McLean, CBC. 33 min. b&w.

1970 **Goin' Down the Road** (En roulant ma boule). Prod: D. Shebib, Evdon Productions, 90 min. col.

1971 **Rip-Off**. Prod: Bennett Fode, Phoenix Films. 90 min. col.

1972 **Paul Bradley**. Prod: Sam Levine, CBC "Telescope". 26 min. b&w.

1973 **Get Back**. Prod: Chalmers Adams, Evdon Productions. (Feature in progress.)

BIBLIOGRAPHY

Take One, Vol. 1, No. 10, "Toronto Letter", an interview by Joe Medjuck and Allan Collins.

The New Yorker, November 21, 1970, "About Town", an interview by Eleanor Ross.

The Globe and Mail, October 31, 1970, "It's the Same Don Shebib Despite *Road*", by Betty Lee. Interview.

La Presse, August 15, 1970, p. 31, "Réponse torontoise au défi québécois", interview by Luc Perreault.

Séquences, No. 62, October 1970, pp. 36-37, on **Goin' Down the Road**.

The Montreal Star, August 15, 1970, "The Underdogs Get Their Own Day", by David Allnutt.

Canadian Magazine, March 13, 1971, pp. 18-20, "Of course it will make a great film. It made a terrific comic book, didn't it?", by John Miller.

Ottawa Journal, February 12, 1971, "Produced, Written, Directed and Now Chauffeured by . . . Shebib", by George Williams.

Saturday Night, November 1971, "It's Not the Inherent Grace, It's the Money", by Marshall Delaney.

Maclean's Magazine, January 1972, p. 26, "The Friendly Neighbourhood Cineastes", by John Hofsess.

The Montreal Gazette, February 12, 1972, "Shebib Turns to Youth Cult for his Latest Film", by Dane Lanken.

Le Devoir, February 12, 1972, on **Rip-Off**, *by Jean-Pierre Tadros.*

(l. to r.) Paul Bradley, Cayle Chernin and Doug McGrath in Don Shebib's Goin'
Down the Road.

SHEPPARD, GORDON

Born in Montreal in 1937, Gordon Sheppard worked as a newspaper, television and radio journalist in Montreal and Toronto. In 1961 he and Richard Ballentine formed Inter-Video Productions Ltd. producing a number of short films for public affairs programs, among them, **The Most**, a witty study of Hugh Hefner and the Playboy empire. In 1963 Sheppard was appointed special assistant to the Secretary of State and, until 1966, was a special consultant on the arts. His first feature, **Eliza's Horoscope**, was photographed by Michel Brault, Paul Van der Linden and Jean Boffety.

FILMOGRAPHY

1962 **The Forum**. Prod: G. Sheppard and Richard Ballentine, Inter-Video Productions Ltd. 10 min. b&w.

The Grey Cup. Prod: G. Sheppard and Richard Ballentine, Inter-Video Prod. Ltd. for CBC. 10 min. b&w.

Strip Clubs in London. Prod: G. Sheppard and Richard Ballentine, Inter-Video Prod. Ltd. for CBC "Close-Up". b&w.

The Most. Prod: G. Sheppard and Richard Ballentine, Inter-Video Prod. Ltd. 28 min. b&w.

1963 **JFK and Mr. K**. Prod: G. Sheppard and Richard Ballentine, Inter-Video Prod. Ltd. 8 min. b&w.

1964 **Dream Girl** (La Femme des rêves). Prod: G. Sheppard and Richard Ballentine, Inter-Video Productions Ltd. for CBC. 28 min. b&w.

1967 **Fifty Bucks a Week**. Prod: G. Sheppard, The Wild Oats. 10 min. b&w.

Love. Prod: G. Sheppard, The Wild Oats. 5 min. Tinted.

Dallegret. Prod: G. Sheppard, The Wild Oats. col.

The Marriage. Prod: G. Sheppard, The Wild Oats. 5 min. col.

1968 **The Liberal Party in Ontario**. Prod: G. Sheppard and R. Ballentine, Inter-Video Productions Ltd. for The Ontario Liberal Party. Two films of 15 min. each. b&w.

1969 **Eliza**. Prod: G. Sheppard, O-Zali Films Inc. 10 min. col.

1972 **Eliza's Horoscope**. Prod: G. Sheppard, O-Zali Films Inc. 120 min. col.

BIBLIOGRAPHY

Canadian Cinematography, July-August, 1963, by Richard Ballentine, on the making of **The Most**.

Toronto Daily Star, September 8, 1962, "*The Most* is Also the First".

The Montreal Star, July 25, 1970, pp. 4 & 34, "Montreal Will be a Hectic Summer Film Setting", by Dusty Vineberg, on the making of **Eliza's Horoscope**.

Toronto Daily Star, April 18, 1970, p. 89, "A Lucky Horoscope for Canadian Filmmaker", by Margaret Penman, on **Eliza's Horoscope**.

SPOTTON, JOHN

Born in Toronto in 1927, John Spotton worked as an assistant cameraman with a small company, Shelly Films in Toronto, before joining the National Film Board in 1949. There he has worked as a cameraman and editor in the television series "On the Spot" and later in Unit B with Tom Daly, Wolf Koenig and Roman Kroitor, among others. Some of the films on which Spotton assisted in this period are Colin Low's **The Days of Whiskey Gap**, **Circle of the Sun** and **The Hutterites**, Koenig and Kroitor's **Lonely Boy** and Macartney-Filgate's **The Back-breaking Leaf**; more recently he filmed Gordon Sheppard's **The Most** with John Foster, and Don Owen's **Runner**, **High Steel** and **Nobody Waved Goodbye** as well as editing the latter. As a director, Spotton was involved in the Manitoba Centennial film, **Of Many People** and has worked on assignments for the United States Information Agency and Canadian National Railways.

FILMOGRAPHY

1965 **Buster Keaton Rides Again** (Avec Buster Keaton). Prod: Julian Biggs, NFB. 55 min. b&w.

1966 **The Forest** (Nôtre Forêt canadienne). Prod: Tom Daly, NFB. 21 min. b&w.

Memorandum (Pour mémoire). With Donald Brittain. Prod: John Kemeny, NFB. 58 min. b&w.

1967 **Never a Backward Step** (La Presse et son empire). With Arthur Hammond and Donald Brittain. Prod: Guy Glover, NFB. 57 min. b&w.

1970 **Activator One**. Prod: Barrie Howells, NFB. 58 min. b&w.

BIBLIOGRAPHY

Canadian Cinematography, May-June 1964, pp. 6, 7, 16, "New Film Features Improvisation", by John Spotton, on the filming of **Nobody Waved Goodbye**.

Film Quarterly (Britain), Winter 1966-67, pp. 57-59, by Henry Breitrose, on **Memorandum**.

References in: *Le Cinéma canadien*.

SNOW, MICHAEL

Painter, sculptor, musician and filmmaker, Michael Snow was born in Toronto in 1929, and graduated from the Ontario College of Art in 1953. He began his filmmaking career working as an animator for George Dunning in the late 50s. Much of his film work has been done in New York, sustained by Jonas Mekas' Filmmakers' Cinematheque and the critical atmosphere. The Canadian entry for the 1970 Venice Biennale was dedicated to Snow's multi-media works; Don Owen shot

"Snow in Venice" for the CBC "Telescope" series at this festival. In 1970-71, Snow was Professor of Advanced Film, Yale University and later in 1971, visiting Artist-Filmmaker at the Nova Scotia College of Art. **Wavelength** won first prize at the Fourth International Festival of Experimental Film in Belgium, 1968. Michael Snow lives and works in Toronto and New York.

FILMOGRAPHY

1956 **A–Z**. Prod: Independent. 4 min. col. Silent.

1964 **New York Eye and Ear Control**. Prod: Independent. 34 min. b&w.

1965 **Short Shave**. Prod: Independent. 4 min. b&w.

1966
-67 **Wavelength**. Prod: Independent. 45 min. col.

1969 **Standard Time**. Prod: Independent. 8 min. col.

  Dripping Water. With Joyce Wieland. Prod: Independent. 10 min. b&w.

  One Second in Montreal. Prod: Independent. 26 min. b&w. Silent.

1968
-69 ⟷ or **Back and Forth**. Prod: Independent. 52 min. col.

1970 **Side Seat Paintings Slides Sound Film**. Prod: Independent. 20 min. col.

1970 **La Région centrale** (Central Region). Prod: Independent. 180 min.
-71 col. Designer of special movie equipment: Pierre Abbeloos.

BIBLIOGRAPHY

Michael Snow/A Survey, by Michael Snow, The Art Gallery of Toronto and Isaacs Gallery, 1970, with "Michael Snow's Cinema", an article by P. Adams Sitney.

Michael Snow/Canada, National Gallery of Canada, Queen's Printer, Ottawa, 1970, for the 25th International Biennial Exhibition of Art, Venice, June 24-October 31, 1970.

Film Culture, N.Y., No. 46, 1968, pp. 1, 3, 4, "Conversation with Michael Snow", by P. Adams Sitney; and "Letter from Michael Snow".

Film Culture, N.Y., No. 52, Spring 1971, pp. 58-63, *"La Région centrale".*

Artforum, N.Y., Vol. 9, No. 10, June 1971, pp. 30-37, "Toward Snow: Part 1", by Annette Michelson.

Artscanada, February-March 1971, "Converging on *La Région centrale",* an interview by Charlotte Townsend.

The Village Voice, N.Y., January 27, 1972, p. 65, an article by Jonas Mekas in his "Movie Journal".

Take One, Vol. 3, No. 3, has a complete filmography, an up-to-date interview, and criticism by Jonas Mekas and Bob Cowan.

References and reviews in:

Expanded Cinema, by Gene Youngblood, E. P. Dutton & Co., N.Y., 1970.
Experimental Cinema: A Fifty-year Evolution, by David Curtis, Studio Vista, London, 1971.
Negative Space: Manny Farber on the Movies, by Manny Farber, Praeger Publications Inc., N.Y., 1971.

The soundtrack of **New York Eye and Ear Control**, by Albert Ayler, Don Cherry and others, has been issued by ESP, Disk 1016.

SPRY, ROBIN

Robin Spry was born in Toronto in 1939 but spent his childhood in England. While there, he was involved in the organizational side of theatre, continuing this involvement in Canada with the founding of classes on film acting technique given at the National Film Board. Spry began his film career at Oxford and the London School of Economics where he made a number of short, dramatic films. He first joined the Board in 1964 as a summer student, and in 1965 full-time, to work with John Spotton as an assistant editor. He was later assistant director on Don Owen's **High Steel** and **The Ernie Game**. His feature film, **Prologue**, was the first Canadian feature to be accepted at the main festival in Venice.

FILMOGRAPHY

1966 **Change in the Maritimes** (Métamorphoses dans les Maritimes). Prod: Joseph Koenig, NFB. 13 min. col.
Miner (Une Place au soleil). Prod: John Kemeny, NFB. 19 min. col.
Level 4350 (4350 Pieds sous terre). Prod: John Kemeny, NFB. 10 min. col.

1967 **Illegal Abortion**. Prod: Guy Glover, NFB. 25 min. b&w.
Ride For Your Life (Mourir champion). Prod: John Kemeny, NFB. 10 min. col.

1968 **Flowers on a One-way Street**. Prod: Joseph Koenig, NFB. 57 min. b&w.

1969 **Prologue**. Prod: R. Spry and Tom Daly, NFB. 88 min. b&w.

1972 **Face**. Prod: R. Spry and Tom Daly, NFB. 20 min. col. and b&w.
Downhill. Prod: R. Spry and Tom Daly, NFB. 30 min. col.
Reaction. (Work in progress.)

BIBLIOGRAPHY

La Presse, September 11, 1969; and February 21, 1970, "Prélude à un monde nouveau", by Luc Perreault.

Teléciné (France), December 1969, "Au contact des hippies, je suis devenu plus optimiste".

Le Devoir, February 21, 1970, "Les dilemmes de Robin Spry", by Jean-Pierre Tadros.

The Montreal Gazette, March 7, 1970, *"Prologue:* A Today Film", by Peter Ohlin.

The Montreal Star, January 24, 1970, "Chicago Confrontation", by Dusty Vineberg.

Séquences, No. 61, April 1970, pp. 60-66, "Entretien avec Robin Spry". Interview.

Jeune Cinéma, France, No. 53, March 1971, pp. 3-5, interview by André Tournes.

Ciné & Medios (Argentina), No. 4, 1970, *"Prologo:* Canadienses alertas".

News Clips/Revue de Presse, has the NFB's collection of the reviews of **Prologue**. Available at film study libraries.

TILL, ERIC

Born in England in 1929, Eric Till came to Canada in 1954 as manager of the National Ballet Company of Canada. Like Paul Almond, Till began his film career with CBC "Festival", directing among other dramas, **Great Expectations** and **Pale Horse, Pale Rider** which propelled him into the feature film area. His **A Great Big Thing** was shot in Montreal by Jean-Claude Labrecque with the assistance of Pierre Patry and Coopératio in its production. Since working in England on **Hot Millions** and **The Walking Stick**, Till has returned to Canada to form his Toronto production company, Coquihala Films Ltd.

FILMOGRAPHY

1961 **Great Expectations**. Prod: CBC "Festival". 90 min. b&w.

1962 **The Offshore Islands**. Prod: CBC "Festival". 90 min. b&w.

1963 **Diary of a Scoundrel**. Prod: CBC "Festival". 90 min. b&w.
Pale Horse, Pale Rider. Prod: CBC "Festival". 90 min. b&w.

1964 **The Master Builder**. Prod: CBC "Festival". 90 min. b&w.

1966 **Miss Julie**. Prod: CBC "Festival". 90 min. b&w.
Glenn Gould. Prod: CBC "Festival". 90 min. b&w.

1967 **A Great Big Thing**. Prod: Martin Rosen and Pierre Patry, Argofilms. 100 min. col.

1968 **Hot Millions**. Prod: Mildred Alberg, MGM. 104 min. col.

1970 **The Walking Stick**. Prod: Alan Ladd Jr., Winkast for MGM. 101 min. col.

1971 **Talking to a Stranger**. Prod: CBC. Four plays of 60 min. each. col.

1972 **A Fan's Notes**. Prod: E. Till, Coquihala Films Ltd. for Warner Bros. 100 min. col.

BIBLIOGRAPHY

Toronto Daily Star, November 14, 1964, "The Television Labors of Eric Till", by Antony Ferry.

Toronto Daily Star, October 4, 1965, "Eric won't be happy till he's directing *The Fox* in move away from TV".

La Presse, January 31, 1970, "Le cinéma maudit se porte bien", by Luc Perreault.

The Globe and Mail, October 11, 1968, "Fantasies in a Bargain Grab-bag", by Wendy Michener.

Toronto Daily Star, October 5, 1968, "Maybe It Should be Warm Millions", by Martin Knelman.

The Montreal Star, November 20, 1971, "A Mad World Unveiled", on **Talking to a Stranger**.

WATSON, PATRICK

Born in Toronto in 1929, Patrick Watson has been involved in many aspects of communication as a teacher, journalist, broadcaster, producer and director. Producer and co-host of "This Hour has Seven Days", he also produced for the CBC many earlier public affairs programs — "Explorations", "Close-Up", "Tabloid" and "Document"; he also produced two shows in Ottawa, "Inquiry" and "Nightcap". As a producer, Watson was involved with Jim Carney's **At the Moment of Impact — Flight 831**, which was made in 1965 for "Document", Brian Nolan's **Park on the Next Level** and Heinz Kornagal's **Emptied of All My Dreams**, also for "Document". Allan King's **Warrendale** was originally commissioned by Watson for the CBC. Watson is an editor and host of the American news program, "The 51st State", and has co-founded (with Laurier Lapierre) the film production firm, Immedia.

FILMOGRAPHY

1958 **Our Man in the Space Race**. Prod: CBC, "Close-Up". 2 min. b&w.
   Kingston Penitentiary. Prod: CBC, "Close-Up". 26 min. b&w.

1959 **Castro's First Year of Power**. Prod: CBC, "Close-Up". 26 min. b&w.

1962 **One Step at a Time** (Pas à pas). Prod: Nicholas Balla, NFB. 15 min. b&w.

The Man in the Bowler Hat. Prod: CBC, "Nightcap". 20 one-minute satirical pieces.

Defence Position Paper. Prod: CBC, "Enquiry". 22 min. b&w.

1963 **A Reasonable Doubt**. Prod: CBC, "Enquiry". 22 min. b&w.

The Pull of the South. Prod: CBC, "Document". 58 min. b&w.

The Hustings Revisited. Prod: CBC, "Enquiry". 25 min. b&w.

1964 **The Seven Hundred Million**. With Roy Faibish. Prod: P. Watson, CBC. 88 min. b&w.

1965 **The Cathode Colors Them Human**. Prod: CBC, "Document". 57 min. b&w.

1968 **Search in the Deep**. Prod: P. Watson, Wolper Productions for ABC, "The Undersea World of Jacques Cousteau". 50 min. col.

BIBLIOGRAPHY

The Star Weekly, November 26, 1966, "What's Wrong Inside the CBC", by Watson.

The Toronto Telegram, June 23, 1966, " 'After Four' Talks with Patrick Watson".

The Toronto Telegram, January 7, 1967, "What Watson Wants on Sunday", by Watson.

The Canadian Magazine, November 9, 1968, "The Way It Is (and Always Has Been) with Patrick Watson", by Barrie Hale.

The Globe and Mail, April 14, 1970, "Risks, Safeguards in Big Broadcasting", by Watson.

Take One, Vol. 1, No. 2, "Theatre and Reality: A Convergence of Forms", by Watson.

Artscanada, April 1970, pp. 14-20, "Challenge for Change", by Watson.

How to Make or Not to Make a Canadian Film, La Cinémathèque canadienne, "How Not to Make a Canadian Film", by Watson.

WAXMAN, ALBERT

Born in Toronto in 1935, Waxman studied acting at the Neighbourhood Playhouse in New York and with Lee Strasberg. (His most recent film rôle was in Paul Almond's **Isabel**.) In 1962 he attended the London School of Film and worked largely in television drama before making his first feature in 1971. Waxman lives and works in Toronto.

FILMOGRAPHY

1968 **Master of the House**. Prod: Kirk Jones, CBC "Quentin Durgens M.P.". 60 min. col.

Twiggy. Prod: A. Waxman, Tobaron Productions. 13 min. col.

1969 **Kid from Spanish Harlem**. Prod: Bill Davidson, Manitou Productions and CBC, "Adventures in Rainbow Country". 30 min. col.

Black Phoenix. Prod: Ron Weyman, CBC, "Anthology". 60 min. col.

Walk, Do Not Run. Prod: Ron Weyman, CBC, "McQueen". 30 min. col.

1970 **Father and Son**. Prod: Ron Weyman, CBC, "Canadian Short Stories". 30 min. col.

1971 **The Crowd Inside** (L'Univers de Christina). Prod: A Waxman, January One Films Ltd. 103 min. col.

BIBLIOGRAPHY

The Globe and Mail, October 17, 1970, "The House of Waxman: Ordeals of a Movie Maker", by Kaspars Dzeguze.

Toronto Daily Star, September 5, 1970, "Toronto Filmmaking is all Agony and Frustration", by Urjo Kareda.

Take One, Vol. 2, No. 11, p. 28, on **The Crowd Inside**.

The Ottawa Citizen, January 19, 1970, on **Black Phoenix**.

Variety, January 28, 1970 on **Black Phoenix**.

Financial Post, October 10, 1970, "Want to be a Movie Angel?", by Arnold Edinborough.

The Toronto Telegram, July 3, 1970, "The Crowd Inside Movie Set in Toronto", by Pat Annesly.

The Montreal Gazette, April 17, 1971, "Big Al's Dream Comes True — His First Feature Film", by Dane Lanken.

WIELAND, JOYCE

Born in Toronto in 1931, artist Joyce Wieland has worked as an animator for George Dunning's Graphic Films and a camera woman for Shirley Clarke's film, **Vosnesensky** in 1967. Although much of her work is "personal" in its subject and execution, her later films reflect her involvement with the New York movement of structural cinema. Recently, Wieland has been working on the dramatic feature film, **True Patriot Love** — a story of Tom Thomson, the Canadian painter, and Eulalie de Chicoutimi; set in Canada in 1919, Part 1 is entitled **Birds at Sunrise.** Wieland's films are in numerous film archive collections.

FILMOGRAPHY

1963 **Larry's Recent Behaviour**. Prod: Independent. 18 min. col.

1964 **Peggy's Blue Skylight**. Prod: Independent. 17 min. b&w.
Patriotism (Part One). Prod: Independent. 15 min. col.
Patriotism (Part Two). Prod: Independent. 5 min. col.

1964 **Watersark**. Prod: Independent. 14 min. col.
-65

1967   **Sailboat**. Prod: Independent. 3½ min. b&w. Printed on color
-68   stock.

    1933. Prod: Independent. 4 min. col.

    Hand-tinting. Prod: Independent. 4 min. b&w. Hand-tinted.

1968   **Catfood**. Prod. Independent. 13 min. col.

    Rat Life and Diet in North America. Prod: Independent. 14 min.
col.

    La Raison avant la passion (Reason Over Passion). Prod. Independent. 90 min. col.

1969   **Dripping Water**. With Michael Snow. Prod: Independent. 10 min.
b&w.

1972   **Birds at Sunrise** (Part 1 of **True Patriot Love**).

Joyce Wieland's films are distributed by the Canadian Film-Makers'
Distribution Centre and the Independent Filmmakers' Cooperative.

BIBLIOGRAPHY

Artforum, February 1970, "Joyce Wieland", by Manny Farber.

Artscanada, April 1970, pp. 43-45, "There is Only One Joyce", by P.
Adams Sitney.

The Ottawa Citizen, July 10, 1971, "Joyce Wieland — Her Romantic
Nationalism and Work", by Robert Fulford.

Artforum, September 1971, Vol. 10, No. 1, pp. 36-40, *"True Patriot
Love:* The Films of Joyce Wieland", by Regina Cornwall.

True Patriot Love/Véritable Amour patriotique by Wieland, The National
Gallery of Canada, Ottawa, 1971, with an interview by Pierre Théberge
interpreted by Michael Snow. (Also has Regina Cornwall's article reprinted
in English and French.)

Film Culture, No. 52, Spring 1971, pp. 64-73, has a selection from a film
outline of **True Patriot Love**.

Take One, Vol. 3, No. 2, "Kay Armatage Interviews Joyce Wieland", a feature article in the women's issue.

WILLIAMS, DONALD S.

Don Williams was born in Stony Plain, Alberta in 1938. His varied background in radio, television and theatre has led to unusual and fruitful combinations. In 1967 he won the Centennial Commission Playwright Award for his play, *Danny.* As artistic director of the Hatrack Theatre, a small company set up in Winnipeg to produce original Canadian works, Williams has funnelled its talents into television drama. In 1971 he filmed a cinemascope background for the Royal Winnipeg Ballet's version of George Ryga's *The Ecstasy of Rita Joe.* **Nis'ku**, a study of the Canada goose won Williams his second Wilderness Award (his first was attained for **Death of a Nobody**). Williams works mainly out of the CBC, Winnipeg.

FILMOGRAPHY

1967 **A Bucket of Tears for a Pound of Jam**. Prod: D. Williams, CBC, Winnipeg. 30 min. b&w.

1968 **Death of a Nobody**. Prod: D. Williams, CBC Winnipeg. 30 min. col.

1969 **Who? Me? Never!** Prod: D. Williams, Manitoba Department of Education and Manitoba Department of Health. 30 min. b&w.
One Upsville. Prod: D. Williams, CBC Winnipeg. 30 min.

1970 **I Run the Mile I Walked**. Prod: D. Williams, CBC Winnipeg for "Twenty-Four Hours". 40 min. col.
A Gift for Maggie. Prod: D. Williams, CBC Network. 60 min. col.
Nis'ku. Prod: D. Williams, CBC Winnipeg. 60 min. col.

1971 **The Ecstasy of Rita Joe**. Prod: CBC and The Royal Winnipeg Ballet.

1972 **Independence Day**. Prod: Philip Keatley, CBC, "The Beachcomber", 30 min. col.

The Highliners. Prod: Philip Keatley, CBC, "The Beachcomber", 30 min. col.

Every Night at 8:30. Prod: D. Williams, CBC Winnipeg and Edmonton. 30 min.

Jerry Potts and 74's. Prod: D. Williams, CBC, "This Land". 60 min. col.

Portrait of a Pig. Prod: D. Williams, CBC Winnipeg. 55 min. col.

1973 **La Légende de vent**. Prod: D. Williams, Radio-Canada. 60 min. col.

BIBLIOGRAPHY

The Telegram, Toronto, September 24, 1970, p. 63, "Film on Geese a Labor of Love", by Roy Shields.

Winnipeg Free Press, December 19, 1970, p. 15, *"A Gift for Maggie".*

Winnipeg Free Press, March 6, 1971, p. 21, "Amateur Theatre in Winnipeg", by Peter Crossley.

Winnipeg Free Press, July 3, 1971, "Camera Rolls for Rita Joe Ballet", by Karen Lerch.

Ottawa Citizen July 24, 1971, "Rita Joe Comes to Life Again in New Impressionistic Ballet", by Gordon Stoneham.

WOODS, GRAHAME

Director, cameraman and writer, Grahame Woods was born in London, England in 1934 and worked as a journalist before joining the CBC in 1956. Beginning as an assistant cameraman on a number of public affairs programs, Woods has since photographed numerous documentaries and dramas directed by himself and others. With Douglas Leiterman he worked on **Forty Million Shoes** and **The Chief**; with Allan King, **Dreams**; with Ron Kelly, **Caio Maria, Open Grave** and **The Gift**; with Terence Macartney-Filgate, **Marshall McLuhan** and **Portrait of Karsh**; with Peter Carter, **The Mercenaries** and **The Day They Killed the Snowman**. Woods has also been director of photography for a number of series — "Wojeck", "Corwin" and "Anthology". His scripts include the following productions: **Twelve and a Half Cents, The Disposable Man** and **Kalinsky's Justice**, all directed by René Bonnière, as well as **Strike** and **The Mercenaries** directed by Peter Carter, and his own **Winter's Discontent**.

FILMOGRAPHY

1966 **The Miracle of Terezin**. Prod: G. Woods, CBC, "Sunday Night". 15 min. col.

1968 **Trudeau**. Prod: G. Woods, CBC, "The Way It Is". 30 min. b&w.
Aberfan. Prod: G. Woods, CBC, "Public Affairs". 30 min. b&w.

1969 **Ginette Ravel**. Prod: G. Woods, CBC. 60 min. col.

1971 **Winter's Discontent**. Prod: G. Woods, CBC, "Theatre Canada". 30 min. col.
Thanks for the Ride. Prod: G. Woods, CBC, "Theatre Canada". 30 min. col.
Rodeo Rider. Prod: G. Woods, CBC, "Anthology". 60 min. col.

BIBLIOGRAPHY

Canadian Cinematography, March-April 1964, pp. 11-14, "Film Features Hand-held Camera", by Woods, on the making of **Open Grave**.

2. animation

An international organization of animators with a Canadian chapter is l'Association internationale du film d'animation (ASIFA). Its executive council includes members from all over Europe and North America, and its first president was Norman McLaren. ASIFA offers a number of services to its members: exchanges of programs between member chapters; a quarterly newsletter on world-wide productions and developments in animation (some individual chapters also publish a newsletter); and an annual meeting to take place during an animation festival. Individual membership is $15.00 per year; corporations may become associate members. In Canada, write to Hubert Tison, Animation Department, CBC, P.O. Box 6000, Montreal, Quebec; or ASIFA–Canada, P.O. Box 118, Station C, Montreal 113, Québec.

Aside from the articles and pamphlets on individual animators in Canada, the following animation materials are available:

Cameraless Animation/Cinéma d'animation sans caméra, by Norman McLaren. Available from the Information Division, NFB. (Reprint from *Fundamental Education,* Vol. 1 No. 4, 1939.)

Exposition mondiale du cinéma d'animation. Catalogue published on the occasion of the World Retrospective of Animation Cinema, 1967, by La Cinémathèque canadienne. Available at 50¢ from La Cinémathèque québécoise.

Feuilletoscopes/Flip-Books, published on the occasion of the World Retrospective of Animation Cinema, 1967, by La Cinémathèque canadienne:

1. *Man and His World*
2. *Metamor-Flip*
3. *Le Dompteur*
4. *First Cigarette*
5. *Baccanal*
6. *Gaminerie*
7 *Infidelité*
8. *Le Papillon*
9. *Flix*
10. *The Room*
11. *Nudnik*
12. *Felix*

Available at $1.00 each from La Cinémathèque québécoise.

Origine et âge d'or du dessin animé américain de 1906 à 1941, by André Martin. A chart published on the occasion of the World Retrospective of Animation Cinema, 1967, by La Cinémathèque canadienne. Available at $10 from La Cinémathèque québécoise.

Pot Pourri. Edited by Patricia Thorvaldson. April, 1972 issue is dedicated to National Film Board animators with articles on or by Robert Verrall, René Jodoin, Wolf Koenig, Mike Mills, Co Hoedeman, Don Arioli, Evelyn Lambart, George Geertsen and Yvon Mallette. Available from *Pot Pourri,* Ontario Regional Office, NFB, 1 Lombard St., Toronto 210, Ontario.

Artscanada, April 1970 issue carries two articles which deal with animators: "Six Filmmakers in Search of an Alternative", by Terry Ryan, discusses the work of Arthur Lipsett, Ryan Larkin and Pierre Hébert; "Nine Film Animators Speak", by Guy Glover, contains words and pictures by Laurent Coderre, Ryan Larkin, Sidney Goldsmith, Bernard Longpré and Norman McLaren. Available for $2.00 from *Artscanada,* 129 Adelaide St. West. Toronto 1, Ontario.

FILM ANIMATORS:

NORMAN MCLAREN was born in Scotland and studied at the Glasgow School of Art where he made his first films. John Grierson, at that time head of the British General Post Office (GPO) Film Unit, noticed McLaren's talent and invited him to join the unit under Alberto Cavalcanti and Evelyn Spice-Cherry (who now works out of Regina, Saskatchewan). Later McLaren made some films for the Guggenheim Museum in New York and in 1941, when Grierson came to set up the National Film Board, McLaren joined him here as head of animation. He has had a profound influence on animators and audiences alike and much has been written on McLaren and his work. The following bibliography is not meant to be complete but simply to indicate the kind of material available:

One of the most important items available was published by La Cinémathèque canadienne in 1965, entitled simply *Norman McLaren.* It contains testimonials by André Martin, Alexandre Alexeieff, John Grierson, John Hubley, Dusan Vukotic, Robert Benayoun, Maurice Blackburn, Colin Low, Len Lye, George Dunning and Grant Munro among others. A detailed filmography up to 1965 is also given and an inventory of techniques developed or used by McLaren in specific films. *Norman McLaren* is available in English and in French at 50¢ each from La Cinémathèque québécoise, 360 McGill St., Montreal 125, Quebec.

Two reprinted articles on McLaren and his techniques are available on request from the Information Division, National Film Board, P.O. Box 6100, Montreal 101, Quebec. *Cameraless Animation/Cinéma d'animation sans camera,* written by McLaren and reprinted from *Fundamental Education: A Quarterly Bulletin,* Vol. 1, No. 4, UNESCO, 1949, gives detailed information with plans for setting-up a work table and the procedure for cameraless animation. The second pamphlet, *Norman McLaren: His Career and Techniques,* by William E. Jordan, is reprinted from *The Quarterly of Film, Radio and Television,* Vol. 8, No. 1 and contains a short biography, a filmography up to 1964 and an appreciative study of his techniques.

Other articles include the following: "The Unique Genius of Norman McLaren", by May Ebbitt Cutler, *Canadian Art,* May/June 1965, No. 97;

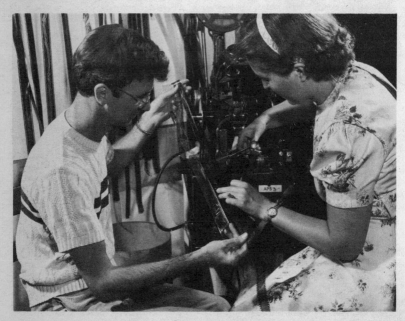

An early picture of Norman McLaren and Evelyn Lambart — the beginning . . .

"Le cinéaste sans caméra", *Perspectives,* No. 43, October 23, 1965, p.28-30; "Multi-McLaren", *Take One,* Vol. 1, No. 1, p.18-23; "Norman McLaren: Personalized Style in Filmmaking", NFB, Toronto, 1970; "McLaren: Je suis un miniaturiste", G. Rheault, *Le Soleil,* Quebec, December 12, 1970, p.51; "Norman McLaren", Germaine Warkentin, *The Tamarack Review,* Autumn 1957, p.42-53; "Mc et Moi: A Spiritual Portrait of Norman

. . . of a long collaboration.

McLaren", Gretchen Weinberg, *Film Culture,* No. 25, Summer 1962, p.46-47; "The Synthesis of Artificial Movements in Motion Picture Projection", by Norman McLaren and Guy Glover, *Film Culture,* No. 48-49, 1970, p.41-48. A mimeographed pamphlet edited by Hardy Forsyth, *Dots and Loops: The Story of a Scottish Film Cartoonist, Norman McLaren,* Edinburgh 1951, is available from the Canadian Film Institute for reference only. Three interviews are available: "Entretien avec Norman McLaren", *Séquences,* No. 42, October 1965, p.52-55; "The Graphic Side of Norman McLaren", by Michael White in *The Montreal Gazette,* March 4, 1972; and (the interview McLaren is said to like best) by Don McWilliams, *McGill Reporter* (McGill University, Montreal), Vol. 1, No. 35, April 28, 1969, pp.3-5. A recent film made by the BBC, **The Eye Hears The Ear Sees**, is an hour-long exposition of McLaren's work and a tribute to him; it is available from the National Film Board. The University of Toronto Press has scheduled a biography of McLaren (by Don McWilliams) to appear (tentatively) in 1973-74.

Along with Evelyn Lambart, **ROBERT VERRALL** was one of the original members of the National Film Board's animation department set up by Norman McLaren. Born in Toronto in 1928, Verrall studied at the Ontario College of Art and worked with Arthur Lismer's Children's Art Centre in Toronto. Collaborating on a number of early films — **Three Blind Mice**, **Family Tree** and **Teamwork Past and Present** — he made his first, **Breadmaking in the Middle Ages**, in 1947. In 1953, with Wolf Koenig and Colin Low, Verrall made the witty **The Romance of Transportation in Canada**; later he made **A is for Architecture** and **Energy and Matter**. Verrall is presently head of the animation group in English production. Among his recent productions are a series of anti-smoking clips, **Where There's Smoke** and **Hot Stuff** by Don Arioli and Zlatko Grgic, **Cosmic Zoom** by Eva Szas and a co-production with Zagreb films, **Man the Polluter**. An interview with Robert Verrall can be found in *Pot Pourri,* April 1972.

EVELYN LAMBART Studied at the Ontario College of Art, joining the National Film Board in 1942. Within this newly-formed organization, everybody's energy was turned to the war effort and Lambart drew diagrams and maps for the "World in Action" series. In her well-known collaboration with Norman McLaren, Evelyn Lambart has worked on **Begone Dull Care**, **Short and Suite**, **Lines Vertical**, **Lines Horizontal**, **A Chairy Tale** and **Mosaic** among many. Her recent work includes stories for children, **The Hoarder, Fine Feathers** and **Paradise Lost**. An interview with Evelyn Lambart can be found in *Pot Pourri,* April 1972.

Born in Hull, Quebec in 1920, **RENE JODOIN** studied at the Ecole des Beaux-Arts, joining the animation department of the National Film Board in 1943. He worked on the series "Let's All Sing Together", directing **Carry On, Alouette** and **Quadrille.** After spending a number of years away from the Board, Jodoin returned in 1954 to work on a series of films for The Department of National Defence and later, a series of scientific films; it was within the latter series that he directed **Comment fonctionne le moteur à jet,** animated by Kaj Pindal and Kenneth Horn. Since 1965, Jodoin has headed up the animation group in French production, directed **Notes on a Triangle** and produced such films as **Le Hibou et le Lemming** by Co Hoedeman, **Catuor** by Judith Klein, **Cycle** by Suzanne Gervais and a series of animated songs, "Les Chansons Contemporaines" including **Fleurs de macadam** by Laurent Coderre and **Tête en fleurs** by Bernard Longpré. Recently his department has begun to experiment with computer animation. Jodoin's work is discussed in *Le Cinéma canadien* and reviews of **Notes on a Triangle** can be found in *La Tribune,* Sherbrooke, March 6, 1968 and *Boxoffice,* April 15, 1968. There is an interview with Jodoin in the April, 1972 issue of *Pot Pourri.*

GRANT MUNRO was born in Winnipeg in 1923 and attended the Winnipeg School of Art and the Ontario College of Art before joining the National Film Board in 1944 as an animator of titles and special effects in the series "Canada Carries On" and "World in Action". Munro has collaborated with a number of other filmmakers in producing many memorable works: as well as acting in and editing McLaren's **Neighbours,** Munro collaborated on its writing; he also acted in and helped write two other McLaren films, **Two Bagatelles** and **Canon.** In 1961 he designed the story board and assisted in the animation of Potterton's **My Financial Career** and later collaborated with Ron Tunis on **The Animal Movie.** He has recently directed and starred in a series of anti-smoking clips and directed a number of 8mm learning loops and a film on the Holmes dance team. An article on Munro, "Ahem! Have you seen any one-minute films lately? (cough, cough)", by Terry Ryan, can be found in the October 4, 1969 issue of *The Gazette.*

GERALD POTTERTON was born in England in 1931 and worked as an actor before joining the company of Halas and Batchelor for which he worked as assistant animator on the feature, **Animal Farm**. In 1954, Potterton joined the National Film Board, collaborating with Grant Munro on **Huff and Puff**; they later collaborated on Leacock's story, **My Financial Career**. Other films which Potterton has directed at the Board include **Fish Spoilage Control**, **It's a Crime** with Wolf Koenig, **The Ride**, **The Quiet Racket** and **The Railrodder**, the latter being a live action film with Buster Keaton. In 1968 Potterton formed his company, Potterton Productions Inc., where he has directed and produced two films combining animation and live action — **Pinter People** and **Tiki Tiki**, a film for children. As a producer, Potterton has been involved in a number of productions, among them, **The Selfish Giant**, designed and directed by **PETER SANDER** who also assisted in the production of **Tiki Tiki**.

An interview with Potterton conducted by Jean-Paul Torok and Hubert Niogret can be found in *Positif,* No. 134, January, 1972, p.41-44. Other articles include "A funny thing happened on the way to the Kremlin", by Martin Bronstein, *The Montreal Star,* March 14, 1970; "How to manufacture dreams and make money: Potterton People", Doris Giller, *The Montreal Star,* January 15, 1972; and "Potterton's Pinter People", by Boyce Richardson in *The Montreal Star,* March 29, 1969.

Born in Montreal in 1943, **RYAN LARKIN** graduated from Montreal's Museum of Fine Arts' School of Art and Design and studied at Montreal's Ecole des Beaux-Arts. He joined the National Film Board in 1964 as a painter and inker, completing a two-minute experimental film, **Cityscape**, in a training course given by Norman McLaren. As well as a number of 8mm loops in a mathematics series and an animated pastel, **Burning Fox**, for the Department of Lands and Forests, Larkin has animated and directed the poetic **Syrinx** and **Walking**. **Street Musique**, a Department of Health and Welfare clip (**ABC of First Aid**) and a clip for a history series bring his work up to date.

Critical reviews of Larkin's work can be found in the following periodicals: *The Montreal Gazette,* September 13, 1969, "Ryan Larkin: painting on film to stir the minds of old and young", by Mark Slade; "Les dessins fantastiques de Ryan Larkin", Pol Chantraine, *Perspectives,* January 31, 1970, p.16-17; *Artscanada,* April 1970 contains Guy Glover's "Nine Animators Speak" and Terry Ryan's "Six Filmmakers in Search of an Alternative". *Positif,* No. 117, June 1970, has a review of **Walking**.

DON ARIOLI was born in Rochester, N.Y. in 1937 and began his career in animation with Jim MacKay at Film Design, Toronto. His first work included animated segments for the CBC children's program "Butternut Square" in 1965. In 1966 Arioli joined the National Film Board where he has written and designed a number of storyboards, among them, **Tax is Not a Four Letter Word**, **The House that Jack Built**, **Best Friends**, **In a Nutshell**, and most recently **Tilt** for the World Bank. Arioli also co-directed (and helped write) **This is a Propaganda Message** with Wolf Koenig, Roman Kroitor and Les Nirenberg, and the anti-smoking clip **Cough Dance** with Grant Munro. He is presently directing the live sequences of an animated film on pollution **Man the Polluter**, and co-directing with Boris Kolar **The Specialists** which is being co-produced by Zagreb Film. Arioli has worked outside the Board as well, animating **Martha** for "Sesame Street" and nineteen short reading clips for The Electric Company. He has completed a storyboard for ABC's "Curiosity Show" and is working on an hour long show concerning love.

An interview with Arioli can be found in the April 1972 issue of *Pot Pourri* along with critical reviews.

BERNARD LONGPRÉ was born in Montréal in 1937. He studied at l'Institut des arts graphiques de Montréal and with the painter-engraver Albert Dumouchel. After joining the animation department at the National Film Board in 1957, Longpré continued his studies in evening classes at l'Ecole des Beaux-Arts in Montreal. As an animator, Longpré worked on Jodoin's **Comment fonctionne le moteur à jet**, **Four-line Conics** by Trevor Fletcher, and Ken McCready's **Glaciation**. He has directed as well as animated a number of government sponsored films — Among them, **Le Poisson denrée périssable**, **An Introduction to Nutmeg**, **The Ball Resolver** and **En février**. In 1968 he directed his experimental film of optical effects, **l'Evasion des carrousels** and in 1969 **Tête en fleurs**, a film animated to Claude Gauthier's song. He is presently working on an animated children's film.

"Nine Animators Speak", by Guy Glover, *Artscanada,* April, 1970, and "Rencontre avec Bernard Longpré", *Le Devoir,* June 27, 1970 are critical interviews, and his work is discussed in *Le Cinéma canadien.*

Working independently out of Vancouver, **AL SENS** has made films for the CBC, the NFB and various commercial clients including International Cinemedia in Montreal. Sens is also a cartoonist and has taught visual arts at Simon Fraser University. Among his films are **A Puppet's Dream**, **An Unidentified Man**, **The See**, **Hear**, **Talk**, **Think**, **Dream**, **Act Film** and **The Sorcerer**. He recently animated a series of anti-smoking clips for the National Film Board and is animating and directing **The Bigot**, produced by John Taylor at the Board. See Sens' article, "Movement is the Message" in *How to Make or Not to Make a Canadian Film.*

Another animator from Vancouver, **JOHN TAYLOR**, studied at the Vancouver School of Art and spent two summers with the animation department, National Film Board. He later founded and taught the Film Workshop at the Vancouver School of Art, directing his **Cadillac** in 1969. Taylor has produced many films for the National Film Board: **Citizen Harold** for the "Challenge for Change" program, **B.C. Centennial Clips**, **Hazardous Products Clips**, **The Bigot**, **Fish Clips**, as well as being involved in **Tilt** and **Hot Stuff**. He is presently producing, and co-directing with Ken Klassen, **The Prairie Film**; this will combine animated and live footage using the rotoscope technique. Taylor is also producing Hugh Foldes' **Bear's Christmas** and Ernie Schmitt's film on drug abuse.

The Vancouver School of Art has been instrumental in developing a number of animators, among them **MEL HOSKINS** and **DAVE ROBERTS**.

Born in Copenhagen in 1927, **KAJ PINDAL** began as an underground cartoonist during the German occupation of Denmark. After the war, Pindal did a comic strip for a daily newspaper and cartoon film clips for an advertising agency; later he worked on a number of UNESCO films and film strips, the latter while in the Army film unit. In 1957 Pindal joined the National Film Board animating for Jodoin's **Comment fonctionne le moteur à jet** and Derek Lamb's **I Know an Old Lady Who Swallowed a Fly**. In 1966 Kaj Pindal directed the witty **What on Earth?** with Les Drew.

Pindal has recently animated a series of anti-smoking clips, directing as well **King Size**. He designed the storyboard, **Journey to the Centre of the Earth** and collaborated once again with Les Drew on its animation. He is also animating **Horsepower**.

MIKE MILLS was born in London, England in 1942. In England he worked for the BBC and Associated Rediffusion for which he directed shorts and commercials for Germany, Italy and Africa. As a free-lance animator/director/producer, he has been involved in over 160 television commercials. Before joining the National Film Board in 1966, Mills worked as series director for NBC's "The Lone Ranger". His work at the Board includes the animation and direction of **Tax is Not a Four Letter Word** and the co-direction with Les Drew and Don Arioli of **In a Nutshell**; he later animated and directed his own storyboard, **Evolution** and the anti-smoking clip, **Dynamite**. Mills is presently working on two feature productions, **The Island** and **Man the Polluter**.

An interview with Mills can be found in the April, 1972 issue of *Pot Pourri*.

Born in Montreal in 1937, **RON TUNIS** studied at the Pratt Institute in New York. He joined the National Film Board in 1961 as a designer-animator where he assisted Norman McLaren, Kaj Pindal and René Jodoin in designing the New York Light Board for the Canadian Tourist Bureau. Among his films are **The Animal Movie** which he animated and co-directed with Grant Munro, **Perception of Orientation** (also co-directed), and **The House That Jack Built** which he directed and animated from a storyboard by Don Arioli. Since leaving the Board in 1967 Tunis has animated Potterton's **The Trade Machine** for Place Bonaventure and a section of his **Pinter People**; he also animated sections of **The Yellow Submarine** and **Tiki Tiki**. Tunis has recently directed and animated two short films for "Sesame Street" and a promotional clip for American Motors. Within the National Film Board's French animation unit, he is presently working on **The Wind**.

CARLOS MARCHIORI was born in Italy in 1937 and studied art in Padua and Venice. He has worked in advertising in Tokyo, and at the National Film Board made the anti-smoking film, **The Drag**. Much of his work has been done with the CBC Graphics Department — "promo" films such as **Man to the Moon**, **Winter Safety**, **Ciné-club** and **Boom**. In Japan, Marchiori made **Paper Paradise** independently, and with Al Guest Animation, **Crunch Crunch**.

Born in Montreal in 1936, **ARTHUR LIPSETT** studied at the Montreal Museum of Fine Arts before joining the National Film Board in 1958. His experiments with scraps of sound from other films to form a composition became the basis of his collage of photographs, **Very Nice, Very Nice** made in 1960. Lipsett went on to shoot, direct and edit two more films of animated photographs, **21-87** and **Free Fall**. Other titles by Lipsett include **Time Capsule**, **Fluxes**, **A Trip Down Memory Lane** and **N-Zone**.

For critical comment on Lipsett's work see "Six Filmmakers in Search of an Alternative", by Terry Ryan, *Artscanada* April, 1970; *Objectif,* July 1962 pp.32-34; and *Artscanada,* August-September 1971, pp.54-57.

Born in Ottawa in 1931, **LAURENT CODERRE** studied at the Ontario College of Art, Ecole des Beaux-Arts and the University of Montreal before joining the CBC and later the NFB in 1960. He has worked on numerous films, and animated **Triangle**, **Electronic Fish Finders** and **Métamorphoses**. He directed and animated **Fleurs de macadam** in the series "Chansons contemporaines" and **Zikkaron**.

See "Nine Animators Speak", by Guy Glover, *Artscanada* April, 1970, p.33.

PIERRE MORETTI was born in Montreal in 1931, studied at l'Institut des Arts Appliqués in Montreal and worked experimentally in the theatre before joining the animation department of the National Film Board in 1964. His first film, **Un Enfant . . . Un Pays** was made in 1967 and in 1969 Moretti animated a song by Claude Dubois in **Greveau gelé**. His **N'ajustez pas**, made in 1970, has taken, as its name suggests, images from television. He completed a film with Peter Foldes in 1971, **Matadata**. He is presently a director-producer in the French animation section of the National Film Board.

President and Creative Director of the advertising agency Ogilvy and Mather (Canada) Ltd., **JOHN STRAITON** is an accomplished animator working out of Toronto. His **The Banshees** (1966) is a film of animated objects, while **Portrait of Lydia** and **Eurynome**, the latter telling of the creation of woman, came from Straiton's own drawings and sculptures. **Steam Ballet** and **Animals in Motion** complete his filmography. Straiton's films are distributed by the Canadian Film-makers' Distribution Centre and the Coopérative cinéastes indépendants.

Born in Montreal in 1944, **PIERRE HEBERT** joined the National Film Board in 1965 after having studied anthropology at the University of Montreal. Working directly on film, he produced his first pieces of animation, **Histoire grise** and **Histoire d'une bébite** in 1962, and **Op Hop** in 1966 using the same method. His computer experiments with random sequences resulted in his later film, **Around Perception**.

A critical article by Terry Ryan can be found in *The Montreal Gazette,* November 29, 1969 entitled "Pierre Hébert: Explorer in the Land of the Mind". See also "Bandes à part", *Objectif,* November-December 1966, pp.36-38.

CO HOEDEMAN was born in Amsterdam in 1940, joining the National Film Board in 1965 where he works in model animation and puppets. In his homeland, Hoedeman had worked on many films including **Cinecentrum**. His work at the Board includes **Continental Drift**, **Matrioska**, **Maboule** and **Oddball**. He recently completed a number of puppet stories including **Le Hibou et Le Lemming, Tchou-tchow** and **The Owl and the Raven**.

Born in Toronto in 1922, **SIDNEY GOLDSMITH** studied at the Ontario College of Art and joined the National Film Board as an animator in 1948. Among the films on which he has worked are **The Romance of Transportation in Canada**, **It's a Crime**, **Jolifou Inn** and **Universe**. Since 1963 Goldsmith has been producing as well as directing, eg. **Development of a Fish Embryo, Four-line Conics** and **Isotopes in Action**. He has directed **Fields of Space**, **Espolio** from a poem by Earle Birney, **Origin of Life**, and recently, **Experiencing Mathematics** and **Relative Velocity**.
  See: "Going Loopy Over New Math", by Jerry Lee, *The Montreal Star,* February 4, 1967.

LES DREW was born in London, England in 1939, spending over seven years with Halas and Batchelor. His work at the National Film Board includes the witty **What on Earth?** which he co-animated and co-directed with Kaj Pindal, **Rx for Export** for the Department of Trade and Commerce, and **The Underground Movie** which he directed and animated in 1972. He has also directed and animated two clips on the hiring of students, animated **Tilt** from a story by Don Arioli and earlier worked on Hubley's **The Cruise**. Also at the National Film Board are **KEN HORN** who completed **What is Life?**, **EVA SZAS** who animated and directed her **Cosmic Zoom**, and **GEORGE GEERTSON** who has directed and animated highway safety clips and **The Men in the Park**. At the CBC, the work of **LOUIS DE NIVERVILLE** and **WARREN COLLINS** has become familiar through animated promo clips.

Born in Toronto, **JIM MACKAY** worked as a graphic artist before joining the National Film Board in 1942. He left in 1949 to found the free-lance animation company, Film Design, with **GEORGE DUNNING**. Among the many films he has been associated with are: **Teeth Are To Keep, Cine Coronary Arteriography, Abstract Story** and **Little Round Rock**, as well as a number of segments for "Sesame Street".

3. writing and writers

The script is a key element in any film in spite of the myth of the "unscripted" documentary in *cinéma-vérité* film. Producers and backers (including the CFDC) demand a script before proceeding and many of our most impressive films testify to the skills of their writers — **The Drylanders** written by M. Charles Cohen, **La Canne à pêche** by Anne Hébert (she has also scripted Claude Jutra's **Kamouraska**), **Goin' Down the Road** and **Wedding in White** by Bill Fruet, and Clément Perron's delicious work in **Mon Oncle Antoine**.

The CFDC is the central clearing house for feature film scripts and this organization will put writers in touch with directors. Contact them at 800 Place Victoria, Suite 2220, Montreal 115, Quebec, or at the Lothian Mews, 96 Bloor Street West, Toronto, Ontario.

Another clearing house, although largely a source of new Canadian plays, is the Playwrights' Co-op, 344 Dupont Ave., Toronto, Ontario M5R 1V9, 961-1800. A number of writers who work in the film medium have had their stage plays reproduced by the Co-op. Write or telephone the Playwrights' Co-op for a complete catalogue and price list.

The Toronto Film-Makers' Co-op, Room 204, Rochdale College, 341 Bloor St. W., Toronto 181, Ontario conducts courses in all aspects of filmmaking including a course in scriptwriting.

Few film scripts have been published in Canada although Editions Lidec Inc. in Montreal have made available two of Pierre Perreault's transcriptions for **La Règne du jour** and **Les Voitures d'eau**. Don Owen's script for **Nobody Waved Goodbye** was published by Macmillan (Toronto) as part of a collection entitled *Nobody Waved Goodbye and Other Plays*. The National Film Board often print scripts from their productions which can be made available through their reference library. Many of the other film study centres have copies of unpublished film scripts available for reference. See section 10. FILM STUDY CENTRES for addresses and accessibility of material.

If you have written a script and wish to establish copyright in the United States, send a copy of that script and $4.00 to the Writer's Guild of America (West), 8955 Beverly Blvd., Los Angeles 48, California, U.S.A.

A few articles and books on scriptwriting are available as follows:
Write Me A Film?: A Symposium of Canadian Filmmakers, edited by Hugo McPherson, contains a number of articles: "Uneasy Riders" by William Weintraub, scriptwriter and director **(A Matter of Fat)** with the National Film Board; "The Fabled Movie Contract" by Ian MacNeill, director-producer also with the National Film Board; "The Non-Literary Film" by Guy Glover, producer at the National Film Board; and "Le Temps: La Poésie du Cinéma", by Jacques Godbout. This collection of articles can be found in *Canadian Literature,* No. 46, Autumn 1970.

"Hello, 'Caroline', Goodbye", by George Robertson can be found in *How to Make or Not to Make a Canadian Film.* "A Trap: The Script", by Jacques Godbout is in the same book.

A number of articles on scriptwriting can be found in the special issue on film, "Cinéma Si", in *Liberté,* Vol. 8, No. 2-3, March-June 1966.

Script Writing for Short Films/Le Scénario du film de court métrage was written by James A. Beveridge who teaches in the film department at York University, Toronto. It is available in the Unesco series, *Reports and Papers on Mass Communication* No. 57, UNESCO, 1969, for $1.25 from any Information Canada bookshop.

L'Adaptation d'un roman au cinéma, by H. Queffelec, was published in the Collection cinéma et culture by the Centre diocesain du cinéma de Montréal in 1959. Available at film study libraries.

The following list of writers, films and articles, though incomplete, indicates the scope of achievement and the possibility for further work in scriptwriting:

STANLEY R. JACKSON joined the National Film Board on John Grierson's invitation in 1942, working as a researcher for the "Canada Carries On" and the "World in Action" series. As part of the Candid

Eye Unit at the National Film Board, Jackson has been called "the conscience of the unit"; his written and spoken commentaries can be heard in such films as **The Days Before Christmas, Blood and Fire, The Cars in Your Life, Universe** and **Circle of the Sun**. Jackson has since directed, written and narrated for many films; in 1971 he wrote and narrated the commentary for **The Conquered Dream**, a BBC-National Film Board co-production.

M. CHARLES COHEN has worked in radio and television drama as well as film. Contributing the CBC series, "Festival", Cohen wrote **The True Bleeding Heart of Martin D** which was directed by George Bloomfield, **David Chapter 2** and **David Chapter 3** directed by Harvey Hart. Hart also directed Cohen's adaptations of **The Luck of Ginger Coffey** and **The Hostage**. In 1955 and 1956 Cohen joined fellow writers Charles Israel, George Salverson, Stewart Nutter, Arthur Hailey, Lister Sinclair and Joseph Schull in a dramatic series "Perspectives", produced for television by the National Film Board. He later wrote **David Thompson, The Great Mapmaker** in the National Film Board series, "History Makers". Cohen wrote the script for **The Drylanders**, the National Film Board's first English feature; it was directed by Don Haldane.

CLEMENT PERRON wrote the French version of many films produced by the National Film Board: **Glenn Gould – On the Record, Glenn Gould – Off the Record**, and **Caroline** as well as the scripts for **Jour après jour, Marie-Victorin** and **Correlieu**. Though largely active as a director, Perron has written scripts for his own **Taureau**, for Labrecque's **Les Smattes** and Jutra's **Mon Oncle Antoine.**

For further reference to Perron's work, see section 1. FILMMAKERS.

GEORGE ROBERTSON was born in Vancouver and has continued to work there largely with the CBC. As a member of the Vancouver Film Unit Robertson wrote the scripts for Allan King's **Pemberton Valley** and **Rickshaw**. Ron Kelly's **Waiting for Caroline**, a CBC-NFB co-production, was also written by Robertson. As a director and producer Robertson has directed a number of his own scripts in the series "Quentin Durgens" and many other television films – **Felicia is Happy, The Trouble with Fred, Remembrance of Lowry, The Eyes of Children, Running to India, The Islanders** and **Joyceville**. Most recently, Robertson wrote the script for George McCowan's **Face Off.**
See: "Hello, 'Caroline', Goodbye", by George Robertson, *How to Make or Not to Make a Canadian Film.*

BILL FRUET has scripted both of Don Shebib's features, **Goin' Down the Road** and **Rip-Off**. As well, Fruet has written David Acomba's first feature film, **Out** and adapted and directed his own original stage play, **Wedding in White** set in his Prairie homeland. **Wedding in White** was later filmed (Fruet directing) and won the Etrog, as best feature, in 1972. As a member of the Playwrights' Co-op and the Toronto Film-Makers' Co-op, Fruet has led a number of classes in scriptwriting.

See: "Customers are Knocking on Screenwriter's Door", by Urjo Kareda, *The Toronto Star*, January 29, 1972, and "Films" column by John Hofsess, *Maclean's Magazine*, November 1972.)

ROCH CARRIER, Montreal novelist and playwright, wrote the script for **Le Martien de Noël**, a children's film directed by Bernard Gosselin, and adapted his novel **La Guerre, Yes Sir!** for a film.

See: "The Seed of Violence that Lurks Within Us", by Lawrence Sabbath, *The Montreal Star*, November 14, 1970; "Roch Carrier: l'écho d'une épopée silencieuse" an interview by Reginald Martel, *La Presse*, November 21, 1970.

JOHN HERBERT adapted his stage play **Fortune and Men's Eyes** for the film directed by Harvey Hart.

See: "Playwright John Herbert Stays on the Outside", by Dane Lanken, *The Montreal Gazette*, November 7, 1970, p. 37.

TED ALLAN, playwright and novelist *(The Scalpel, The Sword)*, wrote **Sept fois par jour** which was directed by Denis Héroux in an Israeli-Canadian co-production and completed a film script based on his childhood experiences in Montreal, **Lies My Father Told Me**, directed by Jan Kadar.

See: "Ted Allan's many faces", by Randy Newell, *The Montreal Star*, August 13, 1971.

CHARLES ISRAEL, novelist, who had done some scripting for the series "Perspectives", later wrote Ron Kelly's spectacular retelling of the Easter story, **Open Grave**.

4. actors

The Association of Canadian Television and Radio Artists (ACTRA) publishes a Membership List of ACTRA members in Canada. This organization also publishes a 400-page book, *Face to Face with Talent* which is an alphabetical listing, with photographs, of ACTRA members. Both are available to directors and producers on request from:

> ACTRA
> 105 Carlton Street
> Toronto 200, Ontario

> or

> ACTRA
> 1434 St. Catharine St., W.
> Suite 418
> Montreal 25, Quebec

In Quebec: Union des Artistes
> 1290 St-Denis St., 6th Floor
> Montreal 29, Quebec

An alternate listing of actors, film services and studios which serves the west coast is *Vantage: Canadian Media Directory;* published twice yearly, *Vantage* is available to producers and directors. Write:

> *Vantage: Canadian Media Directory*
> Vantage Publications Ltd.
> 509-736 Granville St.
> Vancouver, B.C.

The National Film Board in Montreal offers classes in film acting technique. Four times weekly from September to June, actors work with directors in workshop training. Contact John Strasberg, National Film Board, Box 6100, Montreal 101, Quebec.

The National Theatre School of Canada (5030 St. Denis Street, Montreal 176, Quebec. 842-7954) offers the country's toughest and best acting course (3 years). Fee is $500 per year but scholarships are available. Only 32 students are accepted each year into the acting course (16 English, 16 French) following nation-wide auditions.

5. music in films

Two music trade magazines which keep track of composers in the cinema are:

The Music Scene/La Scène musicale published 6 times yearly by BMI. Available to organizations or individuals interested in the performance of Canadian music. Write:

> The Music Scene/La Scène musicale,
> 41 Valleybrooke Drive,
> Don Mills 405, Ontario.

The Canadian Composer/Le Compositeur canadien is published 10 times a year by the Composers, Authors and Publishers Association of Canada (CAPAC). Free to members, subscriptions are available at $2.00 per year from:

> The Canadian Composer/Le Compositeur canadien,
> 501-1407 Yonge St.,
> Toronto 290, Ontario.   925-5138

FILM MUSIC WORKSHOP

Offered as a service by BMI Canada Limited, the Film Music Workshop is open to professional lyricists and composers to stimulate and encourage new creative talent in the film music field. Started in December 1970, the workshops are led by various composers working in film. For further information, contact:

> BMI Canada Limited,
> 41 Valleybrooke Drive,
> Don Mills, Ontario 405

FILM MUSIC STUDY

La Cinémathèque québécoise has a large amount of information available on Canadian composers who have written scores for films other than those produced by the National Film Board. In 1965, la Cinémathèque published a pamphlet, *Musique et cinéma* on the occasion of their homage to two composers, Eldon Rathburn and Maurice Blackburn; this contains filmographies and articles on a number of composers who have worked within the National Film Board.

The Music Department of the National Film Board keeps detailed records and original recordings of their film music. Contact the Archivist, Music Department, National Film Board, Box 6100, Montreal 101, Quebec.

The Ontario Film Institute has available for students of film music a large number of recordings. Arrangements can be made for access by contacting the Secretary, Ontario Film Institute, c/o Ontario Science Centre, 770 Don Mills Rd., Don Mills, Ontario.

Cine Books — the Toronto bookstore — offers for sale recordings of the soundtracks of a wide variety of major film productions (692A Yonge St., Toronto 5. 964-6474).

The following is a list of some of the composers who have worked in Canadian cinema:

APPLEBAUM, LOUIS

Born in Toronto in 1918, Louis Applebaum attended the Toronto Conservatory of Music and joined the National Film Board as a staff composer in 1941. In 1943 he became the NFB's Music Director and from 1949 to 1953 acted as consultant there. Applebaum spent some years in Hollywood as a composer and later at Stratford and the CBC. Applebaum is now director of the Ontario Council for the Arts. Among the films he scored are the following: **Action Stations!** (Joris Ivens), **Target Berlin, Ordeal By Ice,** and **Fortress Japan** in the "World in Action" series; **The Jolifou Inn, Land of the Long Day,** Bill Mason's **Paddle to the Sea** — all made at the National Film Board; Julian Roffman's **The Bloody Brood, The Mask** and **The Proudest Girl in the World.**

BLACKBURN, MAURICE

Born in Quebec city in 1914, Maurice Blackburn studied at Laval
University and the New England Conservatory in Boston before joining
the National Film Board in 1941 as one of the first staff composers
along with Louis Applebaum. Combined with further studies in Paris
and his concert compositions, Blackburn composed numerous scores
for documentaries and arranged folk songs and sound tracks for animated
films. In 1969 Blackburn set up a research studio for music under the
aegis of the French animation section. Among his work are scores for
the following films: **La Poulette grise, Lines Vertical, Lines Horizontal,
A Phantasy, Blinkity Blank, Le Merle, Pas de deux** (all Norman McLaren);
Notes on a Triangle (René Jodoin), **La Canne à pêche** (Fernand Dansereau),
Les Petites Soeurs (Pierre Patry), **Les Mains nettes** (Claude Jutra),
Pierrot des bois (Claude Jutra), **Jour après jour** (Clément Perron),
Percé on the Rocks (Gilles Carle), **Le Festin des morts** (Fernand
Dansereau), **Cité Savante** (Guy L. Côté), **Huit Témoins** (Jacques
Godbout), **Fine Feathers, The Hoarder** (Evelyn Lambart).

See: "Blackburn: 'Traduire la musique dans l'espace était un défi' ",
by G. Rheault, *Le Soleil*, December 12, 1970, p. 51 (on working with
McLaren). Blackburn's work is critically discussed in *Le Cinéma
canadien.*

FLEMING, ROBERT

Born in 1921 in Prince Albert, Saskatchewan, Robert Fleming studied
at the Royal College of Music in London and on a CAPAC scholarship
in Toronto with Dr. Healey Willan and Ettore Mazzoleni. He joined the
National Film Board in 1946 as a staff composer and became the Board's
music Director in 1958. Fleming has arranged folksongs, composed
original songs and scored over a hundred documentary films, eg.:
City Out of Time (Colin Low), **Télesphore Legare, garde-pêche** (Claude
Fournier), **Les Maître-sondeurs** (Guy L. Côté), **Il y eut un soir, il y eut
un matin** (Pierre Patry), **Phoebe** (George Kaczender), the series "Struggle
for a Border" (Ronald Dick), **The Best Damn Fiddler From Calabogie
to Kaladar** (Peter Pearson), **Paul Tomkowicz — Street-railway Switchman**
(Kroitor), **The Bear and the Mouse** (Rubbo).

See: *Musique et Cinéma,* a pamphlet published in 1965 by La Cinémathèque canadienne. Available at film study libraries.

RATHBURN, ELDON

Born in Queenstown, New Brunswick in 1916, Eldon Rathburn studied at McGill University and with Dr. Healey Willan, joining the National Film Board as a staff composer in 1947. Eldon Rathburn was the first recipient of the Annual Award of the Society of Film Makers for Distinguished Contribution to the Industry. Among the films he scored are the following: **Canon, Short and Suite** (with Norman McLaren), **Circle of the Sun, Universe, Corral, City of Gold, Age of the Beaver** (with Colin Low); **The Romance of Transportation in Canada** (Low, Verrall, Koenig), **My Financial Career, The Railrodder, The Ride** (with Gerald Potterton); **Nahanni** (Don Wilder), **The Back-breaking Leaf** (Terence Macartney-Filgate), **The Shepherd** (Julian Biggs), **The Drylanders** (Don Haldane), **Nobody Waved Goodbye** (Don Owen), **Morning on the Lievre** (David Bairstow), **Le Grand Rock** (Raymond Garceau), **Fields of Sacrifice** (Donald Brittain), **What on Earth?** (Les Drew and Kaj Pindle with Don Douglas).

See: *Musique et Cinéma,* La Cinémathèque canadienne, 1965.

WILLIAM MCCAULEY

McCauley worked as a staff composer for Crawley Films from 1947 to 1958, writing over 125 film scores. Among his recent productions are: **Canada: Land of Infinite Variety** (George Kennedy), **This Vibrant Land** (on the Group of Seven), the CBC'S "Jalna" series directed by John Trent, and **Festival** by Christopher Chapman for the Ontario Pavilion at Osaka.

Many other Canadian composers have scored Canadian films. Among them are the following:

STEPHANNE VENNE

Les Mâles (Gilles Carle), **Seul ou avec d'autres** (Denys Arcand, Denis Héroux, Stephanne Venne), **Jusqu 'au cou** (Denis Héroux). **Yul 871** (Jacques Godbout) with François Dompierre.

ROBERT CHARLEBOIS

Tout l'temps, tout l'temps, tout l'temps . . .?(Fernand Dansereau), **Jusqu 'au coeur** (Jean-Pierre Lefebvre), **Deux Femmes en or** (Claude Fournier), **A soir on fait peur au monde** (François Brault and Jean Dansereau).

JEAN COUSINEAU

A tout prendre, Mon Oncle Antoine (Claude Jutra), **Caïn** (Pierre Patry), **Pour la suite du monde** (Michel Brault and Pierre Perrault) with Jean Meunier.

REG GIBSON

Nis'ku (Don Williams).

PIERRE F. BRAULT

Wow (Claude Jutra), **De mère en fille** (Anne-Claire Poirier), **Le Viol d'une jeune fille douce**, and **Red** (Gilles Carle).

BRUCE MCKAY

High Steel, Notes For a Film About Donna and Gail (both Don Owen).

NEIL HARRIS

The Gift of the Magi (Don Williams).

ROBERT RUZICKA

Sunshine Summertime, and **Five Years in the Life** for CBC.

DON DOUGLAS

A Day in the Night of Jonathan Mole (Don Brittain), **The Great Toy Robbery** (Derek Lamb), **The Days of Whiskey Gap** (Colin Low).

DOUGLAS RANDLE

Evolution (Mike Mills).

KARL DUPLESSIS

Atonement, Big Horn, End of a Summer Day, R_X For Export,

A Question of Immunity, all made at the National Film Board.

GEORGES D'OR

Ou êtes vous donc . . . ? (Gilles Groulx), **Saint Jérome** (Fernand Dansereau).

HARRY FREEDMAN

Act of the Heart, Isabel (Paul Almond).

CLAUDE GAUTHIER

Entre la mer et l'eau douce (Michel Brault).

FRANÇOIS COUSINEAU

La Corde au cou (Pierre Patry), **L'Initiation** and **L'Amour humain** (Denis Héroux).

FRANÇOIS DOMPIERRE

Délivrez-nous du mal (Jean-Claude Lord), **Yul 871** (Jacques Godbout) with Stephanne Venne, **Le Dossier Nelligan** (Claude Fournier) with Marc Gelinas, **Don't Let the Angels Fall** (George Kaczender), **St-Denis dans le temps . . .** (Marcel Carrière), **Tiens-toi bien après les oreilles à papa** (Jean Bissonnette) and **IXE—13** (Jacques Godbout).

RAOUL DUQUAY

Patricia et Jean-Baptiste (Jean-Pierre Lefebvre).

BRUCE COCKBURN

Goin' Down the Road (Don Shebib).

LUCIO AGOSTINI

Train Busters, The War for Men's Minds, The Gates of Italy, Geo Politick—Hitler's Plan and **So Proudly She Marches** — all for the NFB's "World in Action" series.

6. film people

There are many people who do not fit into the foregoing categories but who have made vital contributions to the development of filmmaking in Canada. The cursory nature of this chapter, therefore, is an indication only of the limitations of a book of this scope, and not of the importance of the work of the producers, technicians and critics who are included in this section.

THOMAS VAMOS was born in Hungary in 1938 and studied cinema and theatre in his homeland. A cinematographer, Vamos has filmed Jacques Godbout's **Kid Sentiment** and **IXE-13**, Jean-Pierre Lefebvre's **Jusqu'au coeur** and **la Chambre blanche**, Gilles Groulx's **Où êtes-vous donc?**, Marcel Carriere's **Saint-Denis dans le temps**, Jean Chabot's **Mon Enfance à Montréal** and Raymond Garceau's **Vive la France**. In 1972 he directed **l'Exil**. Also at the National Film Board are the sound engineers **ROGER LAMOUREUX**, **RON ALEXANDER** and **CLAUDE HAZANA-VICIUS**; Hazanavicius was sound engineer on **IXE-13**, **La Chambre blanche**, **L'Exil**, and **Mon Oncle Antoine**, and has produced a short film, **Pollu-sons**, dealing with the relation between sound and image in the cinema. **SERGE BEAUCHEMIN** is a sound engineer whose credits include **On est au coton**, **Le Martien de Noël**, and **Calibre quarante-cinq**; **JOSEPH CHAMPAGNE** was sound engineer on **Caroline**, **La Vie heureuse de Léopole Z**, **Fortune and Men's Eyes**, and **Taureau**. Originally a still photographer, **GUY BORREMANS** was the director of photography for Clément Perron's **Jour après jour**, Gilles Groulx's **Golden Gloves** and **un Jeu si simple** (with Jean-Claude Labrecque) and Arthur Lamothe's **Le mépris n'aura qu'un temps** among others. He has also directed a number of shorts including **la Femme image** and **l'Homme vite**. There are a number of articles on Borremans' work in **Jour après jour**: "Guy Borremans Talks About Filmmaking", *Canadian Cinematography*, May-June, 1963; "Les cameramen de l'ONF" by Jacques Leduc, *Séquences*, No. 33, May 1963; "L'homme observe" in *Objectif* 62, No. 15-16,

August 1962. Also see an analysis of **Jour après jour** in *Dossiers de cinéma: 1,* Edition Fides, Montreal, 1968. **WALLY GENTLEMAN** is a technical wizard who helped to design the National Film Board's **Universe** and **Labyrinth** and later Stanley Kubrick's **2001: A Space Odyssey.** He directs his own company, SPEAC. Two articles on Gentleman are as follows: "Inside 2001", *Take One,* Vol. 1, No. 2 and "The man who made 2001 fly has a little shop in a Montreal suburb . . . and he's very outspoken about Canadian film", Dane Lanken, *The Gazette,* Montreal, December 12, 1970. **ALAIN DOSTIE** was cameraman on **On est au coton, On est loin du soleil,** and **Le Martien de Noël; ROGER MORIDE** photographed **Loving and Laughing;** and **PAUL-CHARLES VAN DER LINDEN** was cinematographer of **High, Facade, Act of the Heart, Eliza's Horoscope** and **Journey. RENE VERZIER** was director of photography on **Pile ou face, Les Mâles,** and **Sept Fois par jour.**

In Toronto, **DONALD WILDER** has recently been director of photography on two feature films, **Face-Off** and **Michael Calls.** He first joined the National Film Board as an assistant cameraman in 1944, becoming a director with the "Perspective" series in 1957 for which he directed **The Editor, The Legendary Judge** and **One Day's Poison,** among others. As a free-lancer, Wilder has been director of photography on Don Haldane's **Nikki, Wild Dog of the North** and photographer/co-director with William Weintraub on **Nahanni.** An article on the shooting of **Nahanni,** "The River and the Old Man: the Saga of Filming Headless Valley", by Don Wilder, is available in the November-December, 1962 issue of *Canadian Cinematography.* Also in Toronto are editor and cameraman **ROBERT CRONE** who founded Film House in 1963, and **DON HAIG,** an editor who has worked on numerous television dramas and documentaries; he was chief editor on the series "This Hour Has Seven Days" and "The Fabulous Sixties". **JOE GRIMALDI,** sound engineer, recently mixed Jean-Claude Labrecque's **les Smattes.**

In Vancouver, **GENE LAWRENCE, JACK LONG** and **DOUGLAS MCKAY,** cameramen, were all members of the Vancouver Film Unit. Long, who worked for a number of years with the National Film Board, photographed Allan King's **Skid Row,** Ron Kelly's **A Bit of Bark** and more recently, Daryl Duke's **West Coast On My Mind.** Douglas McKay also worked for the Board beginning there as John Spotton's assistant; in 1956 he photographed for the series "On the Spot" and later worked in animation. McKay was cameraman on Larry Kent's **When Tomorrow Dies,** Sylvia Spring's **Madeleine Is . . .** and Patrick Watson's **Search in** the Deep. **SHEILAH RELJAC**, Vancouver editor, has taught her skill to a generation of west coast filmmakers and recently worked on Duke's **West Coast On My Mind**.

Four producers with extensive experience are **GUY GLOVER, PHILIP KEATLEY, PETER JONES** and **JOSEPH KOENIG**. Guy Glover joined the National Film Board in 1941. As an executive producer, Glover has been involved in the series "Window on Canada", "Passe-Partout", "Comparisons" and "Lewis Mumford on the City". He also has produced such films as **Angel, Quebec as Seen by Cartier-Bresson** and **The Summer We Moved to Elm Street**. Poet and critic, Glover is presently director of programming at the Board. See Glover's article, "How to Make a Canadian Film", in *How to Make or Not to Make a Canadian Film.* Philip Keatley has had extensive experience in drama, first as an actor and later as a director with the CBC Vancouver drama department which he joined in 1957. Keatley worked closely with Paul St-Pierre in producing and directing the indigenous drama series of the west coast; the Cariboo series included **The Window at Namko, Antoine's Wooden Overcoat** and **Frenchie's Wife**. Some of these dramas were later repeated on film for "Festival". As executive producer of drama at CBC Vancouver, Keatley has produced and directed in the series "The Manipulators" and "The Beachcombers". Peter Jones joined the sound department at the National Film Board in 1945 and later the music department as a music and sound editor. As a producer, Jones has been involved in the early series "Eye Witness" and later was responsible for government-sponsored films as well as the NFB-CBC series "Canada at War". Jones has also produced Don Haldane's **The Drylanders** and **Helicopter Canada**. As regional executive producer in Vancouver, Jones has encouraged and fostered a great deal of quality film production. Joe Koenig joined the National Film Board as a writer-researcher having spent a number of years as a magazine editor. Greatly involved in classroom films while at the Board producing **Every Second Car** and **You Don't Back Down**, among others, he founded and directs Cinemedia, a largely educational film firm in Montreal. Two producers with considerable experience are **PIERRE LAMY** and **GUY FOURNIER**. Lamy produced **Red, Les Mâles, La Vraie Nature de Bernadette, La Mort d'un bûcheron** and **Kamouraska**, and Fournier was the producer of **Deux Femmes en or** and **Alien Thunder**.

Among the critics who have supported Canadian cinema are **GERALD PRATLEY** who founded the Ontario Film Institute, **LEO BONNEVILLE**, editor of *Séquences,* the film criticism journal, and **ANDRE PAQUET** who organized the retrospective of Canadian cinema for La Cinémathèque canadienne in 1966 and edited *How to Make or Not to Make a Canadian Film.* See Paquet's article, "Qu'est-ce que le cinéma Canadien?" in *Arts-canada;* Bonneville's "Le cinéma canadien à l'heure de la révolution québécoise", *Séquences* No. 40, February 1965; and "L'industrie du film au Québec", *Le Droit,* Ottawa, November 3, 1971.

7. emerging filmmakers

From the National Film Board, small companies and cooperative production groups, young filmmakers are emerging. In many cases they are assisted by the Canadian Film Development Corporation. The films mentioned in this section, unless produced by the National Film Board, are obtainable from one of the cooperatives (see COOPERATIVE DISTRIBUTION AND PRODUCTION). The following list of filmmakers and their work is divided into regional areas:

QUEBEC

Born in 1945, **ROGER FRAPPIER** studied political science and wrote criticism for *Le Devoir, Sept-Jours* and *La Presse* before directing his first film, **le Grand Film ordinaire** or **Jeanne d'Arc n'est pas morte, se porte bien et vit au Québec**. It was written by Raymond Cloutier, based on a comic presentation by le Théâtre populaire de Québec entitled *T'es pas tannée Jeanne d'Arc?* Produced independently with the help of Arthur Lamothe, Les Cinéastes associés and the CFDC, **le Grand Film ordinaire** is a document of Quebec life and a fabulous story in a circus round; it is distributed by Faroun Films, Montreal. Frappier also directed **Alain Grandbois** and **Gaston Miron** in the series "Ecrivains québécois" for Les Films Jean-Claude Labrecque Inc. To be completed soon, **Allô tout l'monde**, a feature documentary on poet Raoul Dugay and the group L'infonie. Articles on his work include: "Du mythe à la réalité", by Luc Perreault, *La Presse,* February 6, 1971, p.C.9; "J'ai appris le cinéma en faisant *le Grand Film ordinaire*", by Carol Faucher, *Québec-Presse* February 7, 1971; "Du cinéma en tant que produit de culture et non de consommation", *La Tribune,* Sherbrooke, December 12, 1970; and "Le cinéma libre n'est pas mort mais se porte mal au Québec", by Luc Perreault, *La Presse,* September 16, 1970.

ANDRE THEBERGE was born in 1945 in Saint-Eleuthère, Kamouraska county. After his studies at the University of Montreal, he acted in Lefebvre's **le Révolutionnaire** and Godbout's **Yul 871**. He later assisted in the direction of three Lefebvre films — **Patricia et Jean-Baptiste**, **Mon Oeil** and **Il ne faut pas mourir pour ça**. He directed several short films — **Bravo Georgette**, **Tereleur** and **l'Ile Trébuchante** or **On a tout le temps** — before making his first feature at the National Film Board. Produced by Jean-Pierre Lefebvre, **Question de vie** is a delicate story of a young woman left by her husband to cope with three young children. Three interviews with Théberge are as follows: "*Question de vie:* de la manufacture à l'asile . . . ", *Québec-Presse,* February 14, 1971; "André Théberge", *La Presse,* February 13, 1971, p.D.9; and "Le cinéma, une chose simple", an interview with Paul Roux in *Le Soleil,* Quebec, February 13, 1971. *Image et Son* No. 252 has a review of **Question de vie** on p. 226.

MICHEL AUDY was born in Grand-Mère in 1947. Assistant-director on Jean-Pierre Lefebvre's **Q-bec My Love**, Audy developed his skills in a number of independently produced short documentaries — **Piste, Pelouse, Jeunesse 65, Encore inconnu, Pêche très douce** and **Terre de Charlevoix**. He has also produced a number of features, among them **la Gelure** and **la Marée**, distributed by Coopérative cinéastes indépendants, **A force d'homme** (1969) distributed by Euro Film and **Jean-Francois-Xavier de** . . . (1970). The latter film was produced by Jean-Pierre Lefebvre at the National Film Board in the series "Premières Oeuvres". In 1972 Audy directed **Corps et âmes**, a feature produced by Lefebvre's Cinak Cie. Cinématographie Ltée.
See: "Un film canadien off-Montreal", by Renald Savoie, *La Presse,* August 28, 1969.

WILLIE DUNN made his first film, **Ballad of Crowfoot**, in 1969 under the aegis of the Challenge for Change Unit of the National Film Board. He has since co-directed **The Other Side of the Ledger** with **MARTIN DEFALCO**, also at the National Film Board. Dunn has been particularly active in writing music for films; he wrote the song which accompanied **Ballad of Crowfoot** and "The Merry-Go-Round" for **TANYA BALLENTINE**'s **The Things I Cannot Change**. He has also written songs for Defalco's **Cold Journey**, a feature on an Indian within the world of the white man, and **MIKE MITCHELL'S Who Were the Ones?** The CBC's production of **Louis Riel** and **CLAY BORRIS' Paper Boy** have music written by Dunn. Willie Dunn presently freelances out of the National Film Board.

See: "Un phénomène: le méchant Indien sur les écrans de cinéma", by Alex Binkley, *Le Soleil,* Quebec, September 30, 1971.

YVAN PATRY was born in Abitibi in 1948, grew up in Montreal and later studied at the Centre national de cinéma in Paris. Since returning to Montreal, Patry has written critical articles on cinema for *La Presse* and the collection *Le Cinéma québécois: tendances et prolongements.* His first film, **Octobre 68**, was produced for Radio-Canada in the series "Les Temps changent". His first feature, **un Jour sans évidence** or **Ainsi soient-ils,** was produced for the National Film Board by Jean-Pierre Lefebvre in the series "Premières Oeuvres."

FERNAND BELANGER studied filmmaking in France, joining Radio-Canada as an editor. Born in Rivière-du-Loup in 1943, Belanger made three short films, **Initiation, Via Borduas** and **Ty-coeur**, the latter with Claude Dubois at the National Film Board for the program "Premières Oeuvres." Belanger made his first feature, **Ty-peupe**, in 1971. The same year, with Willie Dunn, Belanger received a grant of $2,500 from the American Academy of Motion Picture Arts and Sciences. Articles include: "*Ty-peupe* et Fernand Belanger en liberté", by Jean-Pierre Tadros, *Le Devoir,* October 27, 1971; A review of **Ty-peupe** in *Cinéma Québec,* Vol. 1, No. 3, September 1971, p.14-15; "Un Dionysos urbain", by Fulvio Caccia, in *Transit,* No. 1, Winter, 1972.

FRANÇOIS BRAULT and **JEAN DANSEREAU** have produced (with the help of les Cinéastes associés) their first feature film, **A soir on fait peur au monde**, a musical documentary on Robert Charlebois. Brault was born in Montreal in 1941 and has directed a number of shorts, among them, **les Visages de clémence** and **la Côte nord à l'autre bout du monde** in 1968. Brault was cameraman on this co-directed first feature. Jean Dansereau was also born in Montreal. Having directed a number of shorts at the National Film Board, he co-founded les Cinéastes associés and now manages the production company, les Ateliers du cinéma québécois. He is currently working on **Floralie où es-tu?** a feature he directed and based on Roch Carrier's novel. An interview with Brault can be found in *La Presse,* March 21, 1970.

GILLES MARCHAND and **HUGUES TREMBLAY** produced their first feature, **T-bone Steak chez les mangeuses d'hommes**, in 1969. Tremblay, born in Chicoutimi in 1946, had collaborated on a feature before making his short films **Aluminiumanie, Des corps nus ou la vie est ronde** and **la Grande Illusion courte**.
See: "Tremblay et Marchand: la fantaisie avant tout", by Luc Perreault, *La Presse,* April 4, 1970, p.44.

RON HALLIS made his first feature **Rainy Day Woman** in 1970 and in 1972, **Toni, Randi and Marie**, a second feature on male prostitution.

MARC DAIGLE, executive director of the film cooperative, l'Association coopérative des productions audio-visuelles (ACPAV), completed his first feature, **C'est ben beau l'amour**, in 1970; produced by the National Film Board, the film was also written and edited by Daigle. Daigle was born in St-Hyacinthe in 1947 and studied literature at the University of Montreal.
See: "Jeunesse désemparée cinéma société incertaine", by Mario Pelletier, *Le Soleil,* Quebec, October 30, 1971.

CLOVIS DURAND, born in 1941, worked with Richard Lavoie in Quebec City and directed newsreels for Radio-Canada. With Jean Chabot, Durand directed **un Bicycle pour Pit** in 1968, and with Jean Saulnier **Taverne** and **Hommage à Pat Lachance**. The two latter films and Durand's **Vroom** are distributed by the Coopérative cinéastes independants. Durand has recently completed a film on the novelist Marie-Claire Blais.
See: *"Un Bicycle pour Pit",* by Jean-Pierre Guay, *l'Action-Quebec,* July 24, 1969, p.13.

CLAUDE BERUBE made his first feature, **Pas de jeu sans soleil**, in Saguenay in 1972, with the collaboration of Hugues Tremblay as editor and cameraman. Bérubé's first film, **Couloirs**, was made in 1966 when he was a student. He also co-directed **Carnaval en chute libre** with Guy Bouchard.
See: "Le cinéma, c'est mon infirmité", by H. L., *Québec-Presse,* February 20, 1972.

At the National Film Board, **FRANCIS MANKIEWICZ** wrote and directed his feature **Le Temps d'une chasse** in 1972. With photography by Michel Brault and editing by Werner Nold, the story revolves around the dreams of a bucolic excursion. Also at the NFB, **ANDRE BRASSARD** directed **Françoise Durocher, waitress** written by Michel Tremblay.

ONTARIO

Born in Montreal in 1944, **DAVID ACOMBA** has combined his interest in film and music to produce some exceptional television shows; the first Anne Murray special, **Straight, Clean and Simple**, introduced network stereo in 1971. Earlier he had produced three other music television shows for CBC — **Mariposa Folk Festival, Rock One** and **Rock Two**. During 1968-69 Acomba directed and produced a 26-week series, "Sunday Morning", a 45-minute show which combined film and live action. In the area of fiction, Acomba directed **Summer's Gone After Today** as his thesis film at the University of California, **Somewhere** for CBC's "Program X" and a feature, **Out**, written by Bill Fruet.

See: "Mariposa on film: cutting 41,000 feet to 2,000 takes a lot of time", by Leslie Millin, the *Globe and Mail*, August 25, 1969; "Acomba, rock and that festival feeling", by Cynthia Gunn, *Montreal Star*, April 11, 1970.

The London Film Coop is a distribution cooperative and a spiritual grouping of filmmakers/artists who live in London, Ontario. As well as **JACK CHAMBERS**, there is **GREG CURNOE** who is also a painter and musician who has made a number of experimental films: **Souwesto** and **Connexions**. Like Chambers and Curnoe, **KEEWATIN DEWDNEY** was born in London, Ontario. Teacher, writer, artist and mathematician, Dewdney has been making short, experimental films since 1965: **Scissors, Four Girls, Malanga, Maltese Cross Movement, Patricia, I, Robot, Wildwood Flower** and **Lundun**. Other members of the London group are **FRASER BOA** (**Black and Blue, Chambers**) and **JOHN BOYLE** (**St. Catharines and Toronto**). Their films are distributed by the London Film Coop and the Canadian Film-makers' Distribution Centre. Articles include: "London Regional Liberation Front", by Dr. R. Woodman, the *Globe and Mail*, July 10, 1969; "Artists as Filmmakers", Ross Woodman, *Artscanada*, June, 1968; and "The New Canadian Cinema: Images from the Age of Paradox", by Gene Youngblood, *Artscanada*, April, 1970.

See also: *Greg Curnoe: Canada*, Queen's Printer, Ottawa, 1969.

JIM ANDERSON and **KEITH LOCK** joined forces at York University after Anderson had made his animated **Scream of a Butterfly** in 1969;

together they directed another animated short, **Base Tranquility**, and later **Touched** for the Junior Red Cross which combined animation and live action. Their third film together, **Arnold**, is a live-action comedy with Philip Schreibman and **Big Wave** with Dave Anderson. All films listed are distributed by the Canadian Film-makers' Distribution Centre.

MICHAEL ONDAATJE is a poet/filmmaker, author of three collections of poetry: *The Dainty Monsters, The Man with 7 Toes* and *The Collected Works of Billy the Kid.* His 35 min. film, **Sons of Captain Poetry** concerns another Canadian poet, b.p. Nichol, and he is presently working on **Carry On Crime and Punishment**. Ondaatje's work is distributed by the Canadian Film-makers' Distribution Centre.

CLAY BORRIS made one other short live action film which starred his family before making **Paper Boy**, produced by Tom Daly at the National Film Board. With music by Willie Dunn. Borris lives and works in Toronto.

THE PRAIRIES

Seven young men have decided to remain in the Prairies as a cooperative film unit: **REEVAN DOLGOY, ALLAN STEIN, MARK DOLGOY, HARVEY SPAK, PETER AMERONGEN, BOB REECE** and **TOM RADFORD**. As Filmwest Associates, they have produced over forty films for the National Film Board, CBC and the Alberta Department of Education, among others. Their talents include animation, music, sound, editing, writing and directing. Among their films are **Beaver Hills, This is a Film About Farming** (for CBC'S "This Land"), **A Lament for Woody, Death of a Delta**, and **The Last Best West. REEVAN DOLGOY's Jablonski**, shown on network CBC, told of a concert pianist who had grown up in the West. A number of projects are under way including **The Life of Ernest Brown**, a pioneer photographer whose work is collected in the Glenbow Foundation, and a feature film from a Sheila Watson novel. The members of Filmwest Associates work out of Edmonton, Alberta.

MARITIMES

RICK HANCOX from Charlottetown, Prince Edward Island made his first film, **Cab 16** in 1969, a short documentary of a Charlottetown cab driver; it won the award for the best documentary at the first Canadian Student Film Festival. He has since directed a number of short fiction

films — **I, A Dog, Next To Me, Rooftops, Rose** and **Tall Dark Stranger.**
Hancox' films are distributed by the Coopérative cinéastes indépendants
and the Canadian Film-makers' Distribution Centre.

WEST COAST

MORRIE RUVINSKY was born in Montreal in 1943 and studied at
McGill University. He has done film criticism for the *Vancouver Province*
and written a number of scripts for the National Film Board, CTV and
for a feature he hopes to direct. Ruvinsky has directed a number of
shorts — **What If You Throw A War And Nobody Shows Up?** and **Joanie**.
His two features **The Plastic Mile** and **The Finishing Touch** were both
made in Vancouver between 1968 and 1970. Ruvinsky now works out
of Montreal.
See: "The moviemaker who made it in Europe, but was banned in
Vancouver", *Maclean's,* October, 1969; "The Night *The Plastic Mile*
Lost 500 Feet", a report by Tom Shandel on the banning of that film
from the Vancouver Film Festival, *Take One,* Vol. 2, No. 4.

SYLVIA SPRING was born in Galt, Ontario in 1943. Her first film,
Madeleine, was a short 14-minute pilot for her feature, **Madeleine Is**.
Photographed by Douglas McKay in Vancouver and edited by Luke
Bennett, **Madeleine Is** is distributed by Phoenix Films. Spring is presently
scripting her second feature.
See: "Sylvia Spring: Canadian Filmmaker", by Wayne Cunningham, *The
Reel Thing,* Vol. 1, No. 2, May 1971, p.20-28; "Refuting the Youth
Movie Fantasy", Martin Knelman, the *Globe and Mail,* April 24, 1971;
"Making a Movie Despite the CFDC", by Betty Lee, the *Globe and Mail,*
March 27, 1971; "The Dilemma of Miss Spring", the *Vancouver Sun,*
May 29, 1970.

AL RAZUTIS lives in Vancouver and makes colorful and poetic films —
among them **Elegy for Rose, Inauguration, Sircus Show Fire** and **Aaeon**.
All under 30 min., Razutis' films are distributed by the Canadian Film-
makers' Distribution Centre in Toronto.
See: "No One Understood But the Viewers Were Thinking", *The Sun,*
Vancouver, July 15, 1970.

GLENN LEWIS is a graduate of the Vancouver School of Art, studied
pottery with Bernard Leach in England and teaches ceramics. Also a

dancer, Lewis has worked with the New York Minimalist Yvonne Rainer. In his second film, **Forest Industry** (photographed by David Rimmer), Lewis dances through the woods, forming a rectangle with a blue tape. Lewis' first film, **Block**, experiments with a revolving projection to produce an environment. His films are distributed by the Canadian Film-makers' Distribution Centre.

See: "Lewis' *Forest Industry* Film a Hypnotic Experience", by Joan Lowndes, *The Sun,* Vancouver, July 3, 1970.

Painter and set designer **JACK DARCUS** has made two feature-length fiction films; the first, **The Great Coups of History**, dealt with a middle-aged divorcée and her relationship with her daughter. The second film, **Proxy Hawks**, deals with the relationship between a man, a woman and their animals. Articles: "Darcus: The Artist as Filmmaker", Neil Arthur, *Vancouver Province,* February 6, 1970; and in the same paper on the same date, by James Spears, "The great coup that Jack built (or) A local movie maker makes good".

DAN SINGER was born in Edmonton in 1945 and attended Simon Fraser University where he majored in theatre and communications. In 1966 he made his first film, **The Beginning**, and in the following year, **Da Vida**, a feature. Singer was a cameraman on Tom Shandel's **Hum Central**, John Juliani's **Hurrah** and Eric Jensen's Alberta travel film, **Under the Sun.** In 1968 Singer directed **Pop Art** for CBC on the work of Robert Rauschenberg and **A Sense of Duty**. He produced Morrie Ruvinsky's **She's a Woman.** Singer presently works for Potterton Productions in Montreal.

SANDY WILSON studied at Simon Fraser's film workshop with Stanley Fox before making her first short film, **Garbage**, which was seen on "Take Thirty" in 1968. In 1970 she made **Penticton Profile**, distributed by the NFB Travel Library and the B.C. Government, and the following year **The Bridal Shower** photographed by Douglas McKay, dealing with the details of that ancient ritual. Wilson is presently directing **747**, produced by Peter Jones in the Vancouver National Film Board office. Her films are distributed by the Canadian Filmmakers' Distribution Centre.

KEITH RODAN is a prolific, experimental filmmaker who has worked with animation, live action and stock shots. Among his animated films which are two to eight minutes in length are the following: **Cinetude 1** (1968), **Cinetude 2** (1969), **Cinetude 3, S I** (1970), **Cinetude 4, Blu-zip Bebop, S2, S3, S4 "Age of Steel", S5 "Streets"** (1971). He has also made **Space Movie, Warfilm, In the Park, Via, SFU** and **Intermedia Dance** in 1971.

See: "Interview with Keith Rodan", by Kirwan Cox, *Rushes,* December, 1971; "The New Canadian Cinema: Images From the Age of Paradox", by Gene Youngblood, *Artscanada,* April, 1970 p.7-13.

A number of artists on the west coast have turned to film and video: **MICHAEL MORRIS, DALLAS SELMAN, GLEN TOPPINGS** and **GARY LEE-NOVA**. Lee-Nova and Selman made **Steel Mushrooms** in 1967 and Lee-Nova worked with Ronald Arnold to produce **When We Were Six** in 1969. His other films are **Pepsi Degeneration, The Pathological Market Place** (1966), **The Ballad of a Wise and Curious Wizard, Magic Circle** (1967), **How the West Was One** (1968).

See: "Films Lure Our Artists from Painting, Sculpture", *The Vancouver Sun,* March 26, 1971; "Lee-Nova is Man of Many Talents", by Ann Rosenberg, *The Vancouver Sun,* October 27, 1967.

PETER SVATEK now works in Montreal at Potterton Productions. His earlier **Harry the Hummer** was produced on the west coast while his later children's film **The Pope's Mule**, was produced by Faroun Films in Montreal. **DAVID CURNICK** and **DON WILSON** directed a feature, **The Life and Times of Chester Angus Ramsgood**, a comedy of youth and manners.

8. professional associations

American Federation of Musicians (Canada)
101 Thorncliffe Park Drive
Toronto 17, Ontario

Association canadienne des distributeurs
indépendants de films d'expression française
1405 Bishop St.
Suite 316-317
Montreal, Quebec

Association des producteurs de films du Québec
1070 Bleury St.
Suite 506
Montreal, Quebec

Association internationale du film d'animation
(ASIFA – Canada)
P.O. Box 118, Station C
Montreal 113, Quebec

Association of Canadian Television and Radio Artists (ACTRA)
105 Carlton St.
Toronto 2, Ontario

Association of Motion Picture Producers and
Laboratories of Canada
Suite 512
55 York St.
Toronto 1, Ontario

Association professionnelle des cinéastes du Québec
3466 St-Denis St.
Suite 7
Montreal 130, Quebec

Association des propriétaires de cinémas du Quebec
5950 Côte-des-Neiges
Suite 110
Montreal, Quebec

Canadian Film Editors Guild
P.O. Box 5686, Terminal A
Toronto 116, Ontario

Canadian Motion Picture Distributors Association
130 Bloor St. W.
Toronto 5, Ontario

Canadian Society of Cinematographers
22 Front St. W.
Toronto 1, Ontario

Directors Guild of Canada
Suite 815, 22 Front Street W.
Toronto 1, Ontario

International Alliance of Theatrical Stage Employees
304 Broadway Ave.
Toronto 12, Ontario

Motion Picture Theatres Association of Canada
175 Bloor St. E.
Toronto 5, Ontario

National Association of Broadcast Employees
and Technicians (NABET)
Suite 31
105 Carlton St.
Toronto 2, Ontario

Société des auteurs dramatiques
1001 St-Denis St.
Montreal, Quebec

Society of Filmmakers
P.O. Box 6100
Montreal 101, Quebec
          and
c/o NFB
1923 Granville St.
Vancouver, B.C.

Syndicat général du cinéma et de la télévision
2450 Athlone St.
Suite 108
Montreal 305, Quebec

Syndicat national du cinéma
3466 St-Denis St.
Montreal 130, Quebec

Union des artistes
1290 St-Denis St.
Montreal 130, Quebec

See also: COOPERATIVE DISTRIBUTION AND PRODUCTION

9. film societies

The Canadian Federation of Film Societies/La Fédération canadienne des ciné-clubs (CFFS/FCCC) is a federated group co-ordinating the efforts of all those interested in the appreciation of the film as art. Among their services are the following: assistance in setting up a film society; information exchanges between national and international societies; group rates on films borrowed from the Canadian Film Institute and other distributors.

The CFFS/FCCC publishes an Index of Feature Length Films, an international listing of 16mm and 35mm prints of interest to societies. Descriptive information, rental sources and prices are included.

Enquiries concerning memberships and publications should be directed to:

> Canadian Federation of Film Societies
> 1762 Carling Ave.
> Ottawa , Ontario   K2A 2H7

Other handbooks of interest to film societies are:

Le Ciné-club: méthodologie et portée sociale, by Léo Bonneville, Fides, Montréal 1968.

Film Society Primer, ed. Cecile Starr. Write to the American Federation of Film Societies (AFFS), 144 Bleecker Street, New York, N.Y. 10012.

10. film study centres

A number of film study libraries exist in Canada, but unfortunately, they are all within a very small geographical area. Recently these specialized libraries have begun to cooperate with one another and are beginning to make their material more accessible to people outside the main centres. For instance, the Canadian Film Institute is now selling its card index on microfilm and maintains a letter and telephone service — as do most of the libraries. The Cinémathèque québécoise makes its most recent information available in its periodical, *New Canadian Film*, and — like the CFI — puts out a number of film study publications. Many local libraries are filling the gaps of film study material and every National Film Board office holds some small collection of printed material for the student; certainly the dedicated people in those offices are willing to assist the student in every way possible.

Film study students should also check under the headings PERIODICALS, FILM AND PHOTOGRAPHY ARCHIVES, EDUCATIONAL MATERIAL, FILM COLLECTIONS and, of course, the names of individual filmmakers for more material which may be of interest.

La Cinémathèque québécoise, 360 McGill St., Montreal 125, Que. 866-4688. First of all, the Cinémathèque is a film archive which aims to preserve films, be they Canadian or foreign. The Cinémathèque also is *the* centre for documentation on Canadian cinema, with vertical files carring information on films, filmmakers, distribution and festivals. It also is the repository for about 90,000 stills, posters, tapes and archival materials. The Cinémathèque specializes in information on animation and possesses a large number of drawings and other materials. The Cinémathèque also has its museum, recently opened to the public (Monday to Friday, 9:30 a.m. to 5:30 p.m.). The first of its kind in Canada, this museum offers a large display of antique and modern cinematographic apparatus, an exhibition of film posters, and drawings relating to animated cinema.

Much of the topical material on new films across the country, festivals around the world and other activity is published in the quarterly, *New Canadian Film/Nouveau Cinéma canadien* which is available on request from the Cinémathèque. They also publish a number of studies of national and international cinema. For a publication price list, contact La Cinémathèque québécoise.

From Tuesdays to Fridays, the Cinémathèque québécoise has twice-nightly showings in the basement of la Bibliothèque nationale du Québec, 1700 Saint-Denis St., Montreal, Quebec. National and international cinema, classics and recent productions offer a complete film education. Entrance fee is 55¢ per show; monthly programs may be obtained at the office of the Cinémathèque, in the theatre, or by mail (include a stamped, 4 x 9 envelope with each request). Information about programs can be had by calling 866-4688 during the day and 844-8734 during projection hours.

Le Conseil québécois pour la diffusion du cinéma, Suites 5 & 6, 3466 Saint Denis St., Montreal 130, Quebec. 842-5079.

Uniting a number of Quebec cinematographic organizations, the CQDC publishes several studies of interest to the student of film: the series, *Cinéastes du Québec* offers, for each filmmaker treated, critiques, interviews and a complete filmography. They also publish *Répertoire des longs métrage produits au Québec 1960-1970,* lists of production and distribution houses, and the *Bottin Cinéma,* a catalogue of Quebec filmmakers. Available to the public for reference are files on Quebec filmmakers, national and international festival information, and production and distribution material. Xerox service is available.

Département de documentation cinématographique, La Bibliothèque nationale, 360 McGill St., Montreal 125, Quebec. 873-5450.

The basis of this library is the rich collection of Guy-L. Côté, founder of la Cinémathèque canadienne (now la Cinémathèque québécoise). The library consists of 1,000 periodical titles, many historical in nature, as well as current titles. The 8,000 books on the cinema cover critical and technical works, biographies and scenarios. Card indexes offer information on filmmakers, films, distributors and critical reviews. Press cuttings, pamphlets and other printed material are available in a vertical file system. Although the library is international in scope, special emphasis is placed on the documentation of Canadian cinema. Other services include microfilm, some photo slides, reproduction of documentation, telex and a reading room. The librarian is Pierre Allard.

Film Study Centre, Canadian Film Institute, 1962 Carling Ave., Ottawa K2A 2H7, Ontario. 729-6193.

The Film Study Centre at the Canadian Film Institute offers a number of services to its members: access to a cross-reference card index which offers information on filmmakers, films, distributors, reviews and criticism; press cuttings, pamphlets and other printed material on films, personalities, production and distribution; an international collection of film catalogues; a collection of over 6,000 volumes on the cinema; over 500 critical and trade journals; a collection of 150,000 stills, photographs and posters, many archival in nature. This material is accessible to members — $5.00 per year for individuals, $25.00 per year for institutions. While most of the material is for reference only in the Institute, they do offer telephone and letter service. Stills can be reproduced for a fee and Xerox service is available; special arrangements can be made for borrowing some books on inter-library loan.

The Canadian Film Institute also publishes a number of studies on Canadian and international directors as well as subject filmographies; their *800 Films for Film Study* is another valuable guide for the student. Furthermore, the Institute acts as a distributor for cinema publications from abroad; in particular they handle the International Film Guide series. For an up-to-date publication and price list, write to the Canadian Film Institute.

Another aspect of the CFI's Film Study Centre is their collection of films for critical study. Among their own collection are copies of films on deposit from the Museum of Modern Art in New York. Descriptive catalogues of films available for rental can be obtained from the Canadian Film Institute. Classical films from the Canadian Film Archives and international archives, and recently produced national and international films are often seen in the National Film Theatre situated in Ottawa or at one of the Regional Film Theatres situated in Calgary, Edmonton, Regina, Winnipeg and Halifax. For further information on these programs, write to the National Film Theatre, c/o the Canadian Film Institute.

National Film Board Information Division, P.O. Box 6100, Montreal 101, Quebec. 333-3452.

The Information Division of the National Film Board handles all requests for information on filmmakers, NFB films and related information. *A Brief History: The National Film Board of Canada* by James Lysyshyn is available on request as is a special edition of *News Clips/Revue de Presse,* a collection of articles on the operations, achievements and aims of The National Film Board of Canada. A monthly edition of *News Clips/Revue de Presse* is available for reference in any local or regional office of the National Film Board.

National Film Board films are available in public showings in every office across the country or may be borrowed from them or from the local public library. Catalogues, English and French, are available without charge from any NFB office. Not all films are listed in each catalogue so it is wise to obtain both; many films listed only in the French catalogue would offer no barrier to an English-speaking student of cinema.

National Film Board Library, 3155 Côte de Liesse Road, Saint-Laurent, Quebec. 333-3141.

The library at the National Film Board's main office is basically an internal resource library to serve the staff of filmmakers, the regional offices and offices abroad. Permission, however, can be obtained for use of the library for graduate students of communications.

While much of the material within the library does not deal with film or related topics, it does offer 20,000 volumes and 100 current periodicals. Press clippings, pamphlets and catalogues offer information on all audio-visual media and, in particular, information on the National Film Board itself. Many periodicals are now on microfilm and photocopy service is available as well as a reading room.

The Library also makes available current specialized bibliographies on many aspects of national and international film and other media.

L'Office des communications sociales, 4635 de Lorimier, Montreal 178, Quebec 526-9165.

The communication library of l'Office des communications sociales is not strictly a film study library but deals with all media and, in particular, the relationship between religion and mass media. Open to the general public, the library offers a book collection and periodical collection international in scope. The vertical file system offers critical reviews and documentation on over 25,000 films, personalities and directors.

L'Office des communications sociales publishes the film periodical *Séquences,* edited by Léo Bonneville and available quarterly for $2.50 per year ($2.00 for students), and *Recueil des films,* an annual listing and synopses of films distributed in Quebec along with artistic and moral criticism. Subscription is $3.00 per year with a year-end cumulative index.

Ontario Film Institute, Ontario Science Centre, 770 Don Mills Rd., Don Mills, Ontario. 429-4100.

Gerald Pratley's personal collection forms the basis of the reference library of the Ontario Film Institute. Over 4,000 book titles and 100 periodical titles offer information on all aspects of national and international cinema. Vertical files and a card index contain information on films, filmmakers and other subjects. An added dimension of this library is the collection of taped interviews with directors, actors and composers. Over 2,000 film music recordings are also available for reference.

The Ontario Film Theatre has twice-weekly showings of classic, international and contemporary films. These showings take place in the auditorium of the Ontario Science Centre where directors frequently attend to introduce their work.

For information on programming and membership rates, contact the Institute.

A number of public libraries are building up impressive film study collections. The **Vancouver Public Library** for example has a good book collection on films and a vertical file on local filmmakers in particular. The **London Public Library** in London, Ontario and the **Metropolitan Toronto Central Library** on St. George Street are also good sources of film study information.

Cine Books (692A Yonge St., Toronto 5, Ontario. 964-6474) is Canada's unique film bookshop, selling books, magazines, pictures and posters. Their catalogue is available for $1.00 and they offer mail and telephone service.

Canadian groups or individuals involved in film study can take out an

Education Membership in the American Film Institute at $6.00 per year.
This entitles one to a variety of useful information and publications. Write
to the Education Division, American Film Institute, 1815 H. Street,
N.W. Washington, D.C. 20006, U.S.A.

11. media and film courses

CANADA

The Canadian Film Institute has compiled a *Guide to Film Courses in Canada* which lists those courses offered by universities and community colleges (CEGEPS in Quebec) across Canada. Organized by province, the guide offers a description of each course, degrees and certificates awarded and addresses for further information. This publication can be obtained for $1.50 ($1.00 for members) by writing to the Canadian Film Institute, 1762 Carling Ave., Ottawa, Ontario K2A 2H7.

The Media Division of the National Film Board conducts screen study seminars in conjunction with educational institutions across the country. Group-influenced, multi-faceted film explorations have begun in Montreal, Vancouver, Winnipeg and Elliot Lake. For further information, write to the Summer Institute of Film and Media Study, National Film Board, P.O. Box 6100, Montreal 101, P.Q.

UNITED STATES

The American Film Institute has compiled a *Guide to College Film Courses.* Over four hundred universities are listed. The pamphlet is available for $2.50 from the American Library Association, 50 East Huron St., Chicago, Illinois 60611, or from the American Film Institute, 1815 H Street N.W., Washington, D.C. 20006.

ABROAD

The *International Film Guide,* edited by Peter Cowie on a yearly basis, gives up-to-date information on the prominent film schools in Europe. A.S. Barnes & Co. is the American publisher and the publication is available for $3.95 in most paperback bookstores.

See: TECHNICAL INFORMATION AND ASSISTANCE; COOPERATIVE DISTRIBUTION AND PRODUCTION

12. free films

Many organizations and companies offer to lend, without charge, films as a means of education and/or publicity. These films are generally deposited in a central clearing house and the borrower is usually expected to pay transportation costs either one or both ways. Crawley Films — the country's largest producer of sponsored films — has gathered together titles and sources of free 16mm films; the ninth edition of their *Free Film Directory* lists almost 500 sources, giving access to over 16,000 free films. The directory can be obtained without charge by writing to Crawley Films Limited at either of the following addresses:

> 19 Fairmont Avenue, Ottawa, Ontario K1Y 385
>
> P.O. Box 580, Station "F", Toronto, Ontario M4Y 2L8

Other sources of free films not mentioned in the *Directory* are the following:

> Sterling Movies Canada
> 4980 Buchan Street
> Montreal 308, Quebec
> 737-1147
>
> Cinemacraft
> 12456 rue des Serres
> Montreal 390, Quebec
> 334-9880

(Write to them, asking for their catalogues.)

Don't overlook the National Film Board libraries which are free again (after a brief attempt at imposing nominal rental fees) and public library collections. Public libraries are also good places to borrow a 16mm projector and indeed, learn how to run one efficiently. Another source of good free films are the foreign embassies and trade offices as well as tourist bureaus. Furthermore, every province produces trade and tourist films usually under the aegis of the Department of Trade or Industry; in Quebec, it is under the Department of Cultural Affairs. Write to your provincial government seat for their source of free films.

See: FILM CATALOGUES

13. children's films

The international organization for children's cinema, **International Centre of Films for Children and Young People**, has its headquarters at 241 rue Royale, Brussels, 3, Belgium. Unfortunately, there is no longer a Canadian branch of this organization so information and reports released by them must be obtained directly.

In Canada, there are two unique organizations involved with children's films: **Child's Own Cinema** is a Vancouver-based organization, founded and administered by The Association for Films in Adult Education, an educational, non-profit society. Their work consists in planning film programs for children in more than thirty locations in British Columbia and Alberta. A child's membership card costs $3.50 and this covers ten yearly programs of an hour and a half of film and a story-teller to assist the children in discussion. In order to receive their catalogues or information on the nearest cine-club in your area of Western Canada, write:

> The Association for Films in Adult Education
> 703 - 318 Homer St., Room 703
> Vancouver 3, B.C.

Faroun Films in Montreal is a commercial organization which not only distributes children's films from all over the world but has been producing Canadian children's films as well. Much in the manner of **Child's Own Cinema**, Faroun has organized **Les Clubs Faroun**, a Canada-wide series of children's film societies for which Faroun provides program notes, technical assistance as well as the films. For catalogues or information regarding **Les Clubs Faroun**, contact:

> Faroun Films Ltd.
> 136 St. Paul St., E.
> Montreal 127, Quebec
> 866-8831

> Telex: Farfilm

The National Film Board has set up a unit, **Films For Children** which is producing children's films under Michael Rubbo's direction.

Cinéma enfants is a catalogue listing children's films available from a number of sources. Contact: Fédération des Centres culturels du Québec, 3100 St-Donat, Montreal 429, Quebec. 354-0320.

14. video and community film

The Challenge for Change/Société nouvelle Unit in the National Film Board is the pivot of most of the video and community action films in the country. Both the English and French units publish information and newsletters which are available on request:

> *Challenge for Change Newsletter*
> National Film Board
> P.O. Box 6100
> Montreal 101, Quebec

> *Medium Media*
> Société nouvelle
> National Film Board
> P.O. Box 6100
> Montreal 101, Quebec

Projects initiated by these two units have been developed in Newfoundland, Vancouver, Winnipeg, Montreal — indeed, in virtually every area of the country. And these projects have encouraged the growth of community media groups and resource services such as In-Media in Montreal and Metro Media in Vancouver. Many Canadian filmmakers already involved in documentary, educational and fiction films have begun to work in this area. Among them are Colin Low who directed the Fogo Island Project, Michel Regnier who has worked on fifteen films about the problems of urbanism, Fernand Dansereau who founded In-Media, and Léonard Forest who made a community fiction film.

The following material will give some indication of the kind of work which is being done in community action film and video:

"Challenge for Change" by Patrick Watson, *Artscanada,* April 1970. A warm evaluation of the work at the National Film Board beginning with the Fogo Island Project.

222

"Cinema as a Form of Protest", by Robert Daudelin, *Challenge for Change Newsletter,* No. 5, Autumn 1970.

"Community Use of Cable TV", by Ron Bashford. A talk to the Canadian Educational Communications Conference, 1971. Available on tape for $3.50 from The Edmonton Audio Visual Association, c/o Educational Media Division, Dept. of Extension, The University of Alberta, Edmonton 7, Alberta.

"Fiction Film as Social Animator". *Challenge for Change Newsletter,* No. 7, Winter 1971-72. An interview with Léonard Forest on the making of **La noce n'est pas finie,** a community-evolved feature.

"Fogo Island Film and Community Development Project". A detailed explanation of the approach and implementation of this project carried out in Newfoundland with remarks by the project director, Colin Low. Available by writing to Challenge for Change, National Film Board.

"Memo to Michelle about Decentralizing the Means of Production", by John Grierson, *Challenge for Change Newsletter,* No. 8, Spring 1972.

"Michel Regnier opte pour un cinéma fonctionnel", *La Presse,* December 7, 1968.

"*Saint-Jérome:* the Experience of a Filmmaker as Social Animator", by Fernand Dansereau, *Challenge for Change Newsletter,* Vol. 1, No. 3, Winter 1968-69.

The American VTR magazine, *Radical Software,* in its No. 4 issue dedicated a large section to Canadian facilities and experience. Available from Raindance Corporation, 8 East 12th St., New York, N.Y. 10003.

Vidéographe, 1604 St. Denis Street, Montreal 129, Quebec (842-9788) is a video theatre and production workshop operated by the Société nouvelle Unit of the National Film Board. The production facilities of Vidéographe are open, through a program committee, to any group that has formulated a clear idea of something it would like to say through VTR. Authors of approved projects get a production budget and necessary technical assistance. Vidéographe is also a distribution centre for videotapes. If you have already made a tape, you can submit it to

Vidéographe for screening in the theatre. If accepted, it will be added to the mailing list of over 900 titles being distributed throughout Quebec. These represent audio-visual departments, film clubs and cultural centres. To receive a print, they simply send a blank tape which is dubbed and returned to the requesting group free of charge. Shows are presented in the theatre on St. Denis Street every evening except Mondays at 8 p.m. Admission is 55¢. The director of Vidéographe is Robert Forget.

Intermedia, in Vancouver, has collated an international listing of materials available on one-inch and half-inch videotape. Anyone producing programs in either of these formats is encouraged to send in details for inclusion in the next issue of the index. Video Exchange Directory, c/o Image Bank, 4454 West Second Ave, Vancouver 8, B.C.

See also: COOPERATIVE DISTRIBUTION & PRODUCTION

15. film festivals and competitions

Those international festivals which fall under official international regulations allow only one film from each country to be submitted. In Canada, the National Film Board's Festival Office handles the details of preselection (though an independent body is soon to be established by the Secretary of State). Involved are two representatives from the art field, named by the Canada Council: four representatives of the Canadian Film Producers Association; two film critics, named by the Secretary of State; one representative from the Department of External Affairs and two knowledgeable people appointed by the Government Film Commissioner. These regulations are laid down by the International Federation of Film Producers Associations. For further information contact the Festival Office, NFB, Box 6100, Montreal 101, P.Q.

There are a number of information sources on national and international film festivals and competitions:

The best available source (and the one used by the NFB) is the *Calendar of International Film & Television Events* published jointly by the International Film & Television Council and UNESCO each year. This calendar, which provides dates, addresses, purpose and specialities of festivals, can be had for $2.00. Write:

> *Calendar of International Film & Television Events*
> Via Santa Susanna 17
> 00187, Rome, Italy

Festival Diary is published monthly in newsletter form. Each issue provides a comprehensive listing of international film festivals for the coming twelve months. Subscription at ₤4 per year is available from:

> Short Film Service Ltd.
> 122 Wardour St.
> London W1, England

Film Festival Directory is a book (now dating fast) which lists over 400 film and television festivals held around the world and the cash awards offered. At $10.00 per copy, it is available by writing:

> Back Stage Publications Inc.
> 165 West 46th St.
> New York, New York 10036

The Canadian International Amateur Film Festival sponsored by the Society of Canadian Cine Amateurs will provide names and addresses of member organizations which sponsor amateur festivals and competitions. For this information, write:

> Canadian International Amateur Film Festival
> P.O. Box 984
> St. Catharines, Ontario

The Canadian Film Awards is an annual competition open to all Canadian films in various categories with presentations made during the first week of October. Public screenings of all films entered take place in Toronto and winning films are shown in cities across the country following the awards. For further information and application forms, write:

> The Secretary
> Canadian Film Awards
> 22 Front St. W.
> Toronto, Ontario

FURTHER SOURCES OF FILM FESTIVAL INFORMATION

Information Officer
Canadian Film Institute
1762 Carling Ave.
Ottawa, Ontario K2A 2H7
729-6193

La Cinémathèque québécoise
360 McGill St.
Montreal 125, Quebec
866-4688

Le Conseil québécois pour la diffusion du cinéma
3466 St. Denis St., Suite 5-6
Montreal 130, Quebec
842-5079

Federation of Canadian Amateur Cinematographers/
Fédération des cinéastes amateur canadien (FCAC)
7485 Fabre St.
Montreal 329, Quebec

Society of Canadian Cine Amateurs
P.O. Box 984
St. Catharines, Ontario

Two periodicals, *Take One* and la Cinémathèque québécois' *New Canadian Film/Nouveau Cinéma canadien* regularly carry detailed information on festivals and competitions.

16. cooperative distribution and production

Basically, four cooperative film collections exist in Canada; together they act as the second largest distributor of Canadian films (the first is, of course, the National Film Board). The cooperative collections include features, shorts, experimental and political films. For those who want to borrow films, the cooperatives maintain close ties with independent filmmakers in Europe and the United States as well as in Canada. Their films may be purchased or rented at reasonable prices (rental fees are usually $1.00 per minute). For independent filmmakers, the cooperatives offer a distribution outlet and a better share of the gross rentals than any other — more commercial — distributor.

Each of the cooperatives listed below handle their own distribution and should be dealt with separately; catalogues can be obtained from each of them.

Canadian Film-makers' Distribution Centre
Rochdale College
341 Bloor St., W., Rm. 204
Toronto 181, Ontario   921-2259

Pacific Cinémathèque Pacifique
1145 West Georgia
Vancouver 5, B.C.   684-2488

London Film Co-op
1055 Lombardo Ave.
London, Ontario   439-9030

Coopérative Cinéastes Indépendants/Independent
Filmmakers' Cooperative
2026 Ontario St., E.
Montreal 133, Quebec   523-2816

The following organization distributes a small number of films on political and social action — community control, Third World, women and labour films:

Newsreel
Box 340, Station E
Toronto 4, Ontario   536-6631

In Montreal, l'Association coopérative des producteurs audio-visuelles (ACPAV), 96 Sherbrooke St. W., Tel: 849-5031, is a collective organization for film production. Director is Marc Daigle.

See: TECHNICAL INFORMATION AND ASSISTANCE.

17. technical equipment and services

The best sources of information on where to procure technical equipment and services are either of the two trade journals:

Canadian Film Digest and *Year Book*
c/o Film Publications of Canada Ltd.
175 Bloor St., E.
Toronto 285, Ontario

Ed: Dan Krendal

Subscription: $5.00 per year covers both publications.

TV-Film Filebook
2533 Gerrard St., E.
Scarborough, Ontario

Ed: Arthur C. Benson

Subscription: $3.00 per yearly or twice-yearly issue.

The Association of Motion Picture Producers and Laboratories of Canada provides a booklet with a list of equipment and technical services available on a commercial basis from certain member companies and a membership list. To attain the booklet at no charge, write:

AMPPLC
55 York St., Suite 1301
Toronto 116, Ontario

In Quebec contact l'Association des Producteurs de films du Québec:

APFQ
P.O. Box 143
Postal Station G
Montreal 130, Quebec

STOCK-SHOT LIBRARIES

Stock-shot libraries consist of filmed materials divorced from their original use, gathered together in a film production library and broken down for possible inclusion in later complete productions. Stock may be extracted from newsreels, from the footage of completed films or from unused footage. UNESCO and the Royal Film Archives of Belgium have compiled the *World Directory of Stockshot and Film Production/Un Répertoire mondial de cinémathèques de production,* Ed: John Chittock, Pergamon Press, Paris, 1969. The directory covers 310 libraries in fifty-nine countries, among them Canada. It should be noted however, that while only seven companies in Canada are listed in this directory, virtually every film production organization (as well as the tv networks) is willing to supply stock material. The restrictions on the use of such material vary as do the prices; however, many companies which use film for public relations provide stock free if not being used for commercial purposes.

Le Conseil québécois pour la diffusion du cinéma has available a listing of the film production houses in Quebec. Write:

> CQDC
> 3466 St-Denis St.
> Suite 5-6
> Montreal 130, Quebec

See TRADE JOURNALS

18. technical information and assistance

One of the best and cheapest guides to the technical and practical aspects of filmmaking can be had for $1.50 at most paperback bookstores: *Guide to Filmmaking* by Edward Pincus, "A Signet Book" W3992, New American Library of Canada Ltd., 1969, illustrated, 256 pp.

Amateur filmmakers may find assistance by joining the **Canadian Society of Cine Amateurs/Société canadienne des ciné amateurs**. Formed to foster and stimulate amateur filmmaking in Canada, the organization is open to amateur movie clubs, film production groups and individuals. Write:

Miss Dorothy Walter	Mr. Armand Bélanger
2619 Lakeshore Blvd. W. or	39 Crochet St.
Toronto 14, Ontario	Laval-des-Rapides, Quebec

The **Federation of Canadian Amateur Cinematographers/Fédération des cinéastes amateur canadien** (FCAC) began in 1964 to give technical service to amateur filmmakers on an individual basis. Membership is $6.00 per year and this includes their journal, *Cinecamera* which is filled with technical information. Membership without the journal is $2.50 per year. This organization also gives help on festivals and competitions to the amateur filmmaker. Write: FCAC, 7485 Fabre Street, Montreal 329, Quebec.

Les Laboratoires de film Québec has published a dictionary of cinematographic terms in which words and terms most commonly used are listed in both French and English. In order to obtain a copy without charge, write:

> Les Laboratoires de film Québec
> 265 Vitré St. W.
> Montreal 128, Quebec

The Technical and Production Services of the National Film Board publish an erratic quarterly report as material becomes available on technical developments. Available on request from:

> The Director of Technical and Production Services
> National Film Board
> P.O. Box 6100
> Montreal 101, Quebec

This same branch also makes technical information and service available to the private sector under the strict circumstance that no commercial service of this kind is otherwise available in Canada.

Most filmmakers' organizations offer technical training within their ranks to upgrade their own members. If, however, you don't have the qualifications to join them, contact your local film cooperative (which often has, as well, an arrangement with laboratories for cheaper rates). In Toronto, the Canadian Film-makers' Distribution Centre offers workshops run by professionals on all aspects of filmmaking. Membership fee is $10.00 per year plus work participation. Contact them at Rochdale College, Room 204, 341 Bloor St. West, Toronto 181, Ontario.

See TRADE JOURNALS; COOPERATIVE DISTRIBUTION AND PRODUCTION; PROFESSIONAL ASSOCIATIONS.

19. film and photography archives

As opposed to film collections, film archives are depositories of public records and historic documents which are held in the public trust. While the National Film Board and the Canadian Broadcasting Corporation maintain archival material produced within and outside those organizations, it is, in fact, selected material reflecting their, rather than the public's, needs and views.

A true public archives has the responsibility of preserving, without pre-selection, films and other related material from its own national heritage and that of other heritages as well if such material is made available. Because such work is part of the national interest, it is carried out without prejudice of copyright laws. Furthermore, the archivist has the responsibility of organizing and researching this material in order to effectively promote the preservation and study of the film heritage.

This work is accomplished by an archives in a number of ways:

1) by membership in FIAF (Féderation internationale des archives du film/International Federation of Film Archives). This organization lays down international standards for archival operations, facilitates cooperation between member organizations and oversees the publication of archival documentation;

2) by publishing and encouraging the publication of film study material which will detail and elucidate the archival material which they and sister archives hold;

3) by providing access to the archives through exhibition, lectures and the discussion of the material held in their trust.

Film material from public and private production is preserved in a number of archives across the country:

CANADIAN FILM ARCHIVES/ARCHIVES CANADIENNES DU FILM is a division of the Canadian Film Institute, 1762 Carling Ave., Ottawa, Ontario K2A 2H7. Established in 1958, it became a full member of

FIAF in 1964. Its international film collection includes silent and sound classics, shorts and feature films, television and classic documentaries. Because the Canadian Film Archives operates a National Film Theatre as well as five regional film theatres, material from their archival collection may sometimes be given public exhibition.

Another aspect of this archives is the Stills Library which numbers over 100,000 pieces; photographs of personalities, productions, theatres and apparatus can be reproduced on payment for non-commercial use.

The Canadian Film Archives also gathers together and disseminates printed material on film information and criticism. Of particular interest is the yearly publication of *FIAF Members Publications.* Begun in 1967, the pamphlet lists recent publications of archives around the world. Each pamphlet is available at $1.00 from the Canadian Film Institute. Other publications and services available in the film study area will be found under the heading FILM STUDY CENTRES.

LA CINEMATHEQUE QUEBECOISE, 360 McGill Street, Montreal 125, Quebec, has archives (which became a full member of FIAF in 1966) specializing in animated and Canadian films. Much like the Canadian Film Archives, La Cinémathèque québécoise exhibits its archival collection and films of other FIAF members in frequent public showings.

Its Stills Library numbers over 80,000 pieces, many archival in nature which are available for reproduction. They also preserve taped interviews and cinematographic apparatus.

Many of the publications of La Cinémathèque québécoise are archival expositions; in particular, *How to Make or Not to Make a Canadian Film, Hommage à Maurice Jaubert* and *Une Exposition Georges Meliès.*

NATIONAL FILM ARCHIVES is a division of the National Library and Public Archives of Canada/La Bibliothèque nationale et Archives publique du Canada, 395 Wellington St., Ottawa, Ontario K1A 0N4. Established in 1969, the National Film Archives holds primarily Canadian material from 1898 to the present. Included in the larger national archives, the film collection is an integral part of the record of a people's history. Historical catalogues divided into decades are presently being prepared.

Unlike the archives at the Canadian Film Institute and La Cinémathèque québécoise, the National Film Archives does not itself exhibit its material but will do so through exhibiting archives. In order to make the material available for legitimate study and research, the Archives is planning to transfer, on demand, films to half-inch video tape so that they may be available cheaply across the country.

The Historical Photo Section is another division of the National Library and Public Archives of Canada, holding many thousands of photographs in its trust.

There are a number of other archives across Canada (at least one exists in each of the ten provinces); while their holdings in this area of interest are generally limited to archival photographs, some few have archival films as well:

Alberta

Provincial Museum and
  Archives of Alberta
12845 — 102 Avenue
Edmonton 40, Alberta

British Columbia

Vancouver Public Library
Historical Photo Section
750 Burrard St.
Vancouver, B.C.

Visual Records
Provincial Archives
Victoria, B.C.

Manitoba

Provincial Archives
Provincial Library
Winnipeg, Manitoba

New Brunswick

Provincial Archivist
Bonar Law — Bennett Building
University of New Brunswick
Fredericton, New Brunswick

Newfoundland

Provincial Archivist
Colonial Building
Military Rd.
St. John's, Newfoundland

Nova Scotia

Public Archives of Nova Scotia
Dalhousie Campus
Coburg Rd.
Halifax, Nova Scotia

Ontario

Department of Public Records
  and Archives
Queen's Park
Toronto, Ontario

P.E.I.

Provincial Archives
Box 1000
Charlottetown, P.E.I.

236

Quebec

Provincial Archives
Department of Cultural Affairs
Quebec, Quebec

Saskatchewan

Archives Division
Legislative Library
Regina, Saskatchewan

Provincial Archivist
Saskatchewan Archives Board
Regina Campus Library
University of Saskatchewan
Regina, Saskatchewan

Western Development Museum
1839 11th St. W.
Saskatoon, Saskatchewan

Three other specialized collections exist:

> Photographic Services
> Canadian Pacific Railways
> Windsor Station
> Montreal, Quebec

Over 300,000 archival photographs taken since the building
of the CPR. Open to the public weekdays from 8:30-1:00 &
2:15-5:00. Photographs can be reproduced for a fee on request.

> Curator of Photography
> Notman Photo Archives
> 690 Sherbrooke St. West
> Montreal 110, Quebec
> 392-4781

Including the Notman collection dating from 1856-1934, which
traces the building of the CPR railway. Also the McCord Collection
dating from 1847. Over 500,000 photos accessible week-days by
appointment.

> Glenbow Archives,
> Glenbow-Alberta Institute
> 902-11th Ave. S.W.
> Calgary 3, Alberta

As well as a few archival films and stills from early films made
in Western Canada, this archives has a large collection of photographs of early Eskimo settlements, the building of the CPR,
ranching and immigration to the West. They hold the collection
of the Lomen Brothers, circa 1900-1945, dealing with western and
south-western Alaska.

20. educational material

Multi-media products and visual education material (other than 16mm films) produced by the National Film Board are distributed by three private companies. Such material as filmstrips, 8mm concept films, multi-media kits, overhead projectuals, slides and film loops can be obtained from the following organizations:

In Ontario, contact: Visual Education Centre
95 Berkeley St.
Toronto 2A, Ontario

East of Ontario, contact: SECAS
400 Notre Dame East
Montreal 1, Quebec

West of Ontario, contact: Harry Smith & Sons
1150 Homer Street
Vancouver 3, B.C.

The Canadian Education Media Council is an information and co-ordinating body for individuals and organizations involved in educational media. Three such organizations involved as resource tools are the Educational Media Association of Canada (EMAC) which concerns itself in the public school area; the Educational Television and Radio Association of Canada (ETRAC) involved in the college and university area; and the Canadian Science Film Association (CSFA).

The Canadian Education Media Council publishes a newsletter, *The Media Message,* 10 times a year, available free to its members. For membership fees and information, contact:

Canadian Education Media Council
252 Bloor St. W. (8th floor)
Toronto 5, Ontario
924-7721

Audio cassettes of talks given at the 1971 Canadian Educational Communications Conference are available at $3.50 each from the Edmonton Audio-Visual Association, c/o Educational Media Division, Department of Extension, The University of Alberta, Edmonton 7, Alberta. The following are some of the talks catalogued:

Canadian Science Films in Higher Education (No. 19) by Dr. Lucien Kops;

Colloque: matériel de média en langue française (No. 7) by P. A. Lamoureux;

Libraries and the Wired City (No. 16) by Thomas Ferguson;

Research Films: Science (No. 18) by Stephen Rothwell;

Selection and Evaluation of Educational Films (No. 6) by Anne Davidson;

Should University Professors Produce their own Science Films without Technical Assistance? (No. 20) by A. Leitner.

A number of books, theses and pamphlets are available to the film educator; the following list is not meant to be comprehensive but rather to act as a guide to the types of material being published and by whom.

A Curriculum in Film, by John Stuart Katz. OISE, Toronto, 1972.

An examination of the current approaches to and effects of screen education in selected schools of the Toronto area, by Lyle Reid Cruickshank. Thesis submitted to the College of Communication Arts, Michigan State University, 1969. Available for reference in the NFB library, Montreal.

Experiments with Film in the Art Classroom, edited by Donald Rutledge and others. OISE, Toronto, 1970.

Getting Out of the Box, edited by Austin Repath. Longman Canada Ltd., Toronto, 1972.

Introduction au cinéma, by Gérard Beaudet and Donald Proteau. Centre de psychologie et de pédagogie, Montréal, 1966.

Inventoriez et classez facilement vos documents audio-visuals/Easy Method for Inventory-Taking and Classification of Audio-Visual Material. Written and published (1972) by Françoise Lamy-Rousseau with the collaboration of Maurice Rousseau. Available at their address: 187 rue Brais, Longueuil, Quebec.

Language of Change: Moving Images of Man, by Mark Slade. Holt, Rinehart and Winston of Canada, Ltd., Toronto, 1970.

Living and Learning, by Justice E. M. Hall and L. A. Dennis. Report of the Provincial Committee on Aims and Objectives of Education in the Schools of Ontario. Ontario Department of Education, Toronto, 1968.

Mass Media and You, by Austin Repath. Longman Canada Ltd., Toronto, 1966.

Mass Media in Canada, by John A. Irving. Ryerson Press, Toronto, 1962.

Media for Discovery, by Dr. Hans Möller. Maclean-Hunter Ltd., Toronto, 1970.

Media study — screen education: a comparison of British, American and Canadian approaches, by Lyle Reid Cruickshank. Report submitted to Michigan State University, College of Education 1970. Available for reference in the NFB library, Montreal.

Non-Book Materials: The Organization of Integrated Collections, by Jean Riddle, Shirley Lewis and Janet MacDonald. Canadian Library Association, Ottawa, 1970.

Perspectives on the Study of Film, edited by John Stuart Katz. Little, Brown and Co., Boston, 1971.

Photo/Ciné/Télé: trois agents de communication, by René Beauchamp. Centre de psychologie et de pédagogie, Montréal, 1970.

"The Quiet Revolution — Film in Education", by Roberta Charlesworth. *Artscanada,* April 1970. pp.21-23.

Screen Education in Canadian Schools, edited by James Nuttall. Canadian Education Association, Toronto, 1969. Ontario Department of Education.

Screen Education in Ontario. Queen's Printer, Toronto, 1970.

To Begin Making Movies, by Dr. Charles E. Phillips, SCCA. Information Division, Canadian Education Association.

Tribal Drums, edited by A. E. Hughes. A collection of contemporary song lyrics and poetry with film and record references. McGraw-Hill Co. Ltd., Toronto, 1970.

Understanding Media: The Extensions of Man, by Marshall McLuhan. McGraw-Hill Co., Toronto, 1964.

The Uses of Film in the Teaching of English, edited by Victor Whatton and others. OISE, Toronto, 1971.

A number of other publications are concerned with film education: *School Progress:* a national monthly periodical listing distributors of educational media, film programs, and hardware as well as articles on educational media. Subscriptions are available for $10.00 per year by writing:

> *School Progress*
> Maclean-Hunter Ltd.
> 481 University Ave.
> Toronto 2, Ontario

Canadian University and College: a bi-monthly journal for administrators and educators at the university and college level. Each issue carries a section on audio-visual equipment and availability, software and printed material. The magazine is available at $10.00 per year from:

> *Canadian University and College*
> Maclean-Hunter Ltd.
> 481 University Ave.
> Toronto 2, Ontario

Media and Methods: an American monthly that stresses — in a lively and diverting way — a multi-media approach in grades 7-12. Lots of reviews. Subscriptions are $7.00 per year, from:

> *Media and Methods*
> 134 North 13th Street
> Philadelphia, Pa. 19107

The CBC offers publications and audio tapes of many of their radio programs. A number of them would be of interest to educators. For catalogues of publications and audio tapes, contact:

> CBC Learning Systems
> Box 500, Terminal A
> Toronto 116, Ontario

Editions Fides, 245 Dorchester Blvd. E., Montreal, has published
Dossiers de cinéma: 1, a twelve-section critique of twelve short films
by Canadian filmmakers. As well as an analysis of the film, the sections
give background of the filmmaker, a filmography, bibliography and an
approach to the film suggested in a series of questions. Among the films
discussed are **60 Cycles** by Jean-Claude Labrecque, **High Steel** and **Runner**
by Don Owen, **Percé on the Rocks** by Gilles Carle and **Corral** by Colin Low.

Educational film producers and distributors are listed in *TV-Film
Filebook,* published twice-yearly at $3.00 per copy.

> *TV-Film Filebook*
> 2533 Gerrard St. East
> Scarborough, Ontario

21. film collections

A large number of specialized film collections exist in Canada; where these collections have been discussed in some detail under other headings, this section will make reference to them without further discussion.

FILM ON THE ARTS

The Canadian Centre for Films on Art is the outcome of the 1963 UNESCO Seminar, *Films on Art*, which was held in Ottawa. The Centre operates under the joint sponsorship of the National Gallery and the National Film Board of Canada in co-operation with the Canadian Film Institute which acts as distributor. The Centre has a number of collections under its aegis:

Films on Art/Films sur l'art. This collection is made up of those films gathered by the National Gallery of Canada and supplemented by other films on art from the CFI's collection, embassies, galleries and universities, totaling over 2,000 films in English and French. Films are borrowed through the Canadian Film Institute at their usual rates, and catalogues and advice on programming or program notes can be obtained by writing to:

> Canadian Centre for Films on Art
> 150 Kent Street
> Ottawa, Ontario K1A 0M9

As an extension of the *Films on Art* collection, films on art have been deposited in each province. Arrangements for borrowing these films should be made with the provincial organization concerned:

Educational Media Division
University of Alberta
Edmonton, Alberta

Extension Department
University of British Columbia
Vancouver 8, B.C.

Film Library
University of Manitoba
Winnipeg, Manitoba

Owen's Art Gallery
Mount Allison University
Sackville, New Brunswick

Audio-Visual Centre
Memorial University
St. John's, Newfoundland

London Public Library
305 Queens Ave.
London, Ontario

Le Centre artistique
Université de Sherbrooke
Sherbrooke, Quebec

Audio-Visual Education
Department of Education
Box 578
Halifax, Nova Scotia

Confederation Art Gallery
Charlottetown, P.E.I.

Film Library
University of Saskatchewan
Saskatoon, Saskatchewan

Films on the Performing Arts/Films sur les arts d'interprétation –In conjunction with the National Arts Centre, a catalogue of over 300 titles of films on the performing arts is available. They can be booked through the Canadian Film Institute. Catalogues and information are available from the Canadian Centre for Films on Art.

Films on the Dance/Films sur la danse – A collection of over 60 titles of films on the dance have been put together in conjunction with the National Arts Centre. They can be booked through the Canadian Film Institute at their going rates. Further information and catalogues are available from the Canadian Centre for Films on Art.

SCIENCE FILMS COLLECTIONS

Two collections of science films exist in Canada. The National Film Board collection is wholly Canadian and films may be borrowed through your local library. Catalogues are also available at the nearest NFB office.

The second collection is at the Canadian Film Institute with The National Science Film Library/La Cinémathèque nationale scientifique, 1762 Carling Ave., Ottawa, Ontario K2A 2H7. This collection has over 3,500 films from all over the world. They are catalogued under the following headings: *The Earth Sciences and Related Subjects, Films on Engineering and Technology, Films on the Physical Sciences, Films on Anthropology and Ethnology.* These catalogues, available for a small fee, give descriptions of films listed (with their nominal rental rates).

CHILDREN'S FILMS: See section 13. CHILDREN'S FILMS.

FILM STUDY COLLECTIONS: See section 10. FILM STUDY CENTRES.

CANADIAN FILMS

The largest collection of Canadian films is produced and distributed by the National Film Board. Many thousands of titles are listed in their English and French catalogues, available from your local NFB office or the local distributor which will be the public library system. With very few exceptions, the NFB does not distribute films other than those it has produced.

Other large collections of Canadian films are held by the four cooperatives in Toronto, London, Montreal and Vancouver. See section 16. COOPERATIVE DISTRIBUTION AND PRODUCTION.

Many Canadian films are found in archival collections; see section 19. FILM AND PHOTOGRAPHY ARCHIVES.

The Travel Film Library is a branch of the Canadian Government Travel Bureau which aims to promote tourism in Canada. Administered by the National Film Board in cooperation with the departments of tourism in each of the provinces, the Travel Film Library distributes provincially made films through 500 outlets around the world.

22. trade journals

Boxoffice is an American publication with a "Canadian Edition";
correspondents report in from across the country. Published weekly by
Associates Publications Inc., 825 Van Brunt Blvd., Kansas City, Missouri
64124. Subscriptions are $7.00 per year, single copies at 35¢ from your
newsstand.

The Canadian Composer/Le Compositeur canadien is a bilingual publication appearing 10 times a year and published by the Composers, Authors
and Publishers Association of Canada (CAPAC). Edited by Richard Flohil,
it covers information for and about their membership including their
activities in film music composition. Subscription is $2.00 per year from:

> *The Canadian Composer/Le Compositeur canadien*
> 501-1407 Yonge Street
> Toronto 290, Ontario   925-5138

Canadian Film Digest is a monthly commentary on the commercial
Canadian and international motion picture scene. The yearly subscription rate is $7.50 which includes the *Canadian Film Digest Year Book.*
It includes the following information: listing of exhibitors and personnel;
a limited listing of both 16mm and 35mm distributors; production and
distribution associations; equipment sales and service; updated industry
statistics; censorship boards and rates; listing of recipients of Academy
and Canadian Film Awards; provincial amusement taxes and theatre
licence fees; studios and producers; laboratories; a listing of television
film studios, their distributors and record companies. Both the *Canadian*

Film Digest and the *Year Book* are edited by Stephen Chesley and can be subscribed to by writing:

> *Canadian Film Digest*
> c/o Film Publications of Canada Ltd.
> 175 Bloor St. E.
> Toronto 285, Ontario

Canadian Photography covers professional cinematography to a large degree. Edited by Irvine A. Brace, it is available monthly at $6.00 per year or $10.00 for two years from:

> *Canadian Photography*
> Maclean-Hunter Ltd.
> 481 University Ave.
> Toronto 2, Ontario

Cinema Canada (second edition) is a bi-monthly magazine published by the Canadian Society of Cinematographers. Edited by George Csaba Koller, *Cinema Canada* features interviews with leading cinematographers, reviews of Canadian films, festival information and profiles of independent filmmakers. It is also an outlet for a number of filmmakers' organizations such as the Directors Guild of Canada, the Canadian Film Editors Guild and the Society of Motion Picture and Television Engineers. Subscriptions are available at $5.00 per year from:

> *Cinema Canada*
> Room 202
> 341 Bloor St. West
> Toronto 181, Ontario

The Music Scene/La Scène musicale are two companion publications of Broadcast Music Inc. Canada Limited (B.M.I.) published six times per year and edited by Nancy Gyokeres. Covering news and information for and about their membership, they carry a regular column on film music. *The Music Scene* is available to organizations and individuals interested in the performance of Canadian music. Write:

> *The Music Scene/La Scène musicale*
> 41 Valleybrooke Drive
> Don Mills 405, Ontario

That's Showbusiness covers all aspects of the entertainment field in a chatty (*Variety*-style) newspaper published twice monthly. Editor is Bette Laderonte. Subscriptions are available at $5.00 per year (single copies at 25¢ from the newsstand) from:

> *That's Showbusiness*
> 189 Church St.
> Toronto 205, Ontario

Fidex is a non-profit publication aimed at film users, which attempts to answer the questions: What films are available? How suitable are the films? and Where can the films be obtained? Edited by Dick and Anneke Schoemaker of the Calgary Film Society, *Fidex* contains information essential to film societies, film teachers and anyone else who regularly programs films. Annual subscription: $10. Write:

> *Fidex*
> 6718 Legare Drive S.W.
> Calgary 10, Alberta

TV-Film Filebook is published yearly or twice-yearly for the television and film industry. The cost is $3.00 per copy; extra ones are $2.00 each or $10.00 for five. This publication is packed with all kinds of well-researched information: films for television and educational film distributors; a listing of syndicated television programs and their distributors; studios and production laboratories; government film departments; sound recording studios; editing services; special effects; music services; talent; post production services; technical services; film equipment rentals; motion picture equipment; listing of equipment and technical services available from member companies of the Association of Motion Picture Producers and Laboratories of Canada; marketing research organizations; associations and guilds, unions; television networks; television stations; British television groups; educational film groups and advertising agencies. The editor of the publication is Arthur C. Benson. Write:

> *TV-Film Filebook*
> 2533 Gerrard St., E.
> Scarborough, Ontario

Variety is the bible of the industry. It carries up-to-date information on international film production and distribution. Published weekly in New York, *Variety* maintains correspondents in major Canadian cities and carries a fair amount of Canadian news. Available at 50¢ per copy from most newsstands.

23. bibliography

The following is a list of publications available on Canadian cinema. This does not include books on filmmakers (they are to be found under the particular filmmaker's name) or directories, catalogues, reports, trade journals or periodicals; they will be found under a separate heading. Some of the publications mentioned below originally appeared as periodicals but they have either been republished as a special edition or, by their very authority, rose to a more permanent status:

Artscanada, No. 142/143, April, 1970 dedicated their whole issue to "The Moving Image — Current Trends in Canadian Film". Thorough and still relevant, the issue has been reprinted and is available for $2.00 from *Artscanada,* 129 Adelaide St. West, Toronto 1, Ont.

Canadian Feature Films 1913-1969. Part 1: 1913-1940, Part 2: 1941-1969. These documents are detailed filmographies giving production credits, synopses, notes on production and extracts from reviews for indigenous and non-indigenous films shot in Canada. Each part is available for $3.00 as Canadian Filmography Series Nos. 106 & 107 from the Canadian Film Institute, 1762 Carling Ave., Ottawa K2A 2H7, Ontario. 729-6193.

Le Cinéma canadien, by Gilles Marsolais, gives an excellent historical background, working up to the present, with a concentration on the interaction of the developments. Productions are listed chronologically in a separate section. Published in 1968 by Editions du Jour, available from Editions du Jour, 1651 Saint Denis St., Montreal 129, Quebec.

Cinéma et société québécoise, by Yves Lever is a sociological appreciation of international cinema in a Quebec context. Lever's articles have been gathered from the Catholic periodical, *Relations.* Available for $3.50 from Editions du Jour, 1651 Saint Denis St., Montreal 129, Quebec.

Cinéma québécois, petit guide. Published by the Conseil québécois pour la diffusion du cinéma. First of a series, this guide has been published to permit a first contact with the cinema of Quebec. Contains a selection of short and feature films, an index and a bio-filmography of the most important cinéastes, addresses and a bibliography. Edited by Lise Walser and Lucien Hamelin. Available at the CQDC, 3466 St. Denis St., Montreal 131, Quebec. Tel: 842-5079.

Le Cinéma québécois: tendances et prolongements is a collection of critical articles on Quebec filmmakers and their films plus discussions of film education and the problems of mass media. Edited by Renald Bérubé and Yvan Patry it was published in 1968 by les Editions Sainte-Marie and is available for $2.50 from les Editions Sainte-Marie, 1029 Beaver Hall Hill, Montreal 128, Quebec.

Comment faire ou ne pas faire un film canadien/How to Make or Not to Make a Canadian Film, edited by André Paquet, was published by la Cinémathèque canadienne on the occasion of a retrospective of Canadian cinema presented in 1967. It contains a chronological history of Canadian cinema, a list of One Hundred Essential Films and a number of articles by filmmakers. Priced at $1.00, it is available in English or French from la Cinémathèque québécoise, 360 McGill Street, Montreal 125, Quebec.

Essais sur le cinéma québécois, by Dominique Noguez. The book is a collection of essays on the relationship of Quebec cinema to the educational, social, cultural and political life of the province. Published in 1970, it is available from Editions du Jour, 1651 Saint-Denis St., Montreal 129, Quebec.

Hommage à M. L. Ernest Ouiment, edited by Guy L. Côté. Though out of print, this pamphlet on Canada's pioneer filmmaker and cinema-operator, published in 1966 by La Cinémathèque canadienne, is available in film study libraries.

Inventoriez et classez facilement vos documents audio-visuals/Easy Method for Inventory-Taking and Classification of Audio-Visual Material. Written and published (1972) by Françoise Lamy-Rousseau with the collaboration of Maurice Rousseau, and available at their address: 187 rue Brais, Longueuil, Quebec.

Jeune Cinéma canadien, by René Predal, gives a background of Canadian cinema but largely concentrates on the individual filmmakers and critiques of their work. Written in 1967 it was published by the review, *Premier Plan* No. 45, now available from *Premier Plan,* B.P. 3, Lyon-Préfecture, 69 — Lyon, France.

Liberté, Montreal, March-June, 1966, Nos. 44-45 is a special issue on Canadian cinema entitled *Cinema Si,* containing reports submitted to government bodies, reflections and opinions. Available from Agence de distribution populaire, 1130 La Gauchetière St. E., Montreal 132, Quebec.

The National Film Board of Canada: The War Years. Edited by Peter Morris, 1965, this 32 page book reviews the formative years under John Grierson giving a complete filmography and articles written by contemporaries. Available for $1.00 from the Canadian Film Institute (Canadian Filmography Series No. 103), 1762 Carling Ave., Ottawa K2A 2H7.

Un Pays sans bon sens ou Wake Up, mes bons amis!!!, by Pierre Perrault, Bernard Gosselin, Yves Leduc and Serge Beauchemin, published by Editions Lidec Inc., Montreal, 1972.

Vingt Ans de cinéma au Canada français, by Robert Daudelin, former director-general of le Conseil québécois pour la diffusion de cinéma and now director of la Cinémathèque québécoise. Beginning with an excellent historical background, the discussion centres around the important directors and technicians in Quebec cinema. As part of the "Collection art, vie et sciences au Canada français", it was published in 1967 and is available at no charge from the Ministère des Affaires culturelles, Québec, Québec.

24. directories

AMPPLC Equipment Directory. Film equipment and technical services available from member companies. For a free catalogue, write: Association of Motion Picture Producers and Laboratories of Canada, Suite 512, 55 York St., Toronto 116, Ont.

Association of Motion Picture Producers and Laboratories of Canada: Membership Lists. Available from AMPPLC, Suite 512, 55 York St., Toronto 116, Ontario.

Bibliography: FIAF Member Publications. Edited annually by the Canadian Film Archives for the International Federation of Film Archives of material published by member organizations; years 1967 to 1971 are available at $1.00 each from the Canadian Film Institute.

Bottin Cinema. A listing (name, address, phone number, recent credits) of Quebec's professional filmmakers. Available from Le Conseil québécois pour la diffusion du cinéma, 3466 Saint Denis St., Montreal 130, Quebec.

Cahier des films visés par catégories de spectateurs/Catalogue of Films Approved by Spectator Category. An annual listing of films categorized by the Quebec Cinema Supervisory Board and the rules governing that Board. Available at no charge from the Bureau de surveillance du cinéma, 360 McGill St., Montreal 125, Quebec, 873-2371.

Canadian Film Digest Yearbook. A handbook for the industry with lists of production and distribution agencies, equipment, taxes, studios, statistics. Available only with subscription to the *Canadian Film Digest* at $5.00 per year from Film Publications of Canada Ltd., 175 Bloor St., E., Toronto 285, Ontario.

Canadian Government Photo Centre Price List/Tarifs du Centre de photographie du gouvernement canadien. A catalogue giving information on ordering, color and black and white services, finishing and special services, commercial and special consultation services. Catalogue available from: Canadian Government Photo Centre, Tunney's Pasture, Ottawa, Ontario K1A 0M9.

Canadian Society of Cinematographers. A membership directory of the CSC available from CSC, 22 Front St. West, Toronto 2B, Ontario.

Canadian Women Filmmakers: An Interim Filmography, compiled by Alison Reid in the Canadian Filmography Series No. 108. Available for $1.00 from the Canadian Film Institute, 1762 Carling Ave., Ottawa, Ontario K2A 2H7. 729-6193.

CFE Directory. An annual directory of members of the Canadian Film Editors Guild available from the Canadian Film Editors Guild, P.O. Box 46, Toronto 116, Ontario.

Cine Books. A catalogue of film books, posters, magazines available from Canada's only film bookshop, available for $1.00 from Cine Books, 692a Yonge St., Toronto 5, Ontario.

Directors Guild of Canada: Directory of Members. Available from the Directors Guild of Canada, 25 Prince Arthur Avenue, Toronto 5, Ont.

A Guide to Film Courses in Canada. A yearly updated guide to courses offered in universities and colleges in Canada. Available for $1.50 from the Canadian Film Institute.

Sociétés de distribution. A listing of distribution companies in Canada who deal with French language films. Available at no charge from CQDC, Suite 5-6, 3466 St. Denis St., Montreal 130, Quebec. 842-5079.

Sociétés de production de films au Québec is a listing of production houses in Quebec with addresses and telephone numbers. Available from CQDC, Suite 5-6, Montreal 130, Quebec. 842-5079.

TV-Film Filebook. A twice-yearly handbook for the television and cinema industries listing services available and a myriad of information. Available at $3.00 per copy for TV-Film Filebook, 2533 Gerrard St., E., Scarborough, Ontario.

UNESCO Publications – Communication. Annual catalogue of books and other publications on communications available from UNESCO through any Information Canada Bookshop.

Vantage: Canadian Media Directory. A listing of actors, studios, production services available mainly on the west coast. Available free from Vantage Publications Ltd., 509-736 Granville St., Vancouver 2, B.C.

25. film catalogues

The Association for Films in Adult Education Catalogue. The Association shows and rents their collection of over 300 films to promote adult education within the province of British Columbia. Available by contacting The Association for Films in Adult Education, 703-318 Homer St., Rm. 703, Vancouver 3, B.C.

British Broadcasting Corporation Catalogue. A 16mm film catalogue giving details of BBC television programs available for purchase or rental. Write: BBC Film Sales, 135 Maitland Street, Toronto 5, Ontario.

Canadian Film-makers' Distribution Centre Catalogue, a listing of films distributed by the Canadian Film-makers' Distribution Centre in Toronto as well as a descriptive listing of films distributed by other cooperatives in Vancouver, Montreal and London. Available at $1.00 per copy from the Canadian Film-makers' Distribution Centre, 341 Bloor Street West, Room 204, Toronto, Ontario. 921-2259.

Catalog of 16mm Educational Motion Pictures. Lists a large collection of films available in western Canada from the University of Alberta. Catalogues are available at $3.00 each from the Educational Media Division, Department of Extension, The University of Alberta, Edmonton 7, Alberta.

Catalogues of Special Libraries. A number of foreign embassies, The Royal Architectural Institute of Canada, the Canadian Centre for Films on Art, Films on the Performing Arts, The Department of National Health and Welfare, and UNESCO have deposited their films with the CFI. Catalogues of these special collections are available at 25¢ each from the Canadian Film Institute.

Cinéma enfants and *Cinéma adultes.* Catalogues listing available films from a number of sources. Available from the Fédération des centres culturels du Québec, 3100 St-Donat St., Montreal 429, Quebec. 354-0320.

Coopérative cinéastes independants/Independent Filmmakers' Cooperative Catalogue. Listing over 600 films, features and shorts, experimental, poetic and political, from Canada, United States and Europe. Available at no charge from the Coopérative cinéastes indépendants/Independent Filmmakers' Cooperative, 2026 Ontario St., East, Montreal 133, Quebec. 523-2816.

800 Films for Film Study, compiled by D. John Turner, is available for $3.00 from the Canadian Film Institute, 1762 Carling Ave., Ottawa, K2A 2H7. 729-6193.

Film Study Collection Catalogues. A number of catalogues for students of film, covering the historical face of filmmaking. Available for a small fee from the Canadian Film Institute.

Free Films Directory. A sourcebook of over 16,000 free 16mm films available in Canada. For a copy of the Directory, write Crawley Films Limited, 19 Fairmont Ave., Ottawa, Ontario K1Y 3B5, or 93 Yorkville Ave., Toronto 180, Ontario.

London Film Coop Catalogue, listing the films made in and around London and distributed cooperatively. Write the London Film Coop, 1055 Lombard Ave., London, Ontario. 439-9030.

National Film Board French Language Films in Ontario is an information bulletin available from National Film Board, 1 Lombard Street, Toronto 210, Ontario. 369-4093.

National Film Board of Canada: Film Catalogue/Office national du film du Canada: Catalogue des films. Available on request from the NFB, P.O. Box 6100, Montreal 101, Quebec and from your local NFB office.

National Film Board 16mm Films Relating to Native Culture is a specialized bulletin available from the National Film Board, 1 Lombard Street, Toronto 210, Ontario. 369-4093.

National Science Film Library Catalogues. A collection of ten catalogues of films dealing with all aspects of science. All films listed and the catalogues are available from the Canadian Film Institute, 1762 Carling Ave., Ottawa K2A 2H7. Catalogues are 25¢ each.

Nursing Media Index. Edited and compiled by Marilynne Sequin & John S. Bradley, Nursing Educational Media Association, 1972. A reference tool for those interested in the health sciences — administration, behavioral sciences and family life. Resumés for over 1200 16mm films and sources, many free. Available for $12.00 from *Nursing Media Index,* 26 Edgar Avenue, Toronto 287, Ontario.

Pacific Cinémathèque Pacifique Catalogue, listing films made on the west coast and distributed cooperatively. Write the Pacific Cinémathèque Pacifique, 1145 West Georgia Street, Vancouver 5, B.C. 684-2488.

Les Productions de l'Office du film du Québec. Under the Department of Cultural Affairs, the Quebec Film Board distributes many free cultural, educational, scientific & fictional films made in Quebec and elsewhere. Write: Office du film du Québec, Service de la distribution, 360 McGill St., Montreal 125, Quebec, or 1601 Hamel Blvd. W., Quebec 8, Quebec for a free catalogue of their productions. For a catalogue of all the films they distribute, send $2.00.

Recueil des films. An annual listing of films distributed in Quebec, with artistic and moral criticism. Available for $3.00 per year, $34.00 for collected works (1956-1970) from Office des communications sociales, 4635 de Lorimier, Montreal 178, Quebec.

Répertoire des longs metrages produits au Québec. Organized in a yearly sequence, complete information on credits and availability plus a resumé is given for each film. Available for $1.50 from the Conseil québécois pour la diffusion du cinéma, 3466 St-Denis St., Montreal 130, Quebec.

16mm Film Directory: Film Federation of Eastern Ontario. A catalogue of film blocks which move around eastern Ontario largely through public libraries. Catalogue available from the Ottawa Film Council, P.O. Box 359, Ottawa 2, Ontario.

Special Subject Catalogues. Covering subjects of available films — Education, Fire Prevention, Human Rights, Labour and Management, Literature, Political Sciences, Old Age, Sports. Available at 25¢ each from the Canadian Film Institute.

Vancouver Film Council Catalogue, listing over 600 films, many of screen study value, available within the province of British Columbia only. Write to the Vancouver Film Council, 1701 West Broadway, Vancouver 9, B.C. 733-3414.

In addition, of course, all of the commercial film distributors issue catalogues (of varying interest) of their "product". Of particular usefulness to film students (because of the thoroughness of its listings and descriptions) is Universal's 16mm catalog (write: Universal Pictures, 2450 Victoria Park Ave., Willowdale 425, Ontario; or call 416-491-3000).

26. periodicals   (see also TRADE JOURNALS)

Challenge for Change Newsletter is published three or four times a year by the Challenge for Change Unit at the National Film Board. Edited by Dorothy Todd Henault, the *Newsletter* covers film and video work in community units. The *Newsletter* is available by writing:

> *Challenge for Change Newsletter*
> National Film Board of Canada
> P.O. Box 6100
> Montreal 101, Quebec

Champ Libre: a critical collection on Quebec and international cinema. Edited by a number of critics including Dominique Noguez and Yvan Patry, *Champ Libre* is available at $3.50 an issue from:

> *Champ Libre*
> P.O. Box 399
> Outremont Station
> Montreal 154, Quebec

Cinema Canada is a bi-monthly magazine published by the Canadian Society of Cinematographers. Edited by George Csaba Koller, *Cinema Canada* features interviews with leading cinematographers, reviews of Canadian films, festival information and profiles of independent film-makers. It is also an information outlet for a number of filmmakers' organizations such as the Directors' Guild of Canada, the Canadian Film editors Guild and the Society of Motion Picture and Television Engineers. Subscriptions are available at $5.00 per year from:

> *Cinema Canada*
> Room 202
> 341 Bloor Street West
> Toronto 181, Ontario

Cinéma-Québec is a critical film magazine published 10 times a year in French with a special emphasis on Quebec cinema. Edited by Jean-Pierre Tadros, *Cinéma-Québec* is available at $6.50 ($5.00 for students) per year by contacting:

> *Cinéma-Québec*
> P.O. Box 309, Station Outremont
> Montreal 154, Quebec

Culture Vivante is a quarterly published in French by Quebec's Ministry of Cultural Affairs. Covering all aspects of Quebec's cultural life, it invariably has articles on film. Subscriptions are available at $2.00 per year ($1.00 for students) from:

> *Culture Vivante*
> Ministère des Affaires culturelles
> Hôtel du gouvernement
> Quebec 4, Quebec

Le Grand Journal illustré is a weekly paper which carries a large centre section on Quebec cinema. Edited by Freida Couture-Levesque, it is available at $15.00 per year from:

> *Le Grand Journal illustré*
> Les Publications Quebecor Inc.
> 4270 Papineau St.
> Montreal 177, Quebec
> 527-3161

Ici Radio-Canada lists programs weekly and carries articles on the French programming of Radio-Canada. Available at $13.00 per year from:

> *Ici Radio-Canada*
> Société Radio-Canada
> P.O. Box 6000
> Montreal 101, Quebec

Impact which calls itself "The Canadian Cinema Magazine" is sold (for 25¢) at the candy counters of the two large theatre chains — Famous Players and Odeon. By and large, *Impact* is a glossy PR job for their product. Ed: Barbara Boyden. Subscriptions: $4.00 for 6 issues. Write:

> *Impact*
> 291 Lakeshore Blvd. East,
> Toronto 1, Ontario.

Medium Media is the information magazine of Société nouvelle, the French counterpart of the Challenge for Change program administered by the National Film Board in conjunction with Federal government departments. The magazine covers the history of the program, its operations and aims, cable and video television. Available on request from:

> *Medium Media*
> Société nouvelle
> National Film Board
> P.O. Box 6100
> Montreal 101, Quebec

New Canadian Film/Nouveau Cinéma canadien, published about four times a year in English and French by the Cinémathèque québécoise, keeps track of film production across the country. The editor, Carol Faucher, encourages filmmakers and producers to send news of their activities. *New Canadian Film* also publishes information on festivals, and on Canadian films which have been released. *New Canadian Film* is available on request from:

> *New Canadian Film*
> La Cinémathèque québécoise
> 360 McGill St.
> Montreal 125, Quebec
> 366-4688

Performing Arts in Canada covers all aspects of Canadian cultural activity and often touches on cinema. Published quarterly, it is available for $3.00 per year from:

> *Performing Arts in Canada*
> 49 Wellington St. East
> Toronto, Ontario

Pot Pourri comes out monthly from the National Film Board's Ontario regional office. Edited by Patricia Thorvaldson, *Pot Pourri* includes film criticism, happenings around Ontario and interviews with filmmakers inside as well as outside the Board. *Pot Pourri* is available by contacting:

> *Pot Pourri*
> NFB
> 1 Lombard St.
> Toronto 210, Ontario
> 369-4093

The Reel Thing is published irregularly by the Ontario Film Association and covers information on new films and often carries interviews with filmmakers. Subscription is free to members of OFA and $1.50 per copy to non-members. Write:

> The Editor
> *The Reel Thing*
> Ontario Film Association
> Box 521
> Barrie, Ontario

Rushes is an erratic monthly published by the Toronto Film-makers' Coop. Edited by Jerry McNabb, *Rushes* offers technical information, local and national film news, festival information and articles on filmmakers. The Coop asks for a $3.00 yearly contribution.

> *Rushes*
> Toronto Film-makers' Coop
> Room 201
> Rochdale College
> 341 Bloor St. W.
> Toronto 181, Ontario
> 921-2259

Screen: an information exchange depot published by the Media Division of the National Film Board. Edited by Christine Assal, *Screen* carries and invites articles, reviews and comments. Irregular, *Screen* is available at no charge from:

> *Screen*
> National Film Board of Canada
> P.O. Box 6100
> Montreal 101, Quebec

Select: Programs and articles on programs of CBC radio and television. Published weekly, available at $5.00 per year from:

> *Select*
> Canadian Broadcasting Corporation
> 354 Jarvis St.,
> Toronto, Ontario

Séquences is a quarterly critical periodical published in French by the Office des communications sociales. Edited by Léo Bonneville, *Séquences* covers international cinema with a particular emphasis on the Canadian scene. Subscriptions are $2.50 per year ($2.00 for students) from:

> *Séquences*
> 4635 de Lorimier St.
> Montreal 178, Quebec

Take One is a critical film periodical with national and international coverage. Edited by Peter Lebensold *Take One* is published bi-monthly; a two year subscription is available for $4.50 by writing:

> *Take One*
> Box 1778, Station B
> Montreal 110, Quebec

Télé-cinéma is a twice monthly paper which covers the popular cinema in Quebec. Edited by Jean-Pierre Nicaise, it is available at 25¢ each, $7.00 per year from:

> *Télé-cinéma*
> 2215 Jean-Talon St. E.,
> Montreal, Quebec
> 728-4537

That's Showbusiness is a new, lively, *Variety*-style bi-weekly newspaper covering developments in the Canadian film industry (as well as in theatre, dance, music, etc.) in a very up-to-date format. Copies are 25¢ each, $5.00 per year from:

> *That's Showbusiness*
> 189 Church Street
> Toronto, Ontario
> 363-6773

Vie des arts covers all aspects of Quebec cultural life and does, though irregularly, carry articles on film. Subscriptions are available at $7.00 per year from:

> *Vie des arts*
> 360 McGill Street
> Montreal 125, Quebec

Of additional interest:

The *International Film Guide* lists about 60 film periodicals and trade magazines around the world. Examples of articles, evaluations, prices, and addresses are given in most cases. Published yearly by The Tantivy Press, the *International Film Guide* is available in most bookstores.

Current Film Periodicals in English is an annotated bibliography listing over 100 magazines and newspapers. It also provides subscription rates, addresses, content and orientation description. Available for $1.25 from:

> Adam Reilly
> 405 Lexington Ave.
> Rm. 4200
> New York, N.Y. 10017

Periodica is an international subscription agency which handles over 40 film periodicals from around the world. Write asking for their cinema list with rate schedules from:

> *Periodica*
> 7045 Park Ave.
> Montreal 303, Quebec

REPORTS

The Canada Council: Annual Report. Available at no charge from The Canada Council, 151 Sparks Street, Ottawa, Ontario K1P 5V8.

Canadian Film Development Corporation: Annual Report/Société de développement de l'industrie cinématographique canadienne: Rapport annuel. Available at no charge from CFDC, Suite 2220, 800 Place

Victoria, Montreal 115, Quebec (283-6363); or from CFDC, Suite 18, Lothian Mews, 96 Bloor Street West, Toronto 5, Ontario (966-6436).

La Cinémathèque: Rapport annuel. Back copies from 1966 available at no charge from La Cinémathèque québécoise, 360 McGill St., Montreal 125, Quebec.

Conseil québécois pour la diffusion du cinéma: Rapport annuel. Available from CQDC, 3466 St. Denis St., Montreal 130, Quebec.

National Film Board of Canada: Annual Report/Office National du film du Canada: Rapport annuel: Available on request from the National Film Board, Box 6100, Montreal 101, Quebec.

27. addresses

CBC Learning Systems
Box 500, Station A
Toronto 116, Ontario

The Canada Council
151 Sparks St.
Ottawa, Ontario K1P 5V8
237-3400

Canadian Centre for Films on Art
150 Kent St.
Ottawa, Ontario K1A 0M9
992-1868

Canadian Education Association/L'Association
canadienne d'éducation
151 Bloor St. W.
Toronto 5, Ontario
924-7721

Canadian Film Archives
1762 Carling Ave.
Ottawa, Ontario K2A 2H7
729-6193

Canadian Film Development Corp.
800 Place Victoria, Suite 2220
Montreal 115, Quebec
283-6363

Canadian Film Development Corp.
96 Bloor St. W., Suite 18
Toronto 5, Ontario
966-6436

Canadian Film Institute (CFI)
1762 Carling Ave.
Ottawa, Ontario K2A 2H7
729-6193

Canadian Film-makers' Distribution Centre
Room 204, Rochdale College
341 Bloor St. W.
Toronto 181, Ontario
921-2259

Canadian Library Association
151 Sparks St.
Ottawa, Ontario K1P 5E3
232-9625

Centre de psychologie et de pédagogie
260 Faillon St. W.
Montreal, Quebec

La Cinémathèque québécoise (formerly La Cinémathèque canadienne)
360 McGill Street,
Montreal 125, Quebec
866-4688

Le Conseil québécois pour la diffusion
du cinéma (CQDC)
3466 St. Denis St.
Suites 5 & 6
Montreal 130, Quebec
842-5079

Coopérative cinéastes indépendants/
Independent Filmmakers' Cooperative
2026 Ontario St. E.
Montreal 133, Quebec
523-2816

Département de documentation cinématographique
La Bibliothèque nationale
360 McGill St.
Montreal 125, Quebec
873-5450

Editions du Jour
1651 St. Denis St.
Montreal 129, Quebec
849-2228

Editions Fides
245 Dorchester St. E.
Montreal 129, Quebec
861-9621

London Film Coop
1055 Lombardo Ave.
London 11, Ontario
439-9030

Ministère des Affaires culturelles
Hôtel du gouvernement
Quebec 4, Quebec

The National Film Board of Canada
Box 6100
Montreal 101, Quebec
333-3333

NFB Regional Offices:

NFB
Atlantic Regional Office
1572 Barrington St.
Halifax, N.S.
426-3120

NFB
B.C. Regional Office
115 West Georgia St.
Vancouver, B.C.
666-1716

NFB
Montreal Regional Office
550 Sherbrooke St. W.
Montreal 111, Quebec
879-4753 or 4823

NFB
Ottawa Regional Office
Suite 642
150 Kent St.
Ottawa, Ontario K1A 0M9
996-4861

NFB
Ontario Regional Office
1 Lombard St.
Toronto 210, Ontario
369-4093

NFB
Prairie Regional Office
344 12th Ave. S.W.
Calgary 3, Alberta
264-3911

National Science Film Library/
La Cinémathèque nationale scientifique
1762 Carling Ave.
Ottawa, Ontario K2A 2H7
729-1593

L'Office des communications sociales
4635 de Lorimier St.
Montreal 178, Quebec
526-9165

L'Office du film du Québec
1601 Hamel Blvd. W.,
Quebec 8, Quebec

L'Office du film du Québec
360 McGill Street
Montreal 125, Quebec
873-4044

Ontario Film Institute and Theatre
Ontario Science Centre
770 Don Mills Road
Don Mills, Ontario
429-4100

Ontario Institute for Studies in Education (O.I.S.E.)
252 Bloor St. W.
Toronto 5, Ontario

Pacific Cinémathèque Pacifique
1145 West Georgia St.
Vancouver 5, B.C.
684-2488

Peter Martin Associates Ltd.
35 Britain St.
Toronto, Ontario M5A 1R7
363-2071

Playwrights' Coop
344 Dupont Ave.
Toronto, Ontario
961-1800

Les Presses de l'Université du Québec
Box 250, Station N
Montreal 129, Quebec

Province of Ontario Council for the Arts
151 Bloor St. W.
Toronto 5, Ontario
961-1660

Relations
1396 St. Catherine St. W.
Montreal, Quebec

index of films

credits

Written and conceived by: Eleanor Beattie

General Editors: Peter Lebensold, Joe Medjuck

Special Researchers: Linda Beath, Carol Faucher

Resource People: Michelle Bischoff, Lyle Cruikshank, Robert Daudelin, Clive Denton, Dan Driscoll, Sandra Gathercole, Raymond Gordy, Denyse Morrow, Colin Neale, David Novek, Gerald Pratley, Danielle Sauvage, Pat Thompson

Production Manager: Carol Martin

Designer: Diana McElroy

Editor: Kathy Vanderlinden

Typesetting: Blain Berdan

Printed by: Web Offset

Photographs supplied by: NFB, CQDC, Faroun Films and Les Films mutuels

Body Copy: Press Roman

Titles: Eurostile Bold Extended

Paper: Sooprint

Case: Linson Buckram, Cream